LIVING FOR TODAY
A MEMOIR

From Incest and Molestation to
Fearlessness and Forgiveness

ERIN MERRYN

Health Communications, Inc.
Deerfield Beach, Florida

www.hcibooks.com

616.8583
Mer

10|12
BAT

Some names have been changed to protect the privacy of the individuals mentioned in this book.

Scripture quotations are taken from the *New American Standard Bible* © Copyright 1960, 1995 by The Lockman Foundation. Used by permission.

Library of Congress Cataloging-in-Publication Data

Merryn, Erin.
    Living for today : from incest and molestation to fearlessness and forgiveness / Erin Merryn.
        p. cm.
    Includes index.
    ISBN-13: 978-0-7573-1419-3
    ISBN-10: 0-7573-1419-8
    1. Child sexual abuse.   2. Incest.   3. Sex crimes.   I. Title.
    HV6570.M47 2009
    616.85'836903—dc22

                                                                          2009017807

Publisher: Health Communications, Inc.
        3201 S.W. 15th Street
        Deerfield Beach, FL 33442–8190

Cover design by Larissa Hise Henoch
Interior design by Lawna Patterson Oldfield
Formatting by Dawn Von Strolley Grove

This book is dedicated to my parents,
who have supported their daughters from day one
and never turned their backs on us.
This book is also dedicated to sexual abuse survivors.

CONTENTS

ACKNOWLEDGMENTS

In a world that often turns its back to the ugly horrors of child sexual abuse, I have been blessed to meet some incredible people who have taken a stand with me to put a face and voice on an epidemic in our world.

God knew when He created me that He was going to work wonders in my life, and He has shown me His purpose for me. He has taught me that He will give me only what I can handle, and I know He is smiling down on me as I discover triumph in tragedy. He is my strength that pushes me forward each day. One day He will be standing on the other side of life's door, calling me home to celebrate the life I lived and conquered because of Him.

None of this could have been possible had it not been for the wonderful people at my incredible publishing company, Health Communications, Inc.: Peter Vegso, Tom Sand, Michele Matrisciani, Kim Weiss, and the entire company of men and women who have taken part in allowing my voice to be heard. When you could have easily looked the other way, you saw my passion, heard my determination, and knew lives would be changed through my words. You all have been a part of changing thousands of lives by allowing me to help people break their silence, find their voices, and wake up society. I am truly grateful for your giving me this opportunity to take a stand and change the way America views sexual abuse.

Without my parents I would not be the person I am today. They have stood behind me when I took my first steps, catching me if I fell, and have continued to stand behind me through breaking my silence and finding my healing. I always had them to fall back on.

They have gone above and beyond for their daughters. Not enough words are in the dictionary to express how truly grateful I am for all they have done for me. I am blessed to call you Mom and Dad.

To my sister and best friend Allie, who shares many memories of an incredible childhood filled with so much laughter and joy that has followed us into adulthood, thank you for taking part in sharing your voice with others and supporting the work I do to reach other survivors like us. You have come a long way in your own healing, and I am really proud of you.

To my sister Caitlin, for the support and love you have shared with your two younger sisters. Thank you for reminding me in times of darkness how much I have overcome in my life and that I can conquer other challenges I am sure to face, and for being at my side when I was vulnerable and helping me let it all out.

To Gayla Elliott, for helping me reach the little girl within me and bring her to the surface. You had faith in my ability to confront and heal the abuse in my life and reminded me that healing is a gradual process: one word, one page, and one chapter at a time.

Thanks go to the Children's Advocacy Centers across America, who help children fight for the justice they deserve. To each and every person who dedicates their lives to these centers, whether it is helping the children who walk through the doors or helping fund these nonprofit centers, you help children to step out of darkness, find their voices, and begin to heal.

To all who have taken part in the course of my life in helping me find my voice and heal, you know who you are, thank you. You have played an important part in helping me get where I am today, whether it was teaching me, counseling me, or being a true friend and supporting me.

Last, to you my readers, I thank you for being a part of my journey. It is my hope that you will jump on board and join me in my fight to make other sexual abuse survivors aware that they are not alone. Each of us has a voice and the power to use it.

PROLOGUE

My Sister's Voice

Looking down the path I have taken in my life, I have changed a great deal. My sister and I took different approaches in dealing with the pain of sexual abuse. Looking at a picture of myself at age ten, I wish I could have given that innocent little girl a voice. I have held in a lot of my pain and suffering, not knowing what to do with it or where to go for help. I had a difficult time expressing my feelings, which I am still working on today, but watching my sister be so brave and speak out has helped me find my own voice.

When Erin asked me to share my voice in this book, I was sort of hesitant. What would I say? How would I say it? What am I feeling right now? I have been hurt by relatives who denied what happened to Erin and I, I have forgiven my cousin for what he did to me, I hate being uncomfortable in certain situations, and I clearly remember my cousin trapping me in dark places and molesting me.

Everyone goes through the steps of pain and grief in their own way. I was in denial when the abuse was going on. I hoped it was all a dream and none of it was real. I tried to sweep the memories of the abuse under the rug, praying it would disappear. As a child it was such a big weight to carry and I did not know where to put it. I thought I was tough enough to deal with it on my own and hold it all in. I soon found out I was not. That spring day will live in me forever when Erin and I realized we were carrying the same secret. Together we knew we had to break our silence. She warned me that our lives would never be the same again.

The day we told our parents of the abuse was unforgettable. Finally, I could breathe a sigh of relief and feel safe knowing my cousin would never again lay a hand on us. My parents wrapped their arms around Erin and I that night, telling us how much they loved us and that they believed us. I thank God for the parents He gave me and how loving and supportive they have been through it all.

Years have passed now since that day, and I have grown so much. My sister has accomplished much as an author and speaker, and she has inspired so many. Erin is an advocate for other survivors of abuse. She has helped many people and saved several from years of pain and suffering. I wish I were that strong. Watching Erin on her crusade has helped me grow and find my own voice. It took me a little longer to process and learn how to deal with sexual abuse. I just wanted the memories to go away, but then they all hit me when I got to college. Different situations would trigger memories, pain. But each time I learned something new about myself. Sexual abuse affected me at different stages of my life: childhood, teen years, and now into my twenties. The truth is no matter how much time has gone by, it does not erase the memories of what happened. Since being at college, the abuse has affected me in a more powerful way.

Trust has been the hardest issue for me to deal with. I tend to back away from relationships because I get scared and I do not know how to deal with it. I always go to God for guidance, to show me the right path. I could not have survived any of this without Him, my parents, sisters, and friends. The supportive people in my life have helped me deal with my feelings.

Along with the trust issues, one of the hardest parts to deal with is the feeling of not being believed or supported, especially by your own grandparents and extended family. When I have been through so much pain and hurt and have to live with the scars every day, I get angry knowing that others think it is all made up or they brush it off because my cousin was a teenager. I was ten when I was first sexually abused by my cousin, and a majority of my relatives have taken the perpetrator's side. I have cried many times about everything and how my relatives gave no support or love to me as a kid when this all came out. Not one relative ever came up to that innocent little girl I was and said "I am sorry for what you went through" or "I am here for you." Instead, they said hurtful things: "Oh he was young." "That is what kids do." "It is not like he was some older man you didn't know." Why does age make a difference? It is a sick way of thinking. Sexual abuse is sexual abuse. What is wrong with this picture? It brings tears to my eyes the way my relatives have reacted to this and cannot accept the truth. Denial is where they would rather stay.

Even ten years after breaking my silence, some days I wish I had never broken my silence and instead carried it alone so I would not see the people I love hurting. My parents, sisters, and I have been on an emotional roller coaster over the years, but in the end we will only grow stronger and become better people because of it.

God is all about forgiving, and I have done that. I am just now at a place in my life where I can address my anger about what happened and its outcome. Erin and I are more than sisters; we are best friends who have risen above a tragic event in our childhoods and hold on to and cherish the good memories. We look forward to creating many more in the future.

It seems like it was just yesterday I sat in the waiting room of the Children's Advocacy Center, filled with so much anxiety and fear. My sister came to me just after being interviewed to reassure me that this was a safe place and that the people here truly cared about us. When my family's life was in crisis, the advocacy center opened their doors with people ready to begin our family's journey in healing and allowing my sister and I to break free of silence.

Erin graduated with a master's degree in social work and I am going into emergency management. We both chose a career that will help people in crisis because of our own crises, and we wanted to help others the way people at the center helped us during that difficult time of our lives.

I am a lot healthier by sharing my pain. I have learned so much about others and myself by opening up. Finding my voice has helped me continue to heal. Opening up has taught me to look at myself in the mirror and see who the real me is. My relatives who are in denial cannot hold me down and dampen my spirits. I thank God every day for the people He has put in my life and for teaching me that even when I am at my lowest, I have plenty of time and space to get back on my feet and discover who I am.

I am glad I have finally found my voice and that my sister has been able to use hers to help so many. Everyone has a purpose in life, and I believe Erin found hers. I am not a public speaker—it is not for everyone—but I am glad I have found my purpose, and I am finally free to let out my emotions, knowing I have nothing to be ashamed of.

Allie

INTRODUCTION

District Attorney of Alabama Robert (Bud) Cramer wanted a better system to help abused children. Prior to 1985, the social service and criminal justice systems were not effective in doing what was best for children who came forward with abuse allegations. The process caused them great emotional stress and was a frightening experience for the children. Investigations and interventions into these serious cases of child abuse seemed without purpose—the children had to repeat over and over their stories. These children were retraumatized by the system's process.

Robert Cramer had a vision for a better system: provide a safe place and secure environment for children to tell their stories. He founded the first Children's Advocacy Center in Huntsville, Alabama, in 1985—the year I was born. In one child-friendly environment, the center brought together a coordinated team: law enforcement, child protective service, and medical and mental health workers. Word spread to other states; soon many of them opened their own centers.

According to the National Children's Alliance, 139 Children's Advocacy Centers in the United States helped 75,047 abused children in 1998. Behind this number are the faces of innocent children whose childhoods were shattered by some form of abuse or trauma inflicted on them by evil and sick people. Remember, this number reflects only the number of children who found the courage to break their silence that year. My sister and I were two of those children.

Ten years after we broke our silence in a Children's Advocacy Center, 251,000 children in 2008 received services at these centers across the United States. This massive number is proof that we need advocacy centers. Without them, countless children's voices would remain silent, and they would never have a chance at the justice they deserve. Of this number, 174,090 children reported they were sexually abused. In 2008, a total of 204,390 alleged offenders of some form of abuse were reported to Children's Advocacy Centers. Over 136,000 were 18 and older. Juveniles aged 13–17 made up 24,452 of the alleged offenders. Another 14,284 were under the age of 13, while another 32,000 were an unknown age.

Do I have your attention now? If these numbers do not alarm you, go back and read them again and let the reality sink in. More shocking is that the figures represent only *one year* in America and *only* those cases that came into Children's Advocacy Centers. What about the thousands of children who did not have the opportunity to have their voices heard in 2008? Their abusers come from all backgrounds and ages. Behind these numbers is the force of evil that caused these children harm.

When a child walks through the doors of a center and is interviewed, his or her healing begins. In 2008, Children's Advocacy Centers conducted more than 161,000 forensic interviews and 75,000 medical exams, 67,000 children received therapy, and 85,000 children were referred to therapy. I do not throw these numbers at you to scare you but to show you just how important it is that we have a safe place for children in America to tell their secrets so they can begin to heal.

Today there are over seven hundred centers, including one outside America. Each and every center has its unique presence, although they all share the same mission to reduce trauma and provide support for abused children and their families, and to hold the guilty accountable for their crimes. A vision by Robert Cramer nearly twenty-five years ago has allowed children to come out of darkness and find their voices in a safe and friendly environment, where justice and the first steps in healing begin for children.

America is not the only country affected by child sexual abuse. Millions of children across the world have gone through the horrors of sexual abuse and must live the rest of their lives carrying their invisible scars. Children in America are fortunate to have places like the Children's Advocacy Centers, where they can get counseling, support, and justice. Unfortunately, many other countries lack services for abused children who want to break their silence. They have nowhere to turn.

By opening the door to my life, it is my hope and mission to shed light on the hidden wounds of abuse, to end the stigma and shame associated with abuse, and to show survivors true courage, strength, inspiration, and determination. I can only hope that sharing my personal and private story will help others open the doors to their pasts, allowing their wounds to be exposed without shame and guilt but instead with courage and determination. As you take this walk with me, think of the pains you carry in your heart and soul. Whether you are a survivor of childhood sexual abuse or not, we all have faced trials in life that have caused great pain. I hope by the time you reach the final page of my journey, the hurts and wounds in your heart no longer hold you down, causing you to suffer; rather, you will be standing up ready to push forward and grow. I risked taking my first steps forward. I share my journey from raw emotional pain to inner strength and ultimately to finding my purpose in life. Once you begin that process of healing, the work begins; it is then you will experience an unbelievable transformation taking place within you.

chapter one

INNOCENCE LOST

At age thirteen, I thought I was carrying my secret alone. I never imagined my little eleven-year-old sister was carrying the same dark secret. It was a clear blue Sunday near the end of March 1998. While the sun was shining, darkness loomed over my sister and I. She had just shared with me that our teenaged cousin Brian was "gross." The instant Allie uttered that word, my secret became our secret. It is every parent's worst nightmare, especially when the abuser is someone in the family.

A stillness hung in the air. I felt as if someone had punched me in the stomach. My sister's words echoed through my head. For nearly two years I had felt alone, fearful, confused, lost, empty, dirty, and silenced. With my sister's revelation, all those feelings were pushed aside for one consuming emotion: guilt. I blamed myself for my sister's abuse because I had not spoken up.

For the next several hours, we sat on our trampoline at our lake house and shared with each other the disturbing things our cousin Brian did to us. We used words like *disgusting, dirty, gross,* and *trapped* to describe his actions. Our word choices show how innocent we really were. The words *sexual abuse, molestation,* and *incest* would be added later to our vocabulary—words no children should ever have to identify with.

I learned Brian abused my sister when he could not get his hands on me. One particular time, I did escape my cousin's abuse at a family confirmation party for another cousin. He had tried to corner me all night and followed me down to the basement. I hid behind the washer so he would not find me. Eventually I came out and escaped up the stairs. Though he did not pursue me, I felt the intensity of his gaze follow me. He stayed in the basement with our other cousins and my sister Allie. It was then he took Allie behind the furnace, trapped her, and molested her. Hearing her tell me this angered me.

Though I was certain we had to break our silence, I had no idea how to do it. We struggled the rest of the day, trying to come up with a way to tell our parents. I warned my sister that this would divide our extended family once they heard about what Brian had been doing to us. Brian always told me that no one would believe me because I had no proof, so I feared he was right. Why would anyone believe me? While I was feeling overwhelming guilt for not telling sooner to protect my sister, I thought that with two of us coming forward, someone would believe us.

Growing up with only sisters, I looked up to my male cousins, including Brian. Our families lived within walking distance of one another. Brian is the oldest of four boys. My aunt did not have daughters, so my sisters and I often looked up to Aunt Mary as a second mom. Dad and Aunt Mary were from a family of seven children, giving us a large extended family. While I had many aunts, uncles, and cousins, I felt the closest to Uncle Scott, Aunt Mary, and their four sons. Besides all the holidays and birthday celebrations, our two families got together all the time. We would go places together like Great America, miniature golf, bowling, movies, ice skating, and our summers were spent in Wisconsin on a lake. We would go boating or play out on the raft in the water. Brian and his brother Mike, who was my age, both played hockey. They often went on trips to their hockey tournaments and Aunt Mary would ask me if I would come along and help with my two younger cousins. She knew I loved spending time with them and I loved watching ice hockey. So I went with them on many overnight trips.

It was normal for my younger sister and me to stop after school at their house to play with my little cousins, bake cookies with our aunt, or help her make dinner. Many times we were invited over for dinner. Often both families would get together for dinner. The parents would play cards all evening while my sisters and I would watch movies or play Nintendo, board games, hide and seek, or foosball in their basement. We also played a game our uncle came up with that he called "tickle monster." Brian would go under a blanket and the object of the game was for him to crawl around the basement and try grabbing our feet and tickling us. Sometimes he would lie under the blanket and not move, making us go over and tap his back or feet, then he would suddenly come to life, and we all would scream and take off running. To make it scary, he sometimes turned the lights off so we could not see where he was. It was an innocent, fun game and we played all the time when we were at their house. All it took was one night for that fun and trusting relationship with my cousin Brian to change forever. The image of the cousin I looked up to was suddenly an image I was waking up to in the middle of the night, with his hands down my pants sexually abusing me. An image of his face staring at me is burned in my memory from that night—a night I tried to convince myself the next morning was all a bad dream.

The sexual abuse began in September 1996, when I was eleven, and continued for over a year and a half. His sick, twisted behavior was well thought out as he found ways to trap me in basements, closets, crawl spaces, bedrooms, and bathrooms. Most of the abuse was done in darkness during after-school hours when Brian's mom would ask me to watch my two younger cousins while she ran errands. Why she never got Brian to watch his brothers is beyond me, but most of the time Brian was gone when she left, but he would come home while she was gone. It was almost as if he was waiting for her to leave so he could come home and terrorize me. The abuse happened not only while I watched my little cousins but also during the holidays or family celebrations that occurred monthly and sometimes weekly. A once-innocent game of tickle monster that I had played for years with him turned into a new way to pull me under blankets in darkness and sexually abuse me. And when my cousins and I would play hide and go seek, he would back me into a bedroom, bathroom, or closet and molest me.

One time I hid in Aunt Mary's walk-in closet. Brian was already in there waiting for me. Because the closet was dark, I did not see him when I first went in. It was not until I sat down that I felt his hand on my shoulder. I screamed because he startled me. He clenched his hand around my mouth to silence me. Sitting right behind me, he quickly wrapped his legs around me, trapping me with him. Then it began: He forced his hands down the front of my pants and underwear and up my shirt. He did not say anything; he just breathed heavily against the back of my ear. My sister Allie came close to finding us when she walked into the closet and walked right out, not spotting us because of the darkness. I sat frozen, wishing I would have screamed out to her. I later learned that on this same day, while my sister was hiding in my aunt's bathroom, Brian had trapped her and molested her in the bathroom. Yet we both had no idea when we walked home that day that we both carried the same secret.

I saw a different look in Brian's eyes after the abuse began. I avoided eye contact with him at family gatherings. He terrified me. I will never forget January 4, the night we celebrated Grandpa's birthday at Aunt Mary and Uncle Scott's house. All night I stayed in the kitchen, fearing Brian, who kept coming in and staring me down. His eyes seemed to scream, "I am going to get you!" Eventually, he put on his coat, left the house, and went across the street. I assumed he had gone over to his best friend's house, so I began playing with my cousins, feeling much safer when he was gone. For around fifteen minutes I was upstairs playing a board game with my cousins, when we were called down to sing "Happy Birthday" to Grandpa and have cake. My cousins and sister ran downstairs as I put the game away in the closet and turned off the light. As I turned to leave, Brian stood in my way. I tried to walk past him down the hall, but he pushed me back, forcing me into the darkness of his bedroom. He shoved me onto a green beanbag chair then laid on top of me, kissing my neck, feeling my chest, and eventually placing his hands down the front of my pants. I could hear the singing going on downstairs. I stayed calm and did not fight back because it only made Brian more aggressive. When he forced his finger inside me, I begged him to stop and started crying. He eventually stopped and told me to go get cake with him. To this day I cannot stand chocolate cake because the taste of chocolate reminds me of not only the abuse that night but also of returning downstairs and having to sit across from him whiled he glared at me as I ate my cake and he ate his.

Chocolate cake is not the only thing I have stopped eating since I was a child. A snack called Star Crunch by Little Debbie is a cookie topped with caramel and crisped rice, then coated with fudge. This snack was a staple in my aunt's pantry, and Brian often gave me one after he abused me. It was almost like my "reward" for the pleasure he got out of me. One year while I was in college, I was at a fraternity house and one of the guys offered me a Star Crunch. I kindly took his offer, although it immediately triggered something inside me. It was not until I actually put it into my mouth that I felt like I was going to throw up. I couldn't eat it and had to throw it out.

Holidays and family celebrations are supposed to be happy times, but when Brian began locking me behind closed doors, holding me down, and silencing my voice as he molested me, those joyful times turned into fearful ones. My only escape was writing. It was my way to express the horror I was experiencing as a child, so I turned to my diary and began to journal the pain I was suffering from. My cousin was a football player, so he was much stronger than I. Anytime I tried fighting him off by digging my nails into him or kicking him, he would just laugh and call me psycho. He used this nickname around other relatives, but it went right over their heads because they had no idea why he called me that. It was easy for Brian to hold down one of my arms while he forced his other hand down the front of my underwear. I never knew what Brian was fully capable of doing to me. He would stop the act of abuse because my aunt would arrive home from running errands or he feared a relative might walk in on him, which almost happened a few times.

It seemed with time he became more comfortable with abusing me, taking his time and becoming more aggressive. Not knowing what he would do the next time he trapped me scared me the most. Brian was a quiet teenager. Most of the time, even as he abused me, he did not say much. He only laughed in my face or breathed heavy and hard into my ear. He spoke only to warn me to stay silent or to tell me to relax when I fought back.

There came a point when the burden of carrying the abuse became too painful. I began lying to Aunt Mary as I passed her house on my way home from school so that I could avoid having to go over there. One winter Friday afternoon, she called me, panicked because her other babysitter had canceled. She needed me to babysit because she and my uncle had dinner reservations in Chicago. I suggested that she ask one of the older boys, either Brian or his brother Mike, to watch the kids. She told me both of them had hockey games and were spending the night with friends. Because Brian was going to be gone and I could hear the desperation in my aunt's voice, I agreed to come over.

The night went smoothly. I made the young boys macaroni and cheese, played Nintendo with them, and read them stories before bed. I went into Aunt Mary and Uncle Scott's bedroom to watch television because she told me I could stay in there in case four-and-a-half-year-old Jake woke up. While watching TV, I heard noises coming from downstairs, but I figured it was my imagination and I was getting myself freaked out for nothing. It sounded as if someone was walking around. I kept looking at the bedroom door, which was slightly opened. After hearing the sounds three or four times, I convinced myself it was just house noises or the furnace going on. I turned up the television to drown out the noise.

Moments later I heard a noise again but much closer. I shot a look at the bedroom door and saw it closing. Brian stood there. Panic sent me into motion. I jumped off the bed, all the while scrambling for words to ask why he was home. Instant fear set in as I looked across the room at my cousin, a sick grin stretched across his face. He told me his game was canceled so he had decided to come home instead of staying with friends like he had planned. I knew he could sense my panic and hear the fear in my voice. He closed the distance between us. My only chance of saving myself was getting out of the bedroom. I climbed across the bed as Brian shot around it and jumped for my ankle, grabbing it.

I fought on the bed with him as he tried to restrain me. Eventually, he got on top of me. I feared looking into his eyes, for every time he abused me I saw the same thing—a look of a crazed, evil man. I wanted to spit in his face when he laughed at my struggling to fight him off. With one hand still free, I did what I had never done before. I punched Brian in the balls. He fell off me, and I pulled myself together and ran for the door. I did not look back; I just ran downstairs and stopped when I reached the family room. Standing stock-still, I looked out the window toward my house, thinking about running the whole way. But I feared he would chase after me, drag me into the marsh's tall grass, and rape me. I hoped he would just leave me alone and stay upstairs, but five minutes later I heard the sound of his footsteps coming down the stairs . . . the same noise I thought earlier was just the furnace turning on.

I wanted someone to save me. I wanted to curl up into a ball and cry because I knew he was coming for me. I moved into the kitchen, waiting for him. With my heart racing at what seemed a hundred miles per hour, my eyes darted between both kitchen entrances. I did not know which one Brian would appear from. The instant he came around the corner, I ran. In the terror of the moment, I ran in circles: from the kitchen, to the dinning room, living room, and front doorway. It was like being in a horror movie, but this was real. I was living it, and I did not know how to escape.

Without warning, he stopped chasing me and hid somewhere in the living room. It then occurred to me that I had only one choice before he popped out and trapped me: run upstairs, wake my little cousins, and hold them. I believed this would give me protection. Without thinking for another moment, I shot upstairs. I saw Brian pop out around the corner. He chased me up the stairs and stopped me before I completely got the boys' door open. Brian ordered me to close it.

I just wanted to disappear right then and there. He dragged me back into his parents' room and onto their bed. I begged him not to have sex with me. Before I knew it, he was back on top of me. I felt his pounding heart against my chest. His breathing was heavy and hot against my ear. I fought the urge to vomit. He pulled his hands through my hair; the hair on my arms stood straight. Then I felt Brian unzipping my pants. Tears welled in my eyes. I was so scared of what he was going to do.

I glanced at the clock; the red numbers 9:38 are burned into my memory to this day. My aunt and uncle were not going to be home until 1 AM. As he yanked my jeans down around my thighs and began forcing his fingers up inside me, I realized that if I was going to make it through the night, I had to focus on something to distract me from the pain he was putting me through. I gave up on fighting and just lay motionless with my eyes closed. I tried imagining myself somewhere warm, but when that did not work, I focused on the sounds of passing cars, hoping it would be my aunt and uncle. The abuse went on for two hours—two hours while I tried to distract him with the television program that was on. When that did not work, I had to mentally escape from my own body to survive. But the pain made going somewhere else in my head too difficult. The malicious smile never left his face. At one point Brian grabbed my hand and put it down his pants, against his penis. I made a tight fist and kept pulling away and saying "No" or "Stop it."

At 12:05, I heard another car coming down the street, but this one seemed to slow down. I had never been so happy to hear the sound of the garage door opening. I had prayed for nearly two hours for God to bring my aunt and uncle home early, and here they were, pulling into the garage an hour early. Relief swept over me.

At the sound of his returning parents, Brian jumped up. A look of panic replaced his evil grin. He adjusted himself and made his way to the door, then he stopped and turned to face me. "This is our secret and it never happened." He went down the hall and into his bedroom like nothing ever happened.

How could I face Aunt Mary? When she saw me, she said that it looked like I had been crying. I told her I had fallen asleep on her bed and just woke up. When she dropped me off in my driveway, she handed me an extra ten dollars for coming on such short notice. Little did she know I would have given anything to give her back that ten dollars if I could have back the past two and half hours of my life that her son had stolen from me. Moments like those are frozen in time in my memory. Eleven years later I can still remember it as if it took place yesterday.

A day after learning my sister was also being abused by our cousin, we shattered our silence when we told our parents of the true horror we had endured at the hands of a trusted family member. Nothing can prepare a parent for that kind of news and my parents did not take it lightly. It is every parent's worst nightmare, especially when the abuser is a close family member.

My parents embraced my sister and I as tears streamed down our mother's face. Our older sister Caitlin was sixteen at the time and could not believe what she was hearing. She, like our parents, was in complete shock. I will never forget her saying, "I can't picture Brian like that. He is quiet and laid-back." The truth is Brian was a totally different person around others than when he trapped me behind closed doors. Because I saw how Brian could exhibit two sides to his personality, I learned that people from all walks of life are capable of things that may seem out of character or unimaginable.

It was our parents' immediate response that played a major role in my healing process. They made sure Allie and I knew they believed us, loved us, and supported us no matter what. What I was not prepared for was our extended family's reaction when they learned what Brian had been doing: utter disbelief. Brian denied ever laying a hand on us and the family believed him. My parents did not want Brian locked up for what he did; rather, they wanted him to get help. The justice Allie and I wanted was to make sure he got help so he would never hurt another person the way he hurt us. Unfortunately, Aunt Mary and Uncle Scott were not going to get him that help we so badly wanted for him. After a few sit-down meetings between my parents and Brian's, my aunt and uncle eventually stopped returning our parents' phone calls.

The night before my parents called the police, I made my own phone call, which took a great deal of courage. I called my cousin. "Brian, this is Erin; don't hang up. You know exactly what you did. Quit lying and saying you never touched us."

Silence greeted me, but he had not hung up because I could hear his breathing—something I had heard too many times when he abused me. I think he was speechless because he knew he could not lie to me about what he had done. I then told him my parents were going to the police in the morning and would be pressing charges against him.

He finally spoke. "Can you hold on a minute?"

I heard him talking to someone but could not make out what he was saying. He got back on the phone and asked if he could call me back in a few minutes. I went downstairs and told my parents what I had just done. We waited for the phone to ring, but a few minutes turned into a half hour. An hour later we went to bed. I remember lying in bed when I heard the phone finally ring at 10:30. No one got up to answer it. In the morning we discovered a message on the machine from Brian's dad saying they wanted to sit down and discuss this but this time with Brian, Allie, and me present. My parents said no way would they put us through having to be in the same room with Brian. That same day my parents went to the police department and made a report. A detective was assigned to our case.

On Thursday, April 30, 1998, Allie and I were brought to the Children's Advocacy Center of Northwest Cook County, Illinois. Built in 1895 as a summer retreat home, in 1989 it was turned into the center that would open its doors to help abused children break their silence and begin the healing process. It was a long white house that sat up on a hill. It had a homey feeling. Children who come to these centers across America often walk in scared, confused, sad, and carrying a heavy burden of pain. While Children's Advocacy Centers strive to give abused children justice and healing, not every child sees the person who abused them punished for their actions; however, every center gives abused children another sense of justice: helping them break their silence and share their stories.

Though it was a beautiful sunny spring day when I walked into the center with my mom and sister, I was filled with fear and confusion. I did not know what to expect and just wanted to get whatever was supposed to happen over with. We first met a woman who introduced herself as Larissa. She would be our advocate. She brought Allie and me bagels and juice while she talked privately to our mom in an office. We were then introduced to a friendly woman named Meghan, who greeted us in the waiting room and explained that we would be going into a room and talking with her. I went first and was led down a hall into a small colorful room, where I sat on a blue chair across from Meghan. A large mirror was inset into one wall of the room. I did not know that it was a two-way mirror. A police detective sat on the other side listening to and watching me during the interview.

Meghan seemed compassionate, trusting, and understanding. She began by asking me about my friends, school, and my plans for summer. She spent time getting to know me, the sixth grader who sat across the table from her. In the back of my mind I knew that at some point I was going to have to talk about Brian. She then talked with me about the difference between a lie and the truth and asked me if I would agree to tell the truth that day. After agreeing, I looked at her and said, "That is why I did not tell before."

Meghan asked me for clarification.

"I didn't say anything because I was afraid no one would believe me. Sometimes I play jokes on people, so if I told what Brian had done, they would think I was just making another joke."

I told Meghan such wonderful things about my friends and what I liked to do, then all at once I experienced an overwhelming sense of fear and feeling dirty and ashamed. I felt shame as images of the abuse I endured ran through my head. A part of me was afraid to share with Meghan what I went through because I feared she would judge me for not telling when Brian had molested me the first time.

But Meghan gave me the confidence in that moment to share with her what would happen when my cousin Brian got me behind closed doors. I stared at myself in the mirror and then began opening up, revealing details. It was the first time light was being shed on the darkness I carried. At one point in the interview, Meghan pulled two dolls from underneath the table and placed them in front of me. She asked me to use the dolls to show her what Brian had done to me.

My mind was flooded with memories of my childhood that I had tried to bury. At one point, I felt my emotions rising to the surface. I wanted to cry, but I feared allowing anyone to see my tears. So I swallowed them and continued with my story. I shared a great many details throughout the interview, but whenever I felt as if I was going to cry, I closed up.

Meghan leaned down and met my eyes. "You did a wonderful job. Before I take you back to your mom in the waiting room, can you tell me what you'd like to see happen to your cousin?"

Even after all the pain he had put me through, I did not want him to be locked behind steel bars. "I want him to get counseling for what he did, and I think he should do community service."

Detective Deguilio, who watched and heard both my sister and me in our interviews, believed us. After my sister's interview, Mom went upstairs with the advocate, forensic interviewer, and the detective. Allie and I sat downstairs and watched a movie and played a board game while the team discussed the next step, which was to bring Brian into the police department for questioning. A report was also made to Department of Children and Family Services, who sent someone out to interview Brian's little brothers to make sure they had not been abused.

Detective Deguilio called Brian into the police department that weekend while we were vacationing in Colorado. On Tuesday, May 5, my parents received a call informing us that after having been behind closed doors with Detective Deguilio for a few hours, Brian had confessed to three counts of sexual abuse. At that point the detective had stopped questioning him and placed him under arrest, charging him with three counts of child sexual abuse. He was released to his parents, and my mom and dad were given the option of taking the case to trial or doing what we originally had wanted, which was for Brian to get psychological help. My parents did not want Allie and me to endure a trial after all we had already been through. In addition, we did not see anything good coming from punishing him for hurting us. We believed if Brian received the kind of help he needed, it might prevent another child being hurt.

Our extended family did not support my parents' decision to go to the police. An uncle who had married into the family decided to voice his opinion to my mother through an e-mail:

Bekki,

Don't take this as being friendly. Personally, and this is my opinion only, not anyone else's, you should have stayed in Colorado. The crap you pulled with Mary and Scott stinks and considering that your daughter said something was supposed to have happened here at my home has me very upset. You know damn well, or you would have bothered to check your story first, that your kids were never alone in my home. Someone over the age of sixteen was with them at all times. The fact that you called the police and then left town stinks. The call to DCFS was totally unnecessary. If something had happened anywhere, you should have talked to the parents first. The extremely ill feelings that you have caused a lot of us, feelings toward you and Dan and your kids, is your fault and no one else's. Maybe you could explain to all of us why you refused to see the counselor with Mary and Scott? You brought this all on yourself. For the record . . . you and the kids are not welcome in my home. If you were invited here it would not be at my wish, but others in the family whom I respect.

Mike

Reading this letter again more than ten years after he wrote and sent it, I still want to scream at Mike and tell him what a jerk he is. His comment about my sister and me always being around someone sixteen or older had nothing to do with my cousin sexually abusing us. We were around twenty other relatives, well over the age of sixteen, who were in the next room or down the hall the many times Brian abused us.

Then to accuse my mom of being at fault? He had his facts backward. It was Mary and Scott who refused to get their son help, which was the reason my parents went to the police in the first place. The only person at fault for this whole mess was Brian.

Mike's comment about my mother bringing this all on herself was completely untrue. Brian's decision to sexually abuse his cousins is what got our family in this disaster.

Mike's final comment about us not being welcome in his home was so twisted. We were the children abused by our cousin, yet he said we were liars.

It was my mother's letter back that makes me proud she stood up for her girls.

Mike,

I wasn't going to respond to your last e-mail because anyone who would write anything so mean and twisted . . . well, just being you has to be miserable enough! I don't think you realize how transparent your e-mail was on your own issues . . . to have taken it so personally . . . makes me wonder if you must have a few skeletons rattling in your closet! I hope you deal with them . . . I'll keep you in my prayers.

As far as the facts in your e-mail go . . . well, if you choose to be ignorant that is your choice. . . . I feel really bad for Mary and Scott, too, but you have your victims mixed up. Brian is the one who hurt my girls, us, Mary, and Scott. Mary is in so much pain she needs to vent her anger at someone and it is hard to do it when it is your own son. Mike, if you want to be fair you would have asked our side, not assumed and spewed! Mary did not want to work with us. She would not return our phone calls and believed her son was innocent. (And I don't blame her, that would be hard.) Dan and I sought the advice of not one, but ten counselors, including children advocacy, social workers, and a detective, on how we could handle this without reporting it. We did everything in our power and the end result being he [Brian] denied it and Mary and Scott were going to let it be. They were advised to have a family meeting with the girls present, and Dan and I felt that was secondary abuse to our girls and unheard of (if you even care to know). So Dan and I took action to get Brian the help he needed through professionals. The detective told me Mary and Scott felt Brian was innocent and obviously they didn't tell you, Mike, that Brian confessed to the abuse while being interviewed by a detective, including that incident in your house. The sixteen-year-olds must have turned their heads!

Mike, there are over thirteen different accounts of abuse to Allie and Erin that we know of. They are in counseling with Dan and me. It pisses me off and makes me wonder about you and your opinion when little girls get sexually abused and you call them liars and me a jerk for protecting them, and giving them the message that they don't matter. If Brian had stolen a radio from Kmart it would have been a police matter. You obviously think my girls' innocence, bodies, and minds are worth less than that. I feel sorry for you. If an adult woman is sexually assaulted it is a police matter.

Who the hell do you think is supposed to take care of young girls? Yes, their parents. Brian confessed, he will now get help and then he can be restored. Now isn't that better than denying it and holding it in his whole life?

For the record, no one else in the family who Dan and I care about are blaming us. So your little threat has no bearing! As far as me getting help, I did, Mike, and that is why my girls were taken care of when someone hurt them! Statistic shows most child abuse happens within family and that is why it continues. I hope you were just confused, Mike, because if you weren't I'll be praying for you.

Bekki

By September, fifteen-year-old Brian was given six months probation, no unsupervised contact with Allie and me, and mandated counseling at a center for juveniles who have had trouble with the law.

Though no longer living in silence, I continued to carry pain and memories.

While my cousin got a very light punishment for the pain he caused Allie and me, I was grateful for the work Detective Deguilio did for our family. He did not give up until he got a confession from my cousin. His fighting for what our cousin stole from us gave my sister and me a sense of justice. He pulled the truth out of Brian.

As in so many cases of sexual abuse within the family, it is much more complicated than had it been done by a stranger. Nothing could have prepared me for my extended family's reaction. Brian's mother did not want him having a record that could affect his future, including college and a career. She pleaded with the Illinois state's attorney to clear his record. When the state's attorney looked into the matter, she saw the three counts of sexual abuse on his record and no prior trouble with the law. She signed off and agreed to my cousin's getting counseling, and it would not show on his record. Until my mother told her, the state's attorney had no idea how many times our cousin abused us over the course of nearly two years. All she had to go on was the paperwork in front of her, and it showed three counts of sexual abuse. My cousin may have been a juvenile, but he committed the same crime over and over again and should have been held responsible for his actions by receiving more than just a few sessions of counseling and six months of probation. He should have undergone an intense treatment program for sex offenders and six *years* of probation—until he reached the age of twenty-one.

Unfortunately, we do not live in a perfect world, and I had to realize at thirteen that Brian was going to slip through the cracks of the justice system. Imagine the message that sent to my sister and me. A cousin violates us, confesses, and walks away with barely a slap on the wrist. I learned at a young age that if I was ever going to see justice for the wrongs done to me, I had to find it myself. For a year my parents, sisters, and I stopped attending holidays and began the healing process. The pain of learning what happened to Allie and me took a toll on my parents, and we often heard our mother crying to our dad about it. I will never forget the time Allie and I heard our mother downstairs crying in our dad's arms. She was blaming herself for not seeing the signs that her children were being abused. She reminded our father that his family was treating us like we were the perpetrator rather than the victims. My father struggled with what happened to his daughters and how his parents and most of his siblings were not showing us any kind of support. None of my dad's brothers, sisters, or our grandparents once called to see how Allie and I were.

Allie and I sat crying at the top of the stairs. We realized how damaging this was to our once happy, close-knit family. Our sister Caitlin comforted Allie and me, telling us over and over that none of this was our fault, reminding us that Brian had caused this pain, not us. Allie and I were at the vulnerable ages of eleven and thirteen, respectively, and we just wanted to move on with our lives. We did not want to see anyone hurting.

In a sense, neither of us wanted to deal with the uncomfortable topic and wished it would just go away. Some days it seemed easier carrying it alone before we broke our silence. I could handle carrying my own pain, but seeing my parents in pain was ripping me apart inside. While my sister and I were reminded we did not cause this pain, it was knowing that because we broke our silence about what had been done to us, our parents were hurting. That knowledge was hard on us.

My parents made sure our mental health was taken care of. We attended family counseling, and Allie and I joined separate groups at the Children's Advocacy Center for abused girls. My parents also took part in a parent's support group through the Children's Advocacy Center for parents of abused children. They could relate with other parents who were experiencing similar circumstances and effects, and they were able to understand that they were not to blame for what Brian had done to Allie and me. My parents were able to connect with other parents whose child or children had been abused by family members. So often, parents of abused children feel helpless. When a child falls and scrapes her knees, parents can erase the hurt by kissing it and putting a Band-Aid on it, but not so with the pain of sexual abuse.

Through my group with other girls I realized I was not alone in my experiences and pain, and while maybe some of my best friends could not relate, these girls could. I was at a point in my life where I was not ready to discuss the details of what I went through with Brian, but group gave me a place to feel safe with my feelings. It gave me tools to deal with nightmares and flashbacks. Group also gave me a good understanding that I was not at fault for what happened, and I finally stopped blaming myself for not protecting my sister.

I found lifelong friendships through this group. I have stayed very close with some of the girls over the years, often meeting for coffee or lunch. One girl and I graduated from the same university. Our relationship is unique in that we share an understanding of what we went through as children.

The Children's Advocacy Center was the foundation of my healing. It was here that not only I first shared my story but also I was believed by the detective and the staff. I learned at the center to plant seeds in my soul that would eventually bear fruit as I grew and matured. I was no longer carrying my pain alone.

When Allie and I had left the Children's Advocacy Center after our interviews in 1998, the staff told us to pick out a stuffed animal to take home with us. The ground and shelves all the way down the hall were covered with a variety of stuffed animals. A particular bear caught my attention, so I chose it. Years later, when I was in high school, I returned as a volunteer at the Children's Advocacy Center to show my appreciation for what they did for my family and me.

From the same center that I once took a stuffed animal to comfort me, I gave my own stuffed animals that I no longer needed and knew the comfort it would bring to another hurting child. I also found a woman in Florida who donated a shipment of stuffed animals to the center for abused children.

Every year on April 30 I remember that I broke my silence, and I am filled with appreciation and gratitude for the safe place and staff at the Children's Advocacy Center. It was there I was introduced to stepping out of darkness and into the spotlight.

A year and a half later after breaking our silence and not attending any family gatherings because Brian would not apologize, my father received a phone call from his younger brother Bill saying my cousin was going to apologize. My Uncle Bill was trying to be a mediator and bring my family and Brian's family back together and resolve what had happened. He was the only one in our large extended family that would even acknowledge what my cousin did. My parents talked it over with Allie and me and asked us if we wanted to do this. They needed to know if we would be comfortable being in the same room as our cousin. I was ready to hear what he had to say and was curious to see how a man who once threatened me, terrorized me and denied ever abusing Allie and me would apologize in front of his and my parents.

On January 1, 2000, we arrived at my Uncle Bill's house. We gathered in the family room and sat in chairs and couches. Brian sat across from me with his head down. I was not sure if he was ashamed of what he did or if he could not bear to look my parents in the eye. The tension was thick and we all were uncomfortable. Uncle Bill cleared his throat. "Who wants to start?"

Brian lifted his head and looked in the direction of Allie and me. "I'm sorry for what I did to you and Allie. If I could take it all back, I would." He said no more.

I could not tell if he really meant it or if he was forced to apologize so we would go to Grandpa's seventieth surprise party the next day. My mom said a few things on forgiveness to Brian. My Uncle Scott sat silently with nothing to say and my Aunt Mary looked at my mother and expressed anger at her for sharing that her son abused Allie and me to a few mothers they both knew from a group of ladies that had children that attended school with us. Someone from that group must have confronted my Aunt about Brian abusing us for her to know. My mother had a quick response back. "When I told you Brian abused Erin and Allie you asked me to keep this between our families and not let anyone else in our extended family know what was going on. I told you I would not and behind our backs you told everyone in the family that Erin and Allie were making up lies about Brian touching them." My aunt had no response and the room fell silent but the tension between my aunt and my mom was very obvious to all of us in the room.

Uncle Bill turned to Allie and me. "Do either of you want to say anything?"

Allie shook her head. "No."

I looked at Brian. "I really hope you learned your lesson and will never hurt anyone again the way you hurt us." My uncle wanted us to say whatever we wanted so that we did not walk away and wish we had said something when we had the opportunity. At that time in my life I was not yet strong enough to say what I really wanted to say. That confrontation would come three years later.

When we got up to leave, Brian's dad hugged Allie and me, and then Brian stood in front of me. He reached out and hugged me, "I really am sorry for what I did."

My heart raced and I did not know what to think. So many questions flew through my mind: *Is he really sorry? Is this just a way for us to be part of the family again?* And I struggled with his saying he was sorry because a year and a half earlier he had held me down, sexually abused me, and threatened me not to tell.

My parents talked with us girls about our returning to the family for holidays and other celebrations and wanted to leave it up to us. In 2000 we did return because I felt I was not going to let Brian's presence take away my relationship with my other cousins and family.

The next day I saw Brian again at our grandpa's seventieth party. Not far from my mind was the memory of what had happened two years previous on Grandpa's birthday.

I knew that healing from this abuse would not take place overnight, and the journey I was beginning would alter my life forever. I was not prepared for the life-changing events it would bring.

As I faced each tragedy in my life, I learned to reach into the depth of my soul for strength and determination. Through this healing process, I discovered perseverance and resilience. I could not go into the past and use White-Out to erase any events; instead, I had to find a way to use my pain to help me heal and grow. I had to stare darkness in the face and accept that I could not change the past, but I could build a better future.

During my teen years, I was afraid to pour out the emotions I was feeling inside. Every nightmare and flashback robbed me of my peace. It would be years before I would take the steps to find growth and allow the roots of my pain to expose themselves. And even nearly a decade after breaking my silence at thirteen, I still had pain that I needed to pull from the darkness. I had to go back in time, open a door that I had tightly closed, and face again the horror of abuse that had haunted me for years.

I expose my life story because I know many others are where I have been and are searching for meaning, looking for help, and aching for peace. I believe that by sharing the ugly horror of sexual abuse, people will not be ashamed to share their journeys and in the end discover the strength they possess within themselves.

I open my soul to show the growth that results from healing. At some point, all the pain and confusion you have experienced will begin to make sense, and the pieces of your shattered life will come together. You will no longer feel like you are being pulled beneath the surface, drowning in pain and grief, gasping for air. Instead, the storm will pass, light will break through the darkness, and much of the meaning you long for will be directly in front of you.

chapter two

FINDING MY VOICE

Writing is my outlet. When I could not verbally express the pain I was enduring as a child, I opened my diaries and began to journal about it. I filled nearly a dozen diaries over the course of my childhood and teen years. I could freely release my emotions through journaling. I never allowed anyone to know the pain I was carrying.

For years I struggled with nightmares, flashbacks, and panic attacks as a result of the sexual abuse. By high school, I was having suicidal thoughts and eventually turned to self-injury as my outlet to numb the pain. It is hard to imagine why someone would inflict harm to his- or herself, but for me, when the emotional pain was too much and felt as if it was swallowing me and taking over my life, self-injury was the only way to snap me back into reality. My pain was like a tidal wave that dragged me off the shore into the middle of a sea. I struggled for many years to keep my head above water, to keep from drowning in my past. When I felt as though I had reached land, it was like I was on a deserted sandy beach, feeling isolated and afraid to share with anyone the memories that haunted me.

I learned a coping exercise while in girl's group at the Children's Advocacy Center: going to a safe place in my mind. I remember lying in the darkness as the therapist worked us through the exercise. We girls were lying on the ground and the lights were turned off. I was not really thrilled at first with the exercise because we were often abused when it was dark. The therapist told us not to be afraid. We all closed our eyes and created a safe place we could escape to whenever we needed. Mine was the beach I felt I had washed up on when I broke my silence. So whenever I felt I was not in control and something triggered my memories, the beach in my mind became my safe place. It is the same beach I envisioned when Brian held me down for hours as I tried to fight him off. And when I grew too weak to continue to struggle, I escaped mentally to the beach and told myself the sound of Brian's heavy breathing was really waves crashing on the sand.

The mental picture of this beach was like a security blanket in my healing. But deep down I knew I would one day have to leave this deserted island and face my pain. I feared the rough current that could easily pull me back under into denial, which led me to once again bury my pain. But until I embraced it, I would never move forward. I needed a life vest to keep me on the surface so I could process my trauma. My life vest, telling my story, is the greatest tool in healing.

The physical pain was always far more bearable than the emotional pain I struggled with. I had lost control of my life and I desperately wanted it back. I struggled with trusting people because the people I loved had hurt me the most. Not only had my cousin abused me, but also my relatives called my sister and me liars. Denial was much easier for them to accept than my cousin's confession. My relatives would rather brush off Brian's actions, explaining them away with "He was just a teenage boy," or "He was experimenting." He may have been only fourteen or fifteen, but that is no excuse for his twisted behavior. He was old enough to know right from wrong, and he knew what he was doing was not right. Brian used his manipulative, controlling behaviors to silence his two cousins for his own sick pleasure.

By the time I was a junior in high school, I was seeing a therapist and was taking 100 milligrams of Zoloft for depression, 50 milligrams of Trazodone to sleep at night, and 0.5 milligrams of Risperdal, which is a drug for schizophrenia or bipolar disorder. It helps the thought process. My psychiatrist hoped it would help control the nagging flashbacks that haunted me daily. I could be eating in a restaurant or taking a test in school and suddenly I would be flashing back in my head to a time I was trapped in a closet or bathroom and Brian was molesting me.

The medication helped me function and get through the day. The real work of healing would have to come from my own willpower, which I would have to discover on my own. Although a school psychologist and a private therapist gave me the tools to work through my past, I was the one in control of my happiness. And if I was ever going to move beyond my past, I would have to put the tools to work.

I felt trapped, afraid to share how I had hidden my head in a couch as Brian held me down and molested me, or locked me behind a closed door. I was too ashamed to share with anyone the disturbing things my cousin did to me. Journaling is what saved me. It was my only way to pour out my pain. While the medication helped me cope, it did not erase the memories. I continued to struggle to speak about the images of abuse that flashed in my head.

By the end of my junior year of high school, I realized my need to take back the control and power that was taken from me. The only way I would be successful was by confronting the man who took it from me.

One evening I sat in front of my computer for hours and poured years of pain into a letter to my cousin. I started with, "Brian, this letter is probably coming as a complete surprise to you, but I did not feel I should warn you, since you never warned me when you were going to use my body for your own damn pleasures." By the time I was done, I had a five-page letter. I told him that I wanted him to burn in Hell for what he had put me through and that I wondered if he truly was sorry or if he had been forced to apologize. It was late at night by the time I clicked the SEND button. I must say, other than breaking my silence, confronting the man who had torn our family apart and stolen my innocence, was the biggest step in my healing process. I sent it April 30, 2003, five years to the date my sister and I broke our silence at the advocacy center. The insight and strength I had gained helped push me forward in my healing, part of which was confronting my abuser.

To my surprise, Brian responded a few days later. It was a short response to a five-page letter, but he opened the door to communication with me.

For nearly seven months I corresponded in letters with him, trying to show him how his actions affected my life, how I struggled to find answers, and how I was finally able to work through my anger instead of causing more harm to myself.

What I really wanted to know was why he hurt my sister and me the way he did. Through my correspondence with Brian, nothing he said could justify his actions. I had to accept that I might not get all the answers I was looking for. I realized that by confronting my cousin through limited communication in letters, I became empowered. I could tell him I was no longer afraid, and I was the one in control now. For me to find my voice again, I had to confront the man who abused me. Although I may have not received justice from the law (holding my cousin responsible for his actions), I did find justice by confronting him. Doing so I broke free of the stigma and shame I carried.

Once I found my voice, I realized millions in our world suffer from sexual abuse, rape, and incest. It is a topic that people often turn away from. I wanted to help others understand they are not alone and life does get better. I wanted my words and voice to be heard by people who suffer from painful pasts, those who work with children who have been abused, and parents whose children have been sexually abused.

Soon after I confronted my cousin, shortly before I graduated high school, I turned my diaries filled with my hidden pain into a book entitled *Stolen Innocence*. It chronicled my growth from a child to a young adult, from pain and confusion to courage and forgiveness. I went from a girl struggling to survive my past to being a published author. My life story sat on bookstore shelves, inviting strangers to read the past I once could not even mumble the words to my parents about. I took a risk by going public, and thought long and hard about what might come of putting my personal life out for anyone to read. I knew before ever signing on the dotted lines of a contract that my story might further divide the relationship with my extended family.

My goal in going public was not to put my extended family to shame, or to get back at Brian for abusing my sister and me; rather, my mission was to give a face and voice to an epidemic that society stays hushed about. It took me years to be able to openly talk about my pain, and I was not suddenly going to close that door and go on pretending the abuse had never happened. Although some wished that I had.

As strange as it may sound, part of me believes that the tragic events I experienced as a child had a purpose. I came to believe that I was given a gift: to rise above pain and silence and be a face and voice for millions suffering similar pain. I could speak for others who had been silenced, for those drowning in their own pain. It was time I took off the Band-Aid hiding my dirty, disgusting, and painful wounds and expose them. I knew it was not going to be pretty.

I spent many years feeling alone in this journey, being lost in the darkness, searching for my voice, and longing to feel God's presence. I went through a stage of anger at God, feeling like He had abandoned me. It was then I felt the most alone. Years later I would realize He was there all along, guiding me toward the light at the end of the tunnel. Once I had found my faith in God again, He helped me see the big picture. I could have never predicted after suffering for so many years that I would be filled with so much joy, happiness, and appreciation for life. As the saying goes "all bad things turn around for the good." I understood the good I could do for others by speaking out.

Exposing my wound publicly also had its downside. I came across a review about me on Amazon.com from a man using the false identity of a dead family priest. But I discovered that it was really someone in my family. When I clicked on the name it took me to the reviewer's wish list, and it was there his true identity was revealed, including his full name and town. Sure enough, it was Uncle Mike. He was my first guess of who the "reviewer" was because he was known for speaking his mind, just like he did in his letter to my mom when she went to the police. The review had a bold headline that said PLEASE GET HELP.

This is a book of lies written by a disturbed young girl who, along with her mother, thought nothing of destroying her family. Do not be taken in by the other reviews, they were written by friends who do not know the true details of what happened.

Instead of allowing his rude remarks to hurt me, I ignored it and let it add fuel to my mission to not live in silence. Getting help was how I found my voice. His final sentence about reviews "written by friends who do not know the true details of what happened" was twisted. Once again, my uncle was trying to make others think he knew what went on behind closed doors when he was never present.

The truth is I am not a disturbed young girl; Mike is the disturbed old man who used the identity of a dead family priest to write the review. What a sad, pathetic man. Talk about destroying a family. Amazon .com eventually removed his review.

The sad truth of many cases of sexual abuse committed by a family member is how it divides the family. It is too deep and painful for some family members to accept, so many go into denial and often support the perpetrator, calling the victims liars. It happens more than people realize. If incest were not such a taboo topic, society would be more educated and aware of how often it happens within families. Brian was correct when he warned me about telling anyone because it would destroy our tight-knit family. It is one reason I stayed silent, and I will be the first to tell you it does destroy families, or at least changes them forever. When I think back to the day I learned my younger sister was also being abused, I told her something that will never leave me. "Our lives will change forever when our parents and relatives find out what Brian did to us. Our family will never be the same again after our secret is out." Even at the young age of thirteen, no one had to tell me that unveiling the truth about the abuse would change our family. I was unaware though how much it would significantly change our family and lives. I remember looking at my sister sitting across from me feeling so responsible for what had happened to her and how I should have told someone right after it happened the first time. The difference between then and now is that I have learned I was not at fault for our family's falling apart, my cousin was. Brian's telling me over and over that this would destroy our family put fear in me, and I think that is exactly what he intended. He wanted to scare me, his way of keeping me silent.

My sister and I could have easily made a pact that we would keep this a secret between the two of us and watch each other's back, but we did not and I praise God for giving us the courage at eleven and thirteen to rise above evil and break our silence. I cannot imagine what life would have been like had we stayed silent. How much worse would the abuse have gotten, and would it have stopped?

A lot has changed in my life since I went public with my journey, especially my relationship with my extended family, but two things have not: God has remained faithfully at my side, continually pushing me forward on this incredible journey; and the memories of the abuse I endured are all still with me.

I was once trapped in a dark cold basement storage room with no windows. Brian had lured me down there, trapping me and holding me down. The abuse lasted twenty minutes, and the entire time I could not see his face because it was so dark and he had a bunch of blankets covering us up, but I could feel his cold hands touching my skin. I will never forget the complete darkness and the cold basement. When the abuse finally ended, he ran upstairs. I crawled out from under the blankets, shaking and scared. I had to compose myself; then I struggled in the darkness to find the door to escape. I climbed upstairs, where I could see the sunlight shining under the door. I opened the door and daylight hit my face.

Finding the light at the end of the tunnel once seemed an impossible task. I often wondered if my past would haunt me the rest of my life, living in fear to share with anyone the details of what happened. Not sharing only made things worse for myself. I was keeping myself locked up inside and not recognizing the pain I was in. It was as if Brian still had control over me long after he had stopped abusing me. I stayed quiet years after breaking my silence, never going into much detail except once, when I told my story at the Children's Advocacy Center. But even then it was too difficult to tell all the details. Not only was it the fear Brian had planted in me that kept me quiet, but also I believe it is the way society views the subject of sexual abuse. It is taboo and no one wants to talk about in public.

When I found my voice and began using it, I no longer had flashbacks or nightmares. I decided that when I went away to college, I would go off all the medication I was taking for depression, anxiety, and sleep—a very dangerous decision on my part—but I felt I had moved on and did not need the meds. Thankfully, I did not have any reaction going cold turkey. (I would never advise anyone doing this unless under a doctor's orders.) I went off Zoloft, Risperdal, and Trazodone because I was not in control of what it was doing to my body. It freaked me out to be taking prescription drugs and knowing chemicals were controlling me from having nightmares and flash-backs. I wanted to be in control and not have to take pills to make it through each day. At the time I was prescribed these medications, while in my junior year of high school, I needed them. When I went away to college, I was at a new place in my life and not haunted by my past. However, it was more about me wanting to control something I still longed for even after publishing my diary.

When my diary became public, I became a keynote speaker at many conferences, fund-raisers, and community events. Since the age of nineteen, I have addressed audiences filled with students, teachers, therapists, advocates, law enforcement, judges, prosecutors, state attorneys, lawyers, media, mothers, fathers, and most important, sexual abuse survivors. Each time I step up to a podium or in front of a classroom, I pray that the importance of my message will be received and leave an everlasting mark on the listeners.

Although I may not personally know the people who hear my testimony, I do know that everyone has experienced trials. No one breezes through life without hitting bumps in the road. My hope in speaking out is that the people hearing my message, whether they are a survivor of sexual abuse or struggling with difficulties of life, can find meaning and purpose behind pain. Part of healing involves feeling your pain. Granted, it's not easy, but in the end, you will grow and push forward in life. Many in my audiences are men and women who daily work with abused children, and I want them to understand how important their work is and what an impact they have on children's lives. It takes a big heart to work with the sensitive issue of child abuse. My vision in going public has always been and always will be to end the silence and stigma of sexual abuse and help others find their voices. I took a very painful chapter in my life and transformed it into a message of hope and healing.

In May 2006, I sat in the sunroom of my parents' house while visiting with *Good Morning America*'s host Kate Snow. Cameras and cameramen surrounded us. In a nationally televised interview, I shared my journey through pain and confusion to finding my voice and forgiveness. The same camera crew followed me a few days later back to my high school where I shared my story with students, raising awareness on a topic about which they have little or no education.

At my high school graduation, I sang with the choir "You'll Never Walk Alone." The words stuck with me long after graduating. Two years later, with a crew of cameramen taping me, I walked confidently back into my high school. Where once I walked with my head staring at my feet and my headphones blasting music into my ears so I could tune out the world around me, I now walked the halls with my head held high.

I entered my former health classroom. Every day I had come to class, keeping my head on my desk, struggling to make it through each day. One day our class discussed sexual assault, and I had to sit through a video of a girl being raped. It was not easy viewing this, and I could relate to the fear the teen girl expressed in the video. Back then I would have never thought that years later I would return to the same classroom and talk on the same topic.

I greeted my past high school health teacher as the cameramen got into position to tape me telling the students my story. Through each class period, former teachers stopped in to watch. At one point Jeannette Ardell popped in to hear me speak. She was the school psychologist I had spent countless hours with, trying to sort out my past. Once too ashamed to talk about what had happened to me, with her help I found the confidence and strength to speak out. She helped me find my way out of darkness. I know God had her come into my life for a reason.

I told each class that if they did not already know someone affected by sexual abuse, at some point in their lives they would. When we finished taping, Jeannette, Allie, and I were walking the cameramen to the office to sign out. I thanked the crew for everything they did to make this segment happen. One of the cameramen turned to me. "I just want to let you know that my wife and her mother are both survivors of sexual abuse. It takes courage to do what you are doing."

Normally, this kind of information is not shared, but because I had been open and public with my own experience, it allowed this man to share with me that the love of his life had walked in my shoes. That this cameraman could openly share his personal connection to the topic made revealing my story that much more significant.

The segment aired on a Sunday morning. My parents, sister, and I gathered in the family room to watch it. Kate Snow narrated it beautifully. She was articulate and showed compassion for my story. I could not have asked for a better outcome. The music the producers picked to go with the story was moving. The pictures and home videos they used to show my childhood brought the story full circle. To see it on television was bittersweet. It was incredible how editors were able to take my life story and edit it down to a four-and-a-half-minute segment. It brought a sense of joy to me, showing me the strength I have developed over the years. Yet it seemed surreal to see my childhood play out on national television. The piece was remarkable to me and ended with a positive message on overcoming painful abuse. Near the end of the segment, Kate Snow said, "We did reach out to Erin's cousin."

In an instant I went from being emotionally overwhelmed to panicked.

My parents, sister, and I all looked at one other and said the same thing: "What do they mean they reached out to your cousin?" I had not given the producers Brian's contact information or his real name. I discovered it was copies of Brian's e-mails to me that producers took with them when they did the interview that allowed them to find out who he was because his e-mail address was his first initial and last name. One look in the white pages and they would know where to find him.

I scrambled to find the number of the producer and immediately called her but got her voice mail. I left a quick message and she returned it immediately. "Whenever we do stories, we try giving the other side an opportunity to give their side."

"Did you ever speak to Brian?"

"No. We tried for a long time to talk to your aunt. At first she wouldn't return any of our calls. Eventually, I got through to her. She was not happy to talk to me. I asked her if I could talk to Brian. He was never home when we called and all your aunt said was that she'd tell him. But I never heard from Brian."

Of course the producer never did hear back from him. That would have been a total shock if he did willingly call back and have something to say. Had I known the producers wanted to speak with him I would have sent an e-mail to Brian explaining the interview I was doing on *Good Morning America* and see if he would talk to producers.

We did not know what to expect from our extended family once they learned of my appearance on national television. In the past, the family never wanted to acknowledge the abuse. Would they continue to deny it? The following few weeks after the segment on *Good Morning America* aired would once again change the course of my family's relationship with my extended family.

Just days after my appearance on *Good Morning America*, we received an unexpected phone call from my dad's brother John saying he was contacting an attorney to sue me for slander because I had talked about him on my blog and it could put his job in jeopardy. However, what I had put in my blog was information he had already made public on television in an interview with the news station. In all honesty, my blog entry was harsh because I had been hurt by actions he had taken years earlier. My uncle tried to use his authority as a police officer to get the charges against Brian dropped after he confessed. Detective Deguilio told our mother about it after my cousin confessed, and he told me when I spoke with him in 2003. We also learned that this same uncle told someone that what Brian did was a big nothing and that it was blown out of proportion. In my blog, I simply expressed my feelings about his choices, and it upset him; he believed he had been slandered.

I believe Uncle John's threat was a scare tactic to try to get me to quit talking. Many in my extended family would like to point the finger at me, accusing me of destroying the family by going public. But the truth is there never would be a story to tell had Brian never molested his two cousins.

We could still take civil action against Brian because the statute of limitations in Illinois is not up. Brian was charged with only three counts of abuse when he actually could be held accountable for more. When my sister and I were interviewed, we reported a total of thirteen accounts of sexual abuse. All we needed at the time of the investigation was enough to ensure Brian got the mandated help he needed. Taking me to court would only do them more damage, hurting Brian, whom they have been trying to protect all these years. It would make his simple, peaceful life a nightmare and add fuel to my fire in bringing awareness to sexual abuse. Honestly, I would not want to hurt Brian, for I am at peace in my heart with him. I hope the threats of a lawsuit were only out of anger because I know my relatives would regret that decision if they ever pursued it. What I feel many of my relatives cannot see is my purpose in speaking out about this silent epidemic. They think, "This kind of stuff stays in the family," "You do not share family secrets with the world," or, "Erin, why do you have to continue to regurgitate something that happened over a decade ago?" I want other survivors to have the opportunity to reach the same peace I found in my heart toward my abuser. I believe sharing my story will help them.

A few days after my uncle left this message threatening to sue, my dad's younger brother Bill showed up at my parents' lake house in Wisconsin. "Dan, can you come down to my house? Dad and I want to talk to you."

I watched as my dad and his brother got into the car and drove away. My mother and I sat on the front porch and prayed. We put whatever was about to take place in God's hands. My mother and I sat on the front porch waiting for his return home. He was gone for over an hour. When he came back he told us what had happened.

"Your grandpa was quite upset with your appearances on television. He was also angry because you went to the high school and spoke where Brian's younger brother is attending."

I was shocked that Grandpa was so upset. "Dad, when I spoke to the high school classes, I made sure to avoid any that Brian's younger brother was in. Grandpa never reached out to Allie or me. We were molested by Brian, yet Grandpa supports the molester of his granddaughters. It just doesn't make sense."

My father stood leaning against the garage as my mother and I sat listening to him. "Grandpa's generation did not discuss sexual abuse; therefore, he thinks it is not to be discussed even if it happened in our own family. Erin we know the truth of what happened and the truth will set you free."

What I think my relatives do not understand is that what happened in our family is not uncommon. Millions of families have been impacted by sexual abuse. There are an estimated 60 million survivors of childhood sexual abuse in America according to the United States Department of Health and Human Services.

My dad looked down at my mom and I then took a deep breath. "I did more yelling than my dad did."

I have never heard my dad raise his voice in my entire life, so I knew he was standing up for his daughters and Grandpa must have said some hurtful things about us.

"What did Uncle Bill say? Was he agreeing with Grandpa?"

"He did not take sides he was pretty quiet the whole time just listening. Erin, I tried to explain to my brother and dad that your speaking to audiences across the country has turned this negative event in your life into something positive. Your grandpa said he did not mind you going to other states, but he said it was the national attention that was upsetting the family. He told me that if you do not stop, they would seek legal action and take you to court."

My grandpa couldn't care less if a bunch of strangers heard my story, but he feared I would be recognized on national television. All that mattered to him and the rest of the family was myself being recognized and their being embarrassed. I could not believe my relatives would take me to court if I continued to speak out on raising awareness about an epidemic that they did not want to acknowledge. I lived through this horror, and no one can tell me I have to stay quiet.

"I have been silenced long enough, and I will not allow that family to silence me again. I will continue to speak out and make sure my voice is heard."

When I thought I couldn't be hurt any more by my family, my dad delivered the ultimate injury. "Your grandpa believes you and Allie are just as sexually active as Brian, and you were willingly experimenting and engaging in sexual acts with him."

My mouth dropped open. "How dare him! How dare him! How. Dare. Him!" That is all I needed to hear to determine never to want a relationship with my grandpa again. My mother and I stood in disbelief. I felt as if I was going to get sick. I could not believe this man whom I had called Grandpa all my life and had spent nearly all my holidays with said this. Anger came over me, and a part of me wanted to march straight down to my grandparent's home and tell my grandfather how out of line he was.

But then it was as if God whispered in my ear not to allow my grandpa's disrespectful remarks to consume me. I wondered if my grandpa really meant what he said or if he said it out of anger. I did not want to believe he could believe such a thing.

I could tell by the look on Dad's face that he was still keeping things from me, protecting me from being hurt anymore. I sat there in disbelief just staring off. My dad put his arm around me. "Erin we know the truth. I looked grandpa in the eyes and let him know how out of line he was for saying something so sick and twisted like that. I love you girls and will not tolerate anyone talking like that about you."

Mother said, "We do not need them; we have each other. Do not let their nonsense get to your head. Give it to God he will take care of it."

My sisters found out later what happened and were just as angry. Allie wanted to confront our grandpa. Both sisters agreed our grandpa's remarks were out of line and knew a relationship with him was over.

But I needed to confront my grandma. My sister Allie was very upset and needed to also talk to Grandma. I called her and asked if she could go to breakfast with Allie and me. She said she would have to look at her plans and would let me know the following week. When the weekend rolled around, I called her to see if we could go out then. She asked if we could just come down to her house and talk. I think she feared confrontation in a public place. I did not like the idea of going anywhere near my grandpa, but if going to her house was my only way of speaking to her, then I would do it.

When Allie and I arrived, my grandpa was on the deck. Just seeing him made me angry. I wanted to look at him and say, "How dare you," but instead he pointed to the screened-in porch and said, "She is waiting in there."

We did not say a word, Allie and I just walked right past him. Grandma was sitting at the table waiting for us. We both sat down and began some small talk. We knew we were about to get into a discussion she would rather avoid. I needed to quit pretending everything was normal. "Now, for the reason we came over. I did *Good Morning America* to put a face and voice on an epidemic in our world, not to bad-mouth Brian."

Grandma looked at both of us. Tears filled her eyes. "I love both you girls, but you hurt a lot of people by what you did."

I think she was including my sister as hurting people because Allie appeared with me on the *Montel Williams Show* a few months earlier on a show called "Taking Back My Life." We talked about what we went through with Brian and how we found our voices and broke our silence.

I was taken aback by Grandma's comment that we had hurt a lot of people by speaking out but no statement about Brian hurting us by what he did. It was like she only wanted to see one side, blinding herself to the truth. She had no idea the pain Allie and I had endured, and honestly, I do not think she wanted to know. She mentioned how *Good Morning America* producers called my aunt's house, trying to get ahold of Brian and the two younger boys were answering the phone. She then brought up how it was wrong of me to go into the high school and speak where Brian's younger brother is a student. What she did not know is that Brian's younger brother had already come to Allie a year earlier when he heard about what his brother did and asked if it was true. She told him yes but that we had forgiven Brian. He thanked Allie for making sense of everything because he said he never understood how we went from always seeing one another to suddenly never getting together besides at holidays. He said he knew something had happened but did not know what.

Then Grandma started blaming the Children's Advocacy Center. "They had nothing to do with my appearance on television. Grandma, did you even see the piece on *Good Morning America*?"

"No, I didn't want to see it."

I explained to her my purpose for going on it and how I had been able to extend forgiveness to Brian.

She then mentioned my blog and suddenly began bringing up everything I ever wrote, and telling me how upsetting it was for her to read.

I looked at her. "Have you read the nasty things Uncle Mike wrote about me on the Internet?"

"No."

"Well, maybe you should. What he wrote was unpleasant because much of it was untrue."

"I have a copy of every blog you ever wrote."

I found it interesting to note how much interest my relatives took in my work and read what I wrote. What bothered me was seeing how upset my grandma was over a few things I wrote on my blog, yet never once in eight years showed any anger over Brian's sexually abusing Allie and me. She was so upset about a blog that maybe a total of six people read yet had no compassion for her granddaughters who had suffered the physical and emotional pains of sexual abuse and whose lives were changed forever. The two cannot even be compared, yet when someone is in denial about what happened, they cannot perceive what is true. It seemed too hard for her to let her mind go there and believe her grandson could do such terrible things.

"I published my book to help people break their silence and educate society on sexual abuse."

"You are a talented girl. You should use your talent to write children's books." She paused and clasped her hands. "I trust Brian with all of my grandchildren."

I just bit my lip and let her continue.

"What he did was wrong, but you make it sound like some thirty-year-old man did this to you. He was just a teenager."

Her statement was like a slap in the face. I wanted to scream! *How can you make excuses for his behavior just because he was a teenager? I* thought to myself. In other words, if he had robbed a bank or killed an innocent person, it would be okay because he was just a teenager not some thirty-year-old man.

My blood boiled and my ears felt like they were on fire. I took a deep breath, leaned toward Grandma, and fixed my gaze on her. "Do you know the details of what we went through? Do you know the pain we have suffered?" I was about to add, "Do you know what was happening on Christmas, Thanksgiving, or when you were in the room next door sleeping?" But she interrupted me when she broke down crying.

"Grandma, have you read my book?"

She dabbed her eyes. "I've seen it."

"Do you know the details of what we went through?"

"No, and I do not want to know!"

I turned my head from looking directly at her and stared off into the yard, shaking my head and thinking to myself, *Of course you do not want to know.* The words played over and over in my head. *She is in complete denial and there is no changing her.* Her statements to my sister and me confirmed what we already knew: She stands behind my cousin and supports him. Even at that, it was hard to believe what our grandma said.

I had nothing left to say to my grandma. I just wanted to get up, walk away, and never look back because what she said really hurt. But she had more to say.

"We are all getting older now. Grandpa and I are getting older and you grandkids are growing up. It is time we all start doing holidays on our own. We can get together and do our own thing with you girls."

Allie and I both picked up on what she meant: she was kicking us out of the family. She tried to make it sound like everyone would be spending the holidays apart, but we knew that would not happen. I realized there was no hope in changing her views, but I felt good standing up to her and not pretending that everything is peachy, like we have for so many years.

Allie and I got up from our seats and made our way outside. Grandma followed us as we walked toward the driveway. "So from now on, holidays will be spent different; we will do our own thing together."

Allie and I continued down the driveway and out onto the road. The whole way home we talked over everything Grandma had said. We both could not believe the excuses she made for Brian because of his age. I could have easily told Grandma everything he did to Allie and me, but I did not. My grandma had made a choice. She made it very clear to us that she does not want to know what we endured as children and stands behind Brian. She also made another choice: to lose her relationship with her granddaughters.

When we arrived home, our parents were sitting at the table in the kitchen waiting for us. They both just stared at us expectantly, waiting for one of us to speak. I slipped off my shoes and dropped onto a chair. "Well, we have been kicked out of the family."

"We knew that was coming," Mom said.

We sat down and told them all that had happened.

My dad looked at both Allie and me. "I am so proud of you girls."

We all agreed we were glad they did not want us at holidays anymore and that it was time we started doing our own things as a family. We believed we would only grow stronger as a family from this and it was a healthy new direction for us to move forward with our lives.

After my extended family threatened to sue me and my grandmother told my sister and I we were not welcome at family get-togethers, I knew that no longer having them in my life was a decision that should have been made a long time ago. I could not change the way they were reacting. Over the next several months I would come to learn more about the people I once called family.

Several years have passed since our relationship with our extended family was cut off. It is too painful to even think of ever talking to my grandpa again without his first apologizing for his inappropriate remarks to my father about my sister and me. Sometimes my grandparents show up unexpectedly at our house, acting as though nothing ever happened, or they send Christmas presents or birthday cards. My father eventually had to explain to Grandma that we did not want the Christmas presents, for they were painful reminders from the grandparents who had disowned us. The only gift I will accept from my grandparents is an apology for their words and actions, which would show accountability instead of denial. I hope one day they will consider this. Unfortunately, it appears they believe they owe us no apology.

Once we no longer spent holidays with my relatives, they celebrated the first Christmas without us at Brian's parents' house, where much of the abuse my sister and I endured happened. Prior to our being kicked out, each family took turns hosting the Christmas Eve celebration. After the abuse was revealed, neither Brian's parents nor mine hosted the holiday get-together. I am still close with one of my cousins, who told me my family is the only one not there. They did not kick out the perpetrator but the two cousins he abused. It just does not make any sense, and honestly, I do not know if my parents, sisters, and I will ever understand.

The people I once called family may not admit this, but each holiday that passes, my family's absence is felt. My dad said to me one morning in 2008, ten years after breaking my silence, "I often wonder if Brian realizes his actions are the reason we are not in the family and that he is the reason why this family is divided." I know without a doubt Brian understands that five chairs are missing from the Thanksgiving or Christmas dinner table because of his actions, not mine.

Recently, we have heard that more family members are saying that Brian was forced into a confession and my sister and I are liars. Brian confessed to the police, he wrote letters admitting his wrongdoing, and he asked for forgiveness, yet the family still calls my sister and me liars. This is an example of just how strong denial is.

Someone recently told me they were having lunch with my grandparents and the entire conversation was about me, my book, and my family. She informed me that my grandma told her she read my book *Stolen Innocence*. Something my grandma would not admit to Allie and me when we talked with her in 2006. My grandma went on to tell this person that Brian was just a kid. I cannot comprehend how my grandma can say she read my book knowing the details I describe going through and still continue to make excuses for Brian's behavior. This was not a five-year-old boy who happened to look up his cousin's shirt in curiosity, but a teenager who used physical force to sexually assault his cousins over and over again and used threats to silence them. Which leaves me with only one conclusion: that my grandma must have skipped over the diary entries in my book of the detailed abuse I experienced. My grandma went on to tell this person that she thought Children's Advocacy Centers were suppose to help children and that they obviously failed to help me. Both my grandparents mentioned that my mother, sisters, and I were keeping our dad from having a relationship with his parents. My dad is a grown man who can make his own decisions and he made the decision to stand by his wife and daughters because he knows the truth.

When my sisters and I traveled out of state in November 2006, we met up with second and third cousins. While at dinner one of them mentioned that one of our aunts was visiting them and brought up how my book is all a lie and the police forced Brian into confessing something he did not do. This second cousin stood up for us, telling my aunt she was out of line and it is because of people like her that children stay silent. It was refreshing to know other family members supported us.

I wish I could put the memories flashing through my head onto a video then gather the family, sit them down, hit the PLAY button, and show them the horror my sister and I experienced. Maybe then they would understand what a teenage boy is capable of.

I have to let go of the pain and anger my extended family has caused me and move on. I am a forgiving person, but I feel too much damage has been done to go back and repair the relationship. Some major family therapy would be needed to fix that mess. I can forgive them for their ignorance, harsh remarks, and decisions to support the man who hurt my family, but the sting remains.

My aunts, uncles, and grandparents believe that if anyone should apologize for airing the family's dirty laundry, it is me. They blame me for destroying the family, not Brian. But the truth is I would have never gone on national television, filled a diary with the horror I endured, and spoken to thousands had Brian not hurt my sister and me. I can understand my relatives being hurt by me going public, and I can say from the bottom of my heart that I am sorry for any pain resulting from this. But my intentions in speaking out were all good. From day one, when I broke my silence, I never wanted Brian to be punished for his actions; rather, I wanted him to get counseling. My parents could have easily turned Brian's life upside down by taking our case to trial, which would have landed him in prison. But they were looking to Brian's best interest—getting him help. Revenge has never been our intention, nor is it now when I publicly speak about what he did to Allie and me.

Brian's actions have consequences, and while the justice system may have failed my sister and me by not requiring our cousin to get the proper therapy, I was not going to sit back and allow people I once cared about keep me silent. I struggled for many years before I found my voice and decided to use it not to give my family a bad image but to give others strength to use their voices to show people that the devastation of sexual abuse and incest goes much deeper then just the act of abuse.

In life we lose people we love in tragic circumstances like automobile accidents, fires, cancer, natural disasters, and disease. The pain and grief can be overwhelming. Family and friends come together to mourn their loss and celebrate the life of the person who died. I have experienced a different kind of loss. I have lost an entire extended family of aunts, uncles, cousins, and grandparents. I grew up in this extended family and I hold many cherished happy memories. My parents, sisters, and I lost an entire family to a tragedy that many will not talk about, much less recognize. It is the ugly truth about incest. There is no way around it: the majority of the time it destroys and divides families.

Maybe you are going through this same thing right now. You or your child has been victimized and your family members are supporting the perpetrator because he is part of the family. The truth is Brian needs my grandparent's and other extended family member's support where I do not. I have an unwavering amount of strength and can walk with my head held high knowing I have done no wrong. He is the one who must struggle with his choices; choices that follow him daily.

Over the course of the past few years, I have been asked if I speak to Brian at all. I do not. After my last e-mail in November 2003, telling him I forgive him, I asked him if he would be willing to sit down and speak to me in person. Doing so would help me heal. I wanted to know why he abused me and ask him if it happened to him. Seeing him at holidays before we were kicked out of the family gatherings was a reminder of being abused. Now I felt strong enough to face him and replace that monster who had abused me with a man who was trying to show me he had changed.

chapter three

NOVEMBER 22, 2003

Honestly, Erin, I care *that you are healthy and that you are moving on with your life, but I do not think I will ever really want to have a conversation with you in front of everyone or just you and me alone. It is just not a smart thing for me to do. Yeah, you might be thinking that, hey, everyone will be looking at us and everyone will be like, hey, they are having a conversation and the whole family is good now, but in reality they will be thinking what the hell is Brian doing, is he at it again? Is he trying to manipulate her? This might disappoint you or upset you, but when I responded to your e-mails I never had any intentions to talk to you in person and I still do not. If it happens by accident or someday I feel comfortable enough then fine, but for now, I will not. The feeling I get when I think about what I did is sickness. Complete ignorance, selfishness, and curiosity had taken me over and really that is how I let it happen. I did not have any control over an urge of sexuality and I wanted so desperately to know what it was. That is the only way I can explain my actions. There is no more reason than that.*

Brian

This e-mail is all I have to go on as an explanation about why Brian abused my sister and me. It may be the only explanation I will ever get: an urge of sexuality, curiosity, ignorance, and selfishness. He may or may not have been abused as a child. I might never know, but I have received the closure I longed for by confronting my cousin and forgiving him. I am glad he can express to me that when he thinks about what he did, he feels sick. At least he recognizes his behavior was sick. His actions were evil and twisted and any explanation would be hard to understand. I liked this statement "but in reality they will be thinking what the hell is Brian doing, is he at it again? Is he trying to manipulate her?" He is trying to explain how he thinks our family would react if he was speaking to me. I honestly believe they are in so much denial they would not look at it as his manipulating me because they believe either it never happened or it was blown out of proportion. Brian, however, is aware of his actions. He knows what he did, and he remembers clearly how he manipulated my sister and me. I respect Brian's decision not to speak to me and understand his fear of what people might think of him. Also, the police warned him to have no contact with my sister and me. Whether it was an urge of sexuality or his being a victim of sexual abuse, I have found peace with the answers Brian gave.

Brian's look of a crazed man taken over by evil is burned forever into my memory. It was as if a force had taken over his mind and body and found pleasure in watching me struggle, cry, and suffer. I strongly believe Satan had an influence on my cousin's behavior. When I cried and my cousin laughed, I felt I was staring Satan in the eyes. If evil did not exist, the force behind my cousin's actions would never have happened. Satan causes people to sin, and people can be forgiven of their sins as long as they admit their mistakes.

If I cannot forgive Brian, then I allow evil to win. Satan tries to destroy our lives through acts of evil. Each time Brian wrote me in his letters that he destroyed my life, I would always tell him that he did not destroy my life; he destroyed his own. Because of my incredible faith and ability to forgive, I was able to put Satan in his place and show him that he messed with the wrong person. Satan used my cousin to try to ruin my life. Little did he realize my relationship with my heavenly Father is much greater than anything he could throw at me, and God is blessing my life in many ways. I pray that Satan will leave my cousin alone and not tempt him into hurting anyone else.

I will always love my grandparents no matter what they say about me and pray not only for them but for my entire extended family. Though many relatives look at me in disgust and many may never speak another word to me in this lifetime, I will keep them in my prayers, hoping God will give them insight and allow them to see my purpose in sharing my story. If they would let go of the anger they have toward me for going public, they could see the blessing of forgiveness that transpired through letters with my cousin. Instead of telling others what happened to Allie and me was a bunch of lies or that Brian was forced into a confession, I pray that they accept his admission to his mistakes and quit making excuses for his behavior.

I will never know what my life would have turned out to be had my cousin never abused my sister and me. I have often wondered how different our lives would be right now. I am sure I would have chapters filled from over the years of happy memories with my relatives and I might still be looking up to my cousin Brian as a brother figure. Instead, I can only ask, "What if? What if Brian had never abused us?" I cannot change the past, but I can accept what happened. Though saddened by the decisions of many people I love, I continue to move forward on this journey.

In life we make choices. Every day in junior high morning announcements ended with, "Make it a great day or not; the choice is yours." I made a choice to break my silence and forgive. Just as I made the choice to go public with my personal life, my relatives have made their own choices about the circumstances we have faced. I do not judge them, for that is not my place. Instead, I turn it over to God and leave it in His hands. If God does not heal this family in this lifetime, I believe in my heart these very same people will one day walk in green pastures alongside my parents, sisters, and me in Heaven, where the anger, bitterness, and pain from this lifetime will be replaced with God's grace and peace. I guess we will just have to wait and see.

chapter four

PINKY PROMISE

My past has helped me become who I am today. While the abuse I endured had a huge impact on the person I am, many other events in my life shaped me. I have learned how certain things can trigger memories from different times of my childhood. Some are happy memories, others are painful.

People often ask me what it is like to have my life story an open book for anyone to pick up and read. The truth is the girl who grew up to be the outspoken woman I am today, traveling America offering inspiration to others to break their silence, withheld a dark chapter from view—a piece of my past never revealed to anyone, not even my diary.

Though I matured into a strong, determined, courageous, and resilient woman, the little girl within me was trapped behind a door I never thought I would return to. It is the chapter of my life that did not haunt me until I went to college.

I thought moving away to college would allow me to escape the memories of my fragile childhood. I was happy in college, but I faced a new reality. I discovered that my past follows me wherever I go, and it eventually surfaced.

I knew in my heart that one day, when I was strong enough, I would have to visit this chapter of my life and release it. It would take falling into an unhealthy coping habit that would lead me to breaking my silence once again. The very first part in healing is shattering the silence, so when I went public with my story, I figured I was safe. The nightmares and flashbacks had ended, and I felt I had gained a sense of control back and found peace. I got to a place of forgiveness, which I believed was one of the toughest things to accomplish.

I had found working out was a healthy outlet for my frustration, stress, and anger. Working out every day at my college recreation center during my freshman year made me feel good inside and focused. What had been a healthy coping habit soon turned unhealthy because I began to obsess over the labels on everything I was eating. How many calories was I consuming? How much fat was I putting into my body? Before long I was more concerned about the number of calories I burned. I could not walk through the grocery store without checking how many calories were in each serving of the food I was about to purchase.

Working out became a routine for me. It was like taking a shower—something I did every day without thinking about it. I could not give myself a break from it. Then I started making extra trips up and down the nine flights of stairs in the dorm. I would intentionally forget things so I had to make the extra trips to burn more calories.

I was falling back in time and slipping into unhealthy coping habits. This time I was obsessing over my body image and becoming anorexic. I felt I had mastered my past, but unbidden memories threatened to defeat me. I wanted to do anything that would slam the door on them.

What had begun as a healthy way of life turned into a problem, which I tried to deny. Obsessing over my appearance, I pushed myself to work out harder each day. I avoided looking at myself in the mirror because my image haunted me.

Previously I had never even thought about fat, calories, and carbohydrates. Now, food was my way of having control, something that had been taken from me when I was abused.

Being away at college made it easier for me to hide my eating disorder from my family. I never used the bus to get to any of my classes; rather, I always walked. even in the midst of winter. I was the only one crazy enough to walk to class when the wind chill was minus 4 degrees.

When I went home during college breaks, my parents would get on my case, saying I was too skinny and had lost too much weight. I brushed them off, assuring them that I ate. I told them that my weight loss was from working out and being in shape for once. I seemed to eat normally around them, trying not to draw attention to my eating disorder. I told myself I would work out more when I got back to school and burn off any weight I gained while at home.

I struggled through three years of college, trying to bury a deep pain by focusing on my body image and putting all my energy into working out. My attention was on how I looked on the outside and not what I was avoiding deep inside.

I began my freshmen year of college in the fall of 2004 at a healthy weight of 122 pounds. I dropped down to 105 pounds by my sophomore year and it only got worse. By December 2007, during my senior year, I stepped on the scale and the number 92 appeared. I tried wearing baggy clothes and sweatshirts so people would not notice what I was trying to hide. Friends at college who had known about my excessive working out and dieting were becoming concerned, warning me that I was destroying my body. I was burning twelve hundred calories a day at the gym by doing the StairMaster, elliptical, and running laps around the track. The machines state how many calories you burn, and I would rarely stop until I at least reached my daily goal of twelve hundred. Some days I would work out for two hours, other days four hours.

I struggled with giving myself a day off from working out. What was it I was trying to avoid? What was I running from? I saw a deep pain in my heart each time I stared at myself in the mirror. It was not my reflection I was running from but what I held deep inside me. My mother often told my sister and me that if we held on to the abuse our cousin did to us and never told anyone, it would one day haunt us.

If I was ever going to live a fulfilled life, I had to allow this chapter of my life to come to the surface and be revealed. I could not allow myself to graduate with a degree in social work and go out and help others while still holding on to my own demons. So like I did when I was younger, keeping a journal of my experiences of being molested, I decided to return to my childhood and write about a sensitive and tragic event that occurred years before Brian molested me.

Writing has been a very therapeutic and healing process for me. It also shows that I am human and not perfect. I believed if I would open myself up to what I had kept buried, it would help me overcome my obsession with wanting to be thin. In recording my thoughts and perceptions of this past event, I hoped that I could face my pain, embrace it, let it out, then be released from my eating disorder. My mother was right. Holding on to or denying dark secrets won't make them go away; they will always come back to haunt you. Giving voice to them serves a purpose.

The roller coaster of emotions I am feeling right now as I am about to knock down a door I have kept closed for so many years makes me feel vulnerable. I believe using writing to work through pain has helped me recognize that while I am pushing for others to speak out, I still have a little girl silenced inside me who is now ready to be heard. Instead of sharing about moving forward, this chapter of my life is taking you back down a road to my childhood.

Going off to school is a new step in every kid's life. School is a place to find lifelong friends. In September 1990, I made that step forward into a new experience that I would continue for eighteen years. I can still remember that first day of kindergarten, eagerly sitting outside the door to my new classroom and waiting with my mom and younger sister. Right away I got involved with Daisy Girl Scouts, where I met one of my brand-new friends, an African American girl named Ashley. Although we were not in the same kindergarten classroom, we became instant friends. I learned she lived just up the street and around the corner from me. Often after Girl Scouts we would play together at the park near our houses, or I would go over to her house to play with her huge dollhouse she had in her bedroom.

We regularly played at each other's house. She lived with her mother, little brother, and uncle. From what I remember, her father seemed to be missing from her life. My first experience with sleepovers was at Ashley's house. I was excited and felt grown-up at five years old to spend my first night away from my parents. Ashley and I stayed up playing with her dollhouse, coloring, and watching Disney movies. We hoped we would be in the same first grade classroom so that we could sit next to each other and play together at recess.

One Friday night in the spring toward the end of kindergarten, my mom dropped me off at Ashley's house for an overnight. Like so many nights before, we played house, colored, and watched movies. I slept on the floor in a sleeping bag while Ashley slept in her own bed. I woke to the sound of Ashley's door opening. A man came into the room—Ashley's uncle. I figured he was checking to make sure we had gone to bed, just like my parents would do after we were put to bed at home. But he came in and closed the door after him. Ashley lay fast asleep as her uncle knelt by me and pulled a blanket up toward my head. He sat next to the sleeping bag where I lay pretending to be asleep. Then he began pulling his fingers through my hair. I squirmed and looked up at him, trying to figure out what he was doing. He put his index finger on his mouth as a sign to tell me to stay quiet. I remember it so well because it was something my teacher used when students were talking and should not be. He then whispered that I was a beautiful little girl. I was too young to understand something terrible was about to take place. Instead, I just stared at him, confused. I thought about sitting up, thinking he wanted to talk to me. I was a little chatterbox, so talking to grownups was easy for me.

He went from raking his fingers through the back of my hair to rubbing my back in a circular motion. I did not say a word. I just lay in silence, continuing to stare at him, wondering why he was rubbing my back. Without warning, he pushed me from my side onto my back. His cold hands slipped into the sleeping bag as he began pulling my pajama pants down. I felt the tips of his cold fingers touching my legs. He then placed his hand over the top of my underwear. I did not know what he was doing, but it felt wrong. He slipped his hands under my underwear and immediately tried forcing his finger inside me. I immediately starting kicking and telling him he was hurting me, something I would say years later to a cousin doing the same exact thing. He pulled his hand out and whispered for me not to tell anyone or next time he would make sure it hurt a lot more and he would not stop.

It happened so fast. I tried to make sense of it, but I was six years old, so young and innocent.

The next thing I remember is waking up the next morning to Ashley's poking my cheek. As we walked down the hallway and into the kitchen, I got a strange feeling inside. We sat down to eat Lucky Charms and watch cartoons. My mom picked me up soon after having breakfast. I never said a word to anyone about what Ashley's uncle did.

I feared spending the night at Ashley's again. We continued to see each other at Girl Scouts, and she was always asking for me to come over and play. When I did go over, I preferred to stay outside and play. We spent a great deal of time at the park near our houses, we often road our bikes around the neighborhood, or sat on her driveway with sidewalk chalk. She had a small backyard, but we often built forts back there, creating our own childlike fantasies of make-believe. I think repressing what happened is what saved me in my childhood. I was able to use my imagination to create happy events, but a little girl can carry only so much on her own.

Ashley asked me to spend the night along with another friend of hers. By now we were in first grade and in the same classroom. I asked Ashley if we could all sleep on the ground in her bedroom that night. I wanted to feel protected, and having the other girls on the floor with me gave me a sense that her uncle could not hurt me again.

We stayed up late that night doing things little girls do: playing with dolls and watching a movie. The night ended with us all on her bedroom floor. We giggled a lot that night, lying in the dark with light shining in from the streetlight. We made hand shadows on her bedroom walls. The door to her bedroom was closed, but suddenly we heard the knob turning. We looked up and saw her uncle standing in the doorway. He stepped into the bedroom and closed the door.

Shadows of little girls no longer danced on the wall but rather the shadow of a large man. I pulled the covers over my head, afraid to look at him. He did not go to me right away but instead went toward Ashley and her other friend. I could not see what was going on but felt him right next to me. The other girl told him to stop and Ashley asked him to leave. I kept the blankets pulled over my head. I rolled over onto my side with my back facing them, curling into a ball, hoping to fall asleep and not remember any of it. But the sound of the other girl scared me. She begged him to stop. Then she began to cry, and it made him stop whatever he was doing to her.

He made his way toward me.

I felt his hand on my back just like before. I thought he was going to flip me over, but instead he sat on my legs and started putting his hands down the back of my pajama pants. I lay motionless as he began to slide his body up and down on me. The weight of him sitting on me was crushing me, but I did not fight back. I lay frozen in fear, trapped in my own little body with the weight of a large sick man on top of me, overpowering me. I could not see his face because my head was facing into the carpet, and he had my pillow on top of my head. I turned my head, facing Ashley. He went up and down on me in a humping manner. I felt a soft round object go between my thighs.

The last thing I remember is staring at Ashley—an emotionless blank look on her face. Eventually, she turned her head and looked the other way.

The next morning was as if nothing had ever happened. We girls never mentioned anything. It was as if it was all a bad dream, but Ashley's other friend called her mom early to come pick her up and take her home. Ashley's uncle was not around. I stared at his closed bedroom door, afraid he would open it. I did not know if he was sleeping or working, but I feared he would be coming home or getting up soon. I also called my mom to come pick me up and take me home.

Ashley's mom was in the kitchen when I called my mom. Ashley begged me to stay, but I told her I wanted to go home. Even at six years old, I sensed she was afraid to be with him. But I was just a little girl and scared to stay. I told her we would go to the park later, that way we both could get away.

A part of me felt bad leaving her when my mom pulled into the driveway to take me home. Ashley stood staring out the front door, waving good-bye, when her uncle appeared behind her, watching us pull out. His image terrified me, a cold blank stare watching my mom back out of the driveway. I wanted to cry right there, but I hid my pain and acted strong.

Hiding my pain and acting strong, afraid to cry and show my tears I struggle with all this years later.

This night has lived inside me for years. I can close my eyes and go back to Ashley's bedroom, lying on the floor with our hands in the air making shadows and laughing, then see him suddenly standing there. It is scary how much I can remember from such a young age, but then again, the trauma I experienced was horrific.

The school officials did not believe either Ashley or I were emotionally ready for first grade. So instead of putting us in a regular first-grade classroom with twenty-four other students, they put us with eleven students in a classroom called extended readiness first grade. We would spend the year there and then repeat first grade in a regular classroom the following year. Only three girls were in the class, and Ashley and I were two of them.

Statistics say one in three girls will be sexually abused before their eighteenth birthday, and little did anyone know, in a classroom of three girls, two were being sexually abused.

I am not sure why Ashley was held back, because of trauma or behavioral problems like I had, but I have no doubt that both of us being molested had something to do with it. Over the next several years, I asked my mother why I had been held back, hoping she could give me a good reason but knowing deep inside the real one. All she has ever told me was that I was not emotionally ready for first grade.

Though I hid the act of the sexual abuse, its effects came out in other ways. I acted out in school. I knew no other way to express the pain other than through anger and acting out. As far as I know, after three little girls were sexually abused, nothing ever came out. I never saw Ashley's friend again, but I have often wondered if she broke her silence, repressed the memory, or thought it was a bad dream.

I feared spending the night at Ashley's and would go over there to play only during the day, thinking I would be safer. A part of me felt like I was the only friend Ashley had, and I could not just walk away from my best friend.

I feared her uncle breaking into my house. I often lay in bed at night in my house, afraid he would break in through my bedroom windows or I imagined him coming out of my two closets toward me. I was terrified. I even feared running out of my room, thinking he might be under my bed, grab my feet, and pull me under. The abuse had taken its toll on me. I was acting out regularly, not knowing how to express my anger.

One time Ashley and I went to the park near our homes. We were alone and I pulled out empty beer bottles from the garbage can and smashed them on the street. It was my way of releasing the pain and anger I was holding in. A woman who lived next to the park ran over when she heard the sounds of shattering glass, but I was able to escape on my little pink bike. Another time after being abused by Ashley's uncle, I went to the park later that day alone and smashed the beer bottles again, this time on the sidewalk. Unfortunately, the same lady saw who I was. Her daughter was in Girl Scouts with me and knew where I lived. I ran home, but this time I did not have my little pink bike to escape on, so the lady followed me. I ran directly to the backyard and pretended as if I had been playing in the sandbox the entire time. I buried my feet in the sand, just wanting to disappear. Ten minutes later my mom found me in the backyard, grabbed me by the arm, and said she'd had enough of my bad behavior. Then she marched me to the front of the house, handed me a broom and dustpan, and told me I could not come home until all the glass was off the sidewalk and in the garbage can. She stared at me and demanded, "Why are you doing this?" I did not answer and instead just turned and walked toward the park.

Once back at the park, as I swept up all the glass and dumped it back into the garbage can, I was screaming inside that acting out was my only way to express the pain I had endured. I looked up and saw the mother who had told my mom what I had done standing on the sidewalk by her house with her daughter. They watched as I dumped the slivers of glass into the garbage can. The sun was setting, which meant the streetlights would go on, and a rule in our home was we always had to be home by the time the streetlights went on. I quickly finished sweeping, then made my way home.

At school both Ashley and I, along with two other girls, were in a group who met once a week with the school social worker. We would sit in her office and talk about school, family, friends, and life in general. One of the girls was also named Erin. She was moving to New York and I so badly wanted to go with her and escape. On a day that the group met with the social worker, Ashley did not arrive at school. I came so close to telling the school social worker what her uncle was doing to us, but I was too scared to tell and afraid someone would contact him, then he would come after me. Oh, how I wish I could jump back in time and allow myself to speak out.

Another time I spent the night at Ashley's, she and I slept together in her bed. It did not stop her uncle. I woke to his picking me up and bringing me into his bedroom. He first laid me on the floor in his bedroom, but then lifted me up and put me on his bed. I can still remember there being a ton of clothes on the floor. His room was very messy, mostly with clothes everywhere. I remember staring at the sheets of his bed and although it was fairly dark, I could make out they were dark blue. He pulled down my pants and put his face by my crotch. When he was all done he whispered, "You can go back to bed now." I did not say anything but just got up and walked back into Ashley's room. He always acted fast when he sexually abused me, like he was in a rush or was afraid of getting caught. I remember crawling back into bed and holding on to

Ashley's arm as she lay fast asleep. The last thing I remember was being afraid he was going to come back for me.

On a first-grade report card dated November 1991, my teacher put my attitude toward her and others as "inconsistent" and noted that I "can be quite disrespectful and become quite angry." She continued by saying that she and my parents needed to work together with me to help me learn to express myself respectfully and to cooperate. Little did I know that in just two months from then, my anger would reach a new level.

Before I go any further, I need to warn you that if you are not in a good place in your life you might want to close this book now and pick it up later when you are better able to handle what I am about to share. It is from my heart, but it is graphic.

In January 1992, just before my seventh birthday, I had gone over to Ashley's to play. I had not spent the night since her uncle took me into his bedroom. On some occasions I felt safe at her house because her mom would be around. When her mom was there, he never tried anything. In fact, he always stayed away when her mom was around. I always hoped that her mom would be home.

On this particular day, I had spent the afternoon playing with Ashley at her house. When I arrived, we went to her bedroom and began playing with her big dollhouse. Ashley eventually left to use the bathroom.

The images playing out before my mind's eye are haunting, as if it happened yesterday. While Ashley was using the bathroom, her uncle came out of his bedroom and walked into her room. I did not notice him come in until I heard the door close. I thought it was Ashley and looked up from behind the dollhouse to say something to her. But then I saw him standing there.

Ashley's mom was not home and I feared what he might do. He had locked the door—locking Ashley out and me in. I was so scared I thought I might pee my pants. I sat on the floor with two dolls in my hands as her uncle told me to get up onto the bed. I did as he said, afraid of what might happen if I did not obey him. With my head facing the floor, afraid to look at him, I walked to the edge of the bed.

I was angry, but my anger turned to terror. I began to cry, and he told me not to cry. I was even more scared because it was the middle of the day and the sunlight shone brightly in Ashley's room. I was used to being in darkness and not having to see everything. I trembled inside, fearing to look into the eyes of this monster.

As I sat on the edge of the bed with my legs hanging over, he cupped my chin in his hand and lifted my head, forcing me to look up at him. It was as if he wanted to see the fear in my eyes. I feel like it was his way of terrorizing me by making me look up at him.

He moved quickly, lifting my legs up so I was completely on the bed. I was sitting up and he leaned me back and tried to take off my jeans, but I began kicking and telling him to stop. All my squirming and moving made it difficult for him. For a little girl I put up a good fight. I was not going down without a struggle. I called out for Ashley, who was at her bedroom door, trying to get in. I heard her turning the knob, shaking and rattling it. Then she stopped. I hoped she was trying to find something to unlock the door. While her uncle pulled my pants down, I heard her once again messing with the doorknob.

He got my pants down just above the knee. Between my squeezing my legs together and my jeans being up high, he was having a difficult time, but eventually he got my pants down around my ankles. He tried to take them off, but he could not get them around my shoes.

My shoelaces would always come untied, so my dad had taught me how to double knot them. When Ashley's uncle could not untie the shoes, he tried to yank them off, but I continued to struggle and kick. He succeeded in getting my shoes off and told me if I did not lie still he would tie my arms to Ashley's bed. Then he added, "You would not want me to do that, would you?" I got really scared and began to cry. He told me crying is for babies. I feared being tied up. I looked behind me and saw how he could tie me up. His eyes pierced me with a cold look as he told me that he would be gentle as long as I stayed quiet.

I did not know what to call what he put me through that day, but it was the most extreme pain of my life. He pulled down his own pants past his knees. He then lay his entire body on me, his weight crushing me. I panicked and told him I could not breathe. He used one hand to hold himself up and put the other between my legs.

I lay terrified, staring at the ceiling and gripping the sheets as a piercing pain ripped through me. I cried out. Then I began to scream. He covered my mouth with his hand to silence me and warned me to stay quiet or he would make it much worse. His hands were large. I repeated over and over, "I want my mommy and daddy." Tears streamed down my cheeks. He groaned and made a humming noise. I thought the noises were to ignore my crying. He grabbed my hand at one point and put it down on his penis.

I cried the entire time because it was the worst pain I had ever felt, like I was being ripped in half.

I stared up at him, but his face was blurry because of all my tears. The whites of his eyes are burned into my memory. I cannot get those eyes out of my head. He kept pushing my legs apart and using his hands to keep my legs open.

When he got what he wanted, he got up. He pulled my underwear and pants up, opened the door, and walked out of the room, acting like nothing had happened.

I went through unimaginable horror. Horror that I have carried alone all these years. I can clearly remember the details of that day even sixteen years later. I can never erase from my memory the sights or sounds of that traumatic event. Just a few weeks shy of being seven years old, I was raped. It has taken me sixteen years to say those words. At that tender age I did not know the word, much less what it meant.

I was so cold I shivered and my teeth chattered. Although it was January, my shivering had to do with being scared. I lay there for a few minutes before I was able to finally get up. I was so scared I just wanted to run home. I wondered where Ashley had gone. When I walked out of Ashley's bedroom, I saw her sitting outside the bedroom door, holding a hanger she had used to try to unlock the door. She asked me if I was okay. I told her I just wanted to go home.

I headed toward the front door and grabbed my purple coat and walked down her driveway. Every step was painful. She caught up to me as I turned the corner to my street. She said, "My uncle says we cannot tell anyone or else my mom will lose our house."

The thought of my friend losing her house scared me. As I wiped away my tears, I told her I would not tell anyone. She looked at me and said, "You have to pinky promise you will not tell anyone what he did."

I took her pinky and locked it with mine, promising I would not tell.

It was a long, lonely, cold walk home. I felt like I could not walk straight because I was in so much pain, and it still felt like he was inside me. When I got home I was still trembling and scared. My mom was out of town, so my mom's friend was over watching us, since dad was working.

I went to the bathroom because it felt like I had peed my pants on my walk home, but instead I saw blood in my underwear. I was so scared. It seemed like I sat on that toilet for an hour. Thoughts raced through my head as I sat there. I thought I would be in trouble. I wondered if I should tell my mom's friend the man hurt me "down there," but I did not trust her so I stayed silent. I put on new underwear and hid the other ones in the garbage can in the garage so no one would find them.

At six-years-old I was ashamed of what happened, and I tried to hide the truth. I went to bed that night waking to nightmares of my running on Ashley's street and through the other houses, trying to get away from her uncle. It was the same dream I would continue to have for years. In the end he always grabbed me.

The physical pain from the rape itself was awful. I sat on the toilet the next morning afraid to go to the bathroom. It felt as if someone had stabbed me.

The rape took a huge toll on me. Ashley's uncle said something to me that made me keep my guard up against allowing my emotions to overwhelm me. When I began to cry because of being scared and afraid, he said, "You're not a baby; only babies cry." Of all the emotions I struggled with over the years, crying was the most difficult. If I cried, no matter the situation, I felt ashamed and weak. It was like having a wall blocking the stream of tears that so badly wanted to pour out of me.

I already had trouble expressing my anger at six, and through everything I had endured it was just a matter of time before I exploded, spewing all my anger and rage.

A few days after the rape, my older sister, Caitlin, and I were dropped off at my grandparents. For an hour we sat and played one game after another of Uno. Soon my grandma left to go out with a friend and it was just grandpa, my sister, and me. I was sitting on the arm of the couch when my sister pushed me back, making me fall onto the couch. She began pulling my shoes off. I began screaming for her to stop. It was exactly what Ashley's uncle had done. This innocent act of my sister triggered a meltdown, and I cried and yelled for her to give me my shoes.

The entire time my grandpa sat in his chair, reading the paper. I'd had enough of her teasing me and running around with my shoes, so I made two fists and began banging on the glass door that led to the backyard. I kept staring at my grandpa, who was focused on reading his newspaper. I banged louder, then started screaming, trying desperately to get his attention so that he would do something.

My grandpa had finally had enough. He chased my sister into the back of the house and then into the bathroom, where she fell into the bathtub. He retrieved my shoes, but right about then the glass door I had been pounding on shattered. My left hand went through it, and panicked, I quickly pulled it back. I stared at the now glassless opening, afraid I was going to be in big trouble.

Little did I know I had a deep gash in my wrist, though I saw the blood pouring down my arm. As I made my way into the kitchen, I ran into my grandpa and sister coming back to return my shoes. I did not say a word but held up my wrist. Evidently, I was going into a state of shock. My grandpa acted immediately and grabbed a towel, wrapping it around my wrist to stop the bleeding. He put me in the van and rushed me to the emergency room.

Once in the hospital, doctors and nurses surrounded me, poking and pricking me with needles. I stared at my sister, who sat with both our coats in her hand. Each time I lifted my wrist, which was completely cut open, she covered her face.

From where I lay in the emergency room, I had a perfect view of the elevator my dad would walk through. I begged the doctors to tell him I was asleep; I still was afraid I was going to be in trouble for breaking the window. Then I saw the elevator doors open and my dad walked toward me. He had a look any parent would have rushing to see their child in a hospital. But I was calm. For losing so much blood and having such a deep cut into my wrist, it did not hurt. The rape had hurt far worse than this. When he walked up to my side, I told him how sorry I was for breaking the window. He told me the window could be replaced but my life could not.

The doctors stabilized me enough so that I could sleep. They would operate in the morning. That night my dad slept on a tiny couch next to my bed. I got very little sleep because the nurse seemed to come in every two minutes to take my temperature and vital signs. The surgery took place the next day. When I woke, I was in a hospital room with my dad lying on a couch next to me. The surgeon told me I was lucky to be alive. He said I could have easily bled to death, or had the cut gone a little deeper, it could have been fatal. I left the hospital with a bright pink cast on my arm. When I returned home I received a huge envelope containing get-well cards that my classmates, including Ashley, had made while I was in the hospital. My teacher had written a message on the front.

I returned to school two days later. All my classmates signed my cast. Suddenly I had appointments to see the school psychologist and social worker. All had heard about my anger exploding and putting my hand through the window. They were trying to figure out where the anger was coming from and teach me healthy ways of dealing with it. Before going into the office to see them, I started acting out and pouting against the wall in the hallway, saying I was not going to the office. Regardless, they got me behind closed doors. I threw myself crying onto the floor. They told me that this behavior would not fix the problem and that I needed to express my anger in a more appropriate way. They continued to ask me to sit in the chair, but I refused. I wanted to stay on the floor and hide my face from anyone seeing my tears. If only they had the least bit of an idea about what horror I was holding on to.

By the time I had my cast removed, I had a nice scar on my wrist. The doctor said it would fade over the years, but it would never totally fade.

Though I didn't know it at the time, the school officials had devised an annual goal for me. Sixteen years later I stumbled upon the documents stored away in my parent's crawl space. Once I read the fine print, it made sense why I had been evaluated. The annual goal stated that I had to develop more appropriate ways to manage and resolve my anger. It included a list of objectives. While going through these old documents, I found a huge red folder containing tons of pictures I drew in school. I found pictures of rainbows, snow-men, a picture I dedicated to my friends and wrote all their names out, a picture of the hospital where I had my surgery. Then I came across one that hit me hard. On one side of a folded piece of paper were orange, yellow, and blue scribbles. When I opened it, I could not believe my eyes. It was an image of a little girl with a bow in her hair, lying on a bed and a large man leaning over her with his hands at her pants. Two black horns were on top of this man's head. Around the image were dark black circles I assume represent night-time. In childish handwriting I had written below the picture, "I am going to sleep go awey I want mom."

I could not believe what I was seeing, and it had been there for anyone to see. Why was I finding these sixteen years later stored away in my parent's crawl space? A few years earlier I had come across that same folder but took out only one or two pictures as my mom and I laughed at how I drew people when I was little. Had we continued to look at all of the papers, we would have discovered it. I believe God was behind me on that one. Knowing I was dealing with too much from the abuse I suffered because of Brian, He had deter-mined a time and place for this discovery. It was not the time then for my parents to learn the devastating truth of my early childhood.

That was not the only picture I found; the next one was even more disturbing. In one corner of the picture stood a house and two peo-ple playing at a park. The other side of the paper was a drawing of a door and a bed. On the bed lay a little girl with her mouth open and a man with his face in her crotch. It was a very disturbing image. Under the picture I had printed, "I like to play at Ashly hose not wen her ucle home." These were heartbreaking images I had drawn of myself being abused. I dreaded looking at any more pictures, afraid of what I might see.

I found it hard to believe no one ever saw these. I had to have been drawing them in class. I hid my diary when my cousin was sexually abusing me, I did not hide this artwork at ages six and seven. The images brought it all back to me. I knew sixteen years later exactly what was going on in these drawings. If someone had taken a closer look at my artwork, the reason for my anger and acting out were right there.

My next goal in the school's assessment was to develop a positive self-concept and self-image. Coming across this in my life at twenty-two I could not help but laugh. The goal the school was trying to help me achieve at age seven was the same one I was only now trying to achieve as a college student sixteen years later. While I have a strong self-concept of who I am and the strengths I have, I am aware my self-image is poor, resulting in an eating disorder that developed from never working through the abuse from my early childhood and longing for the control that was taken from me at such a young age.

Over the course of the next year, I advanced to a regular level of first grade. I refused to spend any time over at Ashley's house but continued to hang out with her when we had recess or went to Girl Scouts. If we did not play at the park, we played at my house, or we rode our bicycles on the tennis court.

During this second year of first grade I met a brand-new friend named Shannon. She lived a street down from Ashley's. I feared each time I went over to Shannon's that Ashley would see me and want me to come over and play. The first time Shannon asked me to a sleepover, I was terrified. I feared all adult men would hurt me the way Ashley's uncle had. When Shannon promised we would lock her bedroom door, I told her I would stay overnight. I began spending every day after school with Shannon, and as long as she locked her bedroom door at night, I would sleep over. We would spend a great deal of time in her bedroom playing with her pet hamster, doing arts and crafts, or watching television. The first time Shannon's father knocked on the bedroom door in the middle of the night, I panicked. Shannon got up to unlock the door, and I was afraid he was coming to hurt us. But he only wanted to say good-bye. He was a newspaper deliveryman and left at four in the morning. Most parents say good-bye to their children before leaving for work. Her father just had to do it while she was still asleep. He often came in while she was sleeping and kissed her good-bye without waking her, but since we had the door locked, he had to knock and wake us.

I did fairly well in my first year in a regular first grade, but I still struggled with my anger. Like most children who do not forget a horrifying event, my memories stayed with me and I continued to have nightmares—always of Ashley's uncle chasing me through the court he lived in as I ran through the neighbors' homes, or his breaking into my house. Though I avoided Ashley's uncle by not going over to her house, or staying outside if I went there, for the next year I was still haunted by what happened. In October 1992, I received an invitation to Ashley's eighth birthday party. I had not been inside her house in a long time. It was an overnight, but I thought I would be safe surrounded by a bunch of other girls. We played games, ate birthday cake, and stayed up late like any little girls do at a slumber party. Her mom would be home, so I felt safe. I did not see her uncle almost the whole night and her mom eventually went to bed. Before getting into our sleeping bags in the family room, I went into the bathroom to use the toilet before going to bed. Ashley's uncle had his door slightly open and must have seen me go into the bathroom.

I feared coming out, with good reason. I heard what sounded like someone standing outside the bathroom. I waited a little longer until I felt it was safe enough to go back into the family room. When I opened the door, there he stood. At first I froze, then tried making a dash for the family room, but he stopped me, pushed me into the bathroom, and closed the door. Once again he tapped the tip of his nose with his index finger, indicating for me to stay silent. He said nothing, just stared at me. Then he assaulted me. He spread my legs apart. I tried to push his head away. When my cousin Brian trapped me in his parent's bathroom and pushed me up against the wall in their shower, it had brought me back to being seven and remembering Ashley's birthday sleepover.

I stared at myself in the mirror as this grown man was going up my nightgown. I wondered, Why couldn't Ashley's mom walk in on him doing this and catch him? Ever since this, I have hated looking at myself in mirrors. During my interview at the Children's Advocacy Center when I talked about the abuse with my cousin, I stared the entire time into the large mirror, seeing in my mind's eye myself as a little girl.

When it was over I climbed over some girls and crawled under my sleeping bag and silently cried into my bear. I brought my brown teddy bear everywhere with me. I was attached to it. It brought me security. It was the bear my mom bought me for my seventh birthday, just weeks after I cut my wrist while breaking the glass door. It was the teddy bear that brought me comfort when I slept through the nightmares I endured over the years.

I did not understand why Ashley's uncle picked me out of all the girls, but now as an adult I understand. Maybe the fewer victims he had, the less chance he had of being caught. He knew I had not said anything in more than a year and a half and might have assumed I would stay silent. He could have easily been assaulting many of Ashley's friends and they were being threatened just as much as I was.

After a few minutes, Ashley's uncle came into the living room, and I panicked. But instead of talking to any of us, he went out the front door and left. All night I feared his coming back and hurting me. We never saw him again that night.

I was a very outspoken little girl, always asking questions and very honest. If I could tell my first grade teacher she had gray hair or long toenails, I honestly had no problem speaking my mind. But I was silent about being raped and molested. So I could easily see how other little girls could be silenced under this man's power and control. I avoided Ashley's house the rest of the school year.

Ashley and I were in the same second-grade classroom, and we had the same teacher from our first year in first grade, Mrs. Johnson. Ashley daily asked me to play at her house, and I felt horrible telling her no because deep down, even at eight, I knew the horrors she endured at home. A part of me has carried guilt at not being able to help her, but I was just a kid who was carrying my own dark secret. Ashley knew I was afraid and knew why I stayed away. I knew what she carried within her, so it was hard to know that she came to school each day smiling given what she was really hiding. I feel as if I were born with an old soul, and even at eight I was concerned about my best friend's well-being.

My saving grace came when I learned we were moving to a different neighborhood. I would no longer be living in fear. I was going to be able to bury the past and attend a new school with new friends.

A month before I moved away, while outside cleaning the chalkboard erasers, the fire alarms went off. I ran back inside the building and ran into Ashley, who was returning from the bathroom. We kids were lined up single file then escorted down a hall to the outside. After standing outside for what seemed like forever, the fire department gave the all clear after inspecting the school. It was evident that a student had pulled the fire alarms. What I learned later that day shocked me. Ashley had been called into the office after we were all brought back inside. She was suspected of setting off the alarm, since she was out of class when it was pulled. She admitted to pulling the alarm and was suspended from school. Her mother had to come to school and speak with the principal, then she took Ashley home. I believe Ashley pulled the fire alarm as a cry for help. Did she do it out of curiosity, or was it a cry for help? I might never know her motive. I moved shortly after that and buried that chapter of my life until now.

I never stepped foot inside my old elementary school again until junior high, when some male students had put a mixture of chemicals in the toilets, causing several people to get violently sick and needing to be rushed to the hospital. We were escorted to the elementary school down the street, which happened to be the one where I began my school years and met Ashley. It was not easy walking back into the school that held so many troubling memories for me.

Right after I moved during second grade, my behavior improved in my new school, and you would have never known I was the little girl who acted out and had so many emotional and behavioral problems. No doubt when I got to my new home and started attending a new school, I had repressed the abuse and tried forgetting that part of my childhood. I transferred over to the new school with an IEP (Individual Education Plan), but my behavior problems were not an issue. After a year of seeing the school social worker, I no longer needed his services or an IEP. Looking back, it is very telling that something was not correct in my life if you compare my behavior at the first school with my behavior at the new school. It was like two completely different kids. In fact, if you were to see photos of me at ages two, three, or four, I always had a huge smile on my face. But view pictures of me at ages six and seven, or eight, and that smiling girl is replaced with one who looks lost and confused, who constantly sucked her two middle fingers.

It would be three more years before I would see Ashley again. In 1996, while out riding my bike with my sister, we decided to ride to our old neighborhood. It was a five-minute bike ride across the busy intersection and back into our old neighborhood. I was drawn to want to see Ashley because just a month earlier my cousin Brian had abused me for the first time, and it brought back the night I woke to Ashley's uncle coming into the bedroom and abusing me the first time. I felt this urge to see her because I thought I had abandoned my best friend when she needed me the most. Walking up her front door was not easy. Her mother answered and was surprised to see me. She told me it happened to be Ashley's birthday—another reminder of what had happened on her birthday years earlier. Ashley came to the door and invited my sister and me in. I went back to her bedroom, which hadn't changed much. I was very nervous and afraid I would see her uncle and panic. I laughed and pointed at the dollhouse still in her bedroom.

I sat on her bed, and an overwhelming sense of sadness came over me. I remembered too clearly what occurred on that bed, and I needed to get out. I asked Ashley if she had time to go hang out at the park like old days. She said she would love to, so we made our way to the park and played for an hour, just like we did when we were younger. We walked her home and I wished her a happy birthday. Thankfully, I never saw her uncle while I was there.

I found it ironic that moving away was my saving grace from her uncle, but it only brought me that much closer to my next perpetrator. We lived down a path from my aunt and uncle and the cousin who would abuse me for nearly two years. I often wonder, and will never know, if we had never moved, would my cousin still have abused us. I think it would have happened only when we were together at holidays because I would not have stopped regularly to watch my young cousins had I still lived in my old neighborhood. Moving allowed me to escape one sick man but encounter another one in my own family.

A few more years would pass before I crossed paths again with Ashley. I had just left gym class in junior high when I saw Ashley coming down the hall. We walked past each other, then we both stopped, turned, and looked at each other. We spent a long moment of silence just staring at each other before either of us said anything. Everything seemed to go in slow motion as other students rushed around us to get to their next classes. I locked eyes with my childhood friend, one who had made me pinky promise I would never tell anyone what her uncle had done. It was hard seeing her. Once again it brought back our horrible childhood secrets, reminding me of the silence we both shared. She was a year ahead of me in school, which I did not understand because we had both been held back. We began talking and she explained that her mom fixed it so that she was able to skip a grade when she was in elementary school, and she was now at the right grade level for her age. As strange as it was seeing her unexpectedly, I began passing her in the halls frequently, and each time I was filled with an empty, sad feeling. Once Ashley graduated junior high, I never saw her again. I assumed she moved away because had she stayed in the house she grew up in, she would have gone to the same high school with me.

While away at college, I had tried to track her down, wanting to finally discuss the painful events that took place in our childhoods, but my searches always led at to dead ends. I wonder if she ever told anyone.

Many questions lingered about whatever happened to her uncle. Where was he now? How many young girls' lives did he destroy? Was he ever caught? Does he have children of his own he is hurting? I would like to tell that monster many things. I cannot call him a man; he is a dirty piece of scum. No one deserves to be called a man after raping innocent kids and robbing so much from them.

I figured I would have no chance of getting justice, but to my surprise I learned through my own investigation and networking that Illinois law allows victims of sexual abuse to get civil action up to ten years after their eighteenth birthday. As for criminal action, a victim has twenty years after their eighteenth birthday. So even though it happened when I was just a little girl I still have until I am thirty-eight to seek justice, which is plenty of time to hunt down this monster and show him what happens to men who rape little girls. At the same time, I know how the justice system works and am all too aware that because of the lack of evidence, many survivors of abuse do not get the justice they deserve. I have no physical evidence; it is my word against his. My only hope is that Ashley and the other young girls from that night come forward. I always prayed that Ashley would tell what happened, which would lead the authorities to me. I could only imagine what horrors she has lived through over the years. I hoped she had broken her silence and this scum was already behind bars.

I have found a huge amount of strength and courage over the years. Confronting my cousin helped me grow and take back the power in my life. I am ready to put the rest of the pieces of my life together, and confronting Ashley's uncle, standing up to him, and threatening to put him in his place will show a man who thought he was powerful just how pathetic he really is. I would ask him how he lives with himself and show him I am no longer a little girl afraid of his power. I would love for him to see the woman I turned into and to realize he messed with the wrong girl. Hopefully, one day Ashley's uncle will catch me speaking on national television, and he will run and hide realizing I am stronger then the evil he showed me.

The next step was to do something I put off for a very long time: sit my parents down together and share with them this part of my life. It breaks my heart and brings tears to my eyes that I have kept this from them all this time. It will hurt them terribly when they find out what happened. Seeing their pain will be the hardest part because I remember all too well their reaction when they learned of the abuse from our cousin. It will not be easy sharing something I have carried alone for sixteen years. I know they will support me 100 percent, the same way they have in the past.

No parent wants this kind of news, especially after having lived through one nightmare already. Many times I came so close to telling them, but the words were not there or the timing was not right. I do, however, know it will put a lot of pieces together for them on why I am the person I am: Why I struggle with certain things in my life; why I act certain ways; why I never ventured too far away from home, fearing the world around me; and why I am so passionate about speaking out. There is so much about the person I have become because of the pain I endured from six to seven and then again from eleven to thirteen.

My parents have been my rock in life, giving me the best a child could ask for while growing up. Though I did endure a lot of painful events, my parents helped make my childhood magical. If you knew nothing about me and I handed you a photo album of my childhood, you would see just how magical it was. One picture would show my sisters and me opening boxes of presents on Christmas Eve. Another picture would show me at age five at the pumpkin patch, picking out pumpkins with my sisters. Then there is the photo of our camping trips to the sand dunes at ages six and seven. Pictures of an eight-year-old out on snowmobile trails would make you smile. When I see these pictures of me with the Christmas tree, at the pumpkin patch, camping, or on the snowmobile, I immediately recall fond memories from my childhood. The same way photos bring me back to reliving the happy days of my childhood, images burned into my memory remind me of the two men who stole my innocence, destroying a part of my childhood. I am the only one who carries the snapshots in my mind of the horror I experienced. I can only describe in words what I see with my mind's eye: being held down on a bed or locked in a bathroom, and much of the time in darkness.

My mother stayed home to raise her three daughters, teaching us good morals and values. She was involved in our lives: helped out at school, volunteered in PTA, chaperoned field trips, and always took extra good care of us when we were sick. My father has been the hardest working man I have ever met. He started a business that is now very successful, raised a family, and put a roof over our heads. He has always put his daughters and wife first. At different times while my sisters and I were young, my parents opened their arms to three foster babies from the inner city of Chicago, who would live with us during different times.

Had my parents known I was being assaulted at such a young age, I am sure they would have wanted this man dead. A part of me wonders how they would have responded had they learned of the abuse when it first happened. It has been hard enough for me to carry my pain for as long as I have, and it is going to be even harder to see how it affects my parents. I have struggled throughout life, wanting to take care of others, but never taking care of myself the way I should. Avoiding the pain I carry. Now I wanted to protect and shield my parents of the pain for what they could not see.

I have a big heart for others. I came into the world wanting to take away others' pain and bring them happiness. From a young age I reached out to the elderly in senior centers and to the children I babysat. Even at the young age of six, I knew my best friend needed me. I was all she had and did my best to be by her side until my pain became too great.

It has not been easy writing this chapter. I had to dig up memories and feelings from the past that I have kept hidden all these years—even as I stood before large audiences. I had no intentions of sharing this chapter of my life publicly, but then I realized I had nothing to be ashamed of and that by sharing it, others might find the strength to shatter their silence. I often had to stop writing because I became overwhelmed with emotion. I had to step outside and walk around my college campus with my dog, Chance. Writing this chapter has been a giant step forward in my healing. I have met so many incredible people by speaking out. Many have poured out their souls to me, sharing their heartbreaking pasts and asking me how I stand strong with so much courage.

The truth is I was swallowed up in so much pain for such a long time that writing and public speaking has allowed me to release that pain. It is my own therapeutic process of healing. I cannot begin to tell you how many times, as I stood before an audience or looked into a camera as it was rolling, that I have wanted to break my silence on my young childhood abuse. I honestly felt I would keep this chapter of my life private and carry it with me forever. But I also believe that there is a time and place for everything. I had to ask myself, Is it doing any good to keep quiet about the abuse? It has caused me to have body image issues resulting in an eating disorder that is very hard to overcome. Just when I think I am back on the healthy path and at a healthy weight, I relapse into old habits of obsessing about my image and feeling disgusted with my body. It was much easier to break myself of my self-injury habit I struggled with in high school. I also had the support of a therapist and a school psychologist who helped me find healthy ways of coping.

There is a part of me that is still trying to scrub away the dirty feelings I have about my body, a body that has been taken advantage of, used and abused by forces of evil. While I have found happiness and wake each day thankful to be alive, I know I am not perfect and the struggles I face are part of the healing process. I often put too much pressure on myself by denying myself the right to break down and be weak. I feel I should be strong for others. But I know that if I do not take care of myself, I might not be healthy enough to continue to spread my message of courage and hope. Writing this chapter has opened my eyes to the realization that I need to take care of myself before trying to take on the world and help others who are struggling to overcome their pain. So part of my self-care involves being open and honest, with others and myself. I will lean on God to get me through this next phase of my life, knowing my strong faith in God has always pulled me through the tough times.

Although I have traveled down dark roads at a very young age, I have come as far as I have because I am not alone. God has been holding my hand through it all. When I could not find my way through the darkness, He carried me. When I cried myself to sleep, He rocked me in His arms. When I doubted He was even there, He forgave me. He has given me the strength to share this chapter of my life with you. As Friedrich Nietzsche said, "That which does not kill us makes us stronger." And as it says in the Bible, "I can do all things through Him who strengthens me" (Phil. 4:13). I live and breathe and rise above the evil through the strength and courage He has given. The little girl inside me has found her voice. I am no longer the little girl who cannot express her anger.

At six years old, I shattered beer bottles in the street and a glass window as my only way to scream out the pain I was hiding inside. I have gained control over another aspect of my life and opened a door. The child I once was is no longer hiding under the covers in the dark. I will show her the way to the light at the end of the tunnel and the path toward healing.

chapter five

SHATTERING SILENCE

I made a promise to the little girl I once was: when the time was right, I would give her the opportunity to be heard so she would no longer be silenced and the pieces of her shattered childhood would become whole again. On September 13, 2007, I followed my morning routine: I awoke, got ready for class, had my morning cup of coffee, and walked my dog, Chance. Then I headed to my social work class, followed by my psychology class. After my last class I headed home. I had planned this trip home to do interviews around my hometown and Chicago at different agencies for my internship in the spring. I also planned it as the weekend I would share with my parents the secret I had kept from them for over sixteen years.

The entire four-hour drive home I prayed, asking God to give me the strength to break this news to my parents. Some may wonder why my cousin's actions haunted me so much yet the abuse I suffered at six was just now surfacing. Others may think that a lot of my pain from my teen years is rooted in the abuse of my early age. During my high school years I thought only once of the rape, and even then it was not haunting me. It just crossed my mind one day while sitting in the school psychologist's office when I thought of bringing it up to her. But because it didn't haunt me as Brian's abuse had, I decided against telling her or anyone else. I believed I was safer keeping to myself, afraid of what might come of it if I did tell. The main difference between the two events was that I was constantly around Brian, but when I moved away from the old neighborhood, I never crossed paths with my rapist again.

I have said many times that I am speaking out for all the little children who are being abused and have been silenced, yet I still had a little girl trapped inside who had not found her voice or received justice. I used to have a recurring nightmare of my cousin Brian abusing me in his parent's bedroom while a six-year-old me stood or sat in a corner of the room crying and watching. The same week I ran into my friend Ashley in eighth grade, the memory of the rape returned, and it began to eat away at me. That same week I sat down with my mom and told her I had something I needed to talk to her about. For hours she tried to get me to open up and tell her. I wanted so badly to tell her about my pinky promise, but I just could not get up the courage. So after nearly two hours, I just told her that I was feeling really depressed. Once again avoiding what was really on my mind allowed me to bury the secret. It did not haunt me again until my freshman year of college. I knew now that I could not let another day slip by without telling my parents.

I went out to dinner with both my parents. I felt sharing the news with them at dinner was not appropriate. I wanted to do it at home. Yet like so many times in my life, I came so close to telling them but feared the pain they might endure if I told them. I did not want them to feel they had failed to protect me from evil. By the time we got home, my dad stayed up only ten minutes before going to bed. My intentions were to tell them together, but at the same time I had put it in God's hands and knew whatever happened was meant to be.

My mom and I got to talking. "Your grandfather has been showing up to see your dad every weekend at our house in Wisconsin."

I clenched my fists. "That really bothers me, Mom. How is it that he has the nerve to show up at our house after what he said about Allie and me?" Some of my earliest childhood memories are of being raped and molested, and the last thing I wanted in my life was a man who did not support me.

I struggled to know how to share my early abuse with my mom. She herself was a survivor of sexual abuse by numerous people she trusted as a child, including family members. I focused on my well-being and reminded myself not to take on any blame for how the news might affect her. I believed my mother was at a much better place in her life because it had been nine years since she learned what Brian had done to her daughters. She had come to her own place of healing and forgiveness for him.

My mother went to great lengths as a stay-at-home mom to give my sisters and me so many amazing childhood memories with her creative ability. Her number one goal in raising three girls was to protect them from someone hurting them. Yet even she could not break the cycle of sexual abuse continuing from her generation to mine. One reason I suppressed much of my pain as a result of Brian's abuse was because of how much it affected my parents. I hated seeing my mom hurting. I did not work through it until I just could no longer hide the pain.

My father has had to endure heartache at being alienated from his parents and most of his siblings who choose to support Brian. When I have tried to put myself in my father's shoes by imagining that one of my sisters' sons abused my child and my parents and sisters supported my nephew, I got a feeling of abandonment. Although my father does a good job of hiding most of his emotions, I know the pain he feels is deep. Sometimes I feel he pushes himself, over-working, just to avoid feeling the pain. Some days I wish I could fix it, giving him back the family he knew before his children were sexually abused. I know I cannot do that, but I do know that someday my sisters and I will bless my father and mother with grandchildren, bringing a new kind of joy into their lives. I have no doubt they will make excellent grandparents.

As I continued to talk with my mom, the tears of the child I have kept silenced inside me began streaming down my face. I have never cried in front of my mom about the abuse I endured. I always hid my tears. I hated for her to see me hurting so I always hid the aching pain behind closed doors. As I sat with my mom that night, I remembered how sixteen years prior I put on my winter coat and made that chilly painful walk home after being raped.

Mom assumed I was crying because I was upset about how much my grandparents had hurt me. She did most of the talking as I sat and listened and cried, trying to decide when the time would be right. As I sat there listening to Mom talk, I thought, "You have no clue what I'm about to tell you. God, give me the strength to do what I must. I cannot carry this burden another day."

I was a jumble of nerves. I couldn't look my mom in the eye but instead focused on the wall. Thoughts raced through my mind: Is the time right? How will she react? What will Dad say?

I moved to the couch across from Mom. She looked at me and patted my knee. "Well, I need to get to bed. I've got to work in the morning." She pointed to the television she had turned on earlier. "Do you want the TV on?"

I looked down to my clasped hands resting on my lap. "No, you can turn it off."

She aimed the remote and the TV clicked off. "Are you going to bed, too?"

I shook my head. "No."

She was silent. I could feel her eyes resting on me. "Is everything okay?"

"No, Mom, it is not."

She came toward me and knelt by my side. "What is it; is it me?"

"No." I flicked a tear away.

"Is it your dad?"

"No, you and dad have not done anything."

She paused, then asked, "Is it you?"

My throat locked up. I couldn't utter a sound. All I could do was nod my head.

"Is it something horrible?" Her voice was tight. I knew she was worried.

I hung my head. "Yes."

She gently held my arms, trying to get me to look her in the face. But I turned my head, afraid for her to see the pain that I was sure was evident in my eyes. I felt again the shame that had filled me as an abused little girl.

"Erin, I want you to finish this sentence. Mom, I need to tell you. . . . "

All my rehearsed speeches failed me. I blurted out, "Mom, Brian was not the first person to abuse me as a kid."

Her eyes grew big. "What! What do you mean? Who? Oh my God, Erin!"

"My friend's uncle."

She moved onto the couch beside me and pulled me into a hug. "Oh my God. Oh my God." She was obviously so shocked she could not say anything else. Then her tears fell. "You had a horrible childhood. I cannot believe what you have lived through. Whose uncle was it? When did it happen? Why didn't you ever tell us? I don't get it. Your whole mission is to get people to break their silence, yet you have been keeping silent."

"It never haunted me like the abuse I endured with Brian. I felt if I exposed this painful secret, it would be like opening a can of worms and my life would be a lot more difficult. And it's only now coming to surface. Now the memories of what happened are haunting me."

She locked her eyes onto mine. "What exactly did he do? He never raped you, did he?"

I took a deep breath, but before I could say a word, she began wailing. My mother no doubt read the answer in my eyes. She was crying so loud I feared my dad would wake up any second and come to find out what was wrong.

I grabbed her and drew her close to me. We just cried into each other's embrace.

"But, Mom, look at the person I am today. I am not that little girl anymore, and I am now giving her a voice. That little girl inside me is going to help many other people. I have come this far and I won't stop here."

We sat on the couch for the next hour. I relived the horrors I endured at Ashley's house. I looked at my mom. "Does it all make sense now, why I never wanted to spend the night at my friend's house, why I spent so much time at home once we moved? Do you understand why I had so many anger problems those first few years of school? I can see now that anger was my only way of expressing the pain I was holding in, and that is why I struggle today with my body image." I told her how I have felt disgusted with my body that has been used and abused and that the only way I felt I could gain control is through controlling what I ate. "I know it is going to take me time to learn to accept and love the person I am inside. It is not easy."

I told her about my research into the statues of limitations in Illinois. "It's not too late to go after this man."

She cocked her eyebrows. "Oh, you'd better believe we are going to find this scumbag."

"I do not even know his first name. It would be like trying to find a needle in a haystack."

"But the elementary school you went to will have records of the people who picked Ashley up from school and who she lived with. We will put a name with the face that has haunted you." She paused as though thinking back sixteen years. "Did you tell your high school therapist?"

"No, I never told anyone. Not my therapist, school psychologist, or any of my friends."

"What about your sisters, Allie and Caitlin?"

"Mom until about a month ago, nobody knew." I had mentioned it at dinner a few weeks earlier to my friend Kimmy, whom I met through the Children's Advocacy Center group when I was thirteen, but I had not gone into detail with her. I also told a counselor down at college a few weeks earlier. "I told Kimmy because I needed advice on how to tell you and Dad."

My mother found it difficult to believe that after all the therapy I'd had, all the public speaking, and going on national television I had kept this part of my life silenced all these years.

"Why do you think I speak out? One day I knew I would give that little child I once was her voice back." I explained to her that I think a lot of it had to do with being really young. "I did not repress what happened; I was always aware of it. I just bottled it up, and now it is all starting to bubble up and disrupt my life."

I told her about the drawings I did in school that she had kept all these years stored away in our crawl space. "The pictures are in that folder we looked at a few years back, but we never went through the entire thing. The two pictures I came across were toward the back."

"I want to see them, Erin."

"They are disturbing. You may not want to see them."

"I know, but I need to do this. Please, get them."

I went into my bedroom and pulled them out. When I brought them down and gave them to her, she began to sob uncontrollably. She pounded her fist onto the couch.

I pulled her into another hug. When her sobbing subsided, I lifted her chin, "Look at me. I do not want you to blame yourself in any way. You gave me the best childhood; my childhood was not horrible. I just had some horrible things happen to me, but the good times outweigh the bad."

She shook her head. "Why would I save that folder?"

"I have no clue, but why would I be the one to stumble upon it sixteen years later? I guess that's when you have to believe that everything happens for a reason, even when we cannot make sense of it." Tears welled. "First a grown man rapes you, and then a family member molests you. How much more can one kid go through?"

"And look at the person I am today because of it. Do you understand why I have such a passion to raise awareness about childhood sexual abuse? I have lived it my whole life. Why not do something positive with it to help others instead of letting it rob any more of my life from me?"

My public speaking helps me to continue to heal. The least I can do for myself now is to release the silence and let the horror be heard. I also knew how huge it was going to be and how life changing it would be. "We are talking about going back and reliving my rape by an adult man when I was almost seven." Then I added, "A big reason I begged Brian not to rape me the last time he sexually abused me was because the rape I endured as a child all came flooding back to me that moment, and I remembered the pain was unbearable." I punched him in the balls when he sat on top of me because I feared he was going to rape me as Ashley's uncle had. Each time Brian held me down, it reminded me of the times Ashley's uncle sat on top of me. While my cousin did some pretty horrendous stuff to my sister and me, he never raped me, but I was always afraid he would. Punching him in the balls might have been my only way of escaping another rape. I lived through one rape; I could not live through another.

My mother's eyes were puffy and red. "I don't want to leave your side. It feels like it just happened."

"You need to get some sleep. It's really late and we can talk more tomorrow."

"How can I go into work?"

"You need to, Mom. It will be better for you to keep your mind focused on other things. Besides, I have an interview in the morning for my internship placement. I don't want you home by yourself, thinking about what I've just dumped on you."

"Would you leave the drawings on the counter? I will tell your dad in the morning."

"Sure, Mom." I kissed her goodnight. "Everything is going to be all right. I am okay."

I felt like I needed to comfort both the little girl inside me and my mother, assuring them that neither of them could have prevented the rape. I didn't want my mother to blame herself and I didn't want to blame the little girl inside me for not speaking up at six.

When I climbed into bed, I knew Mom was crying herself to sleep. I prayed to God to comfort her and thanked Him for his strength. I knew God was going to walk me through this process, but I worried about the effect it would have on my mom. Then I reminded myself that I needed to take care of myself. I felt God's presence as He helped me stay strong and shatter my silence. I fell asleep with the memory of my shattering the beer bottles on the street and sidewalk. All these years later I am finally facing my childhood and picking up the shattered pieces.

I am a prime example how deep the silence of sexual abuse can go. Though I have stood before crowds since 2004, sharing my journey of finding my voice and breaking my silence, I was still keeping a little girl trapped inside me. But now I let her voice be heard. She will no longer be silenced inside my soul.

I woke the next morning and heard my mom getting ready for work. I lay in bed and began to question myself. Did I just dream talking to Mom? Did none of that happen last night? I really began to wonder if I had dreamed telling my mom everything.

While I was trying to figure this out, Mom walked into my room and whispered, "Erin, I am going to wait until the weekend is over to tell Dad." We did not want to ruin his weekend because one of his childhood friends was coming to Wisconsin to visit him. I knew then that it was not a dream, and I could hear in my mom's voice that she was trying to keep herself together. In the same way that people can remember exactly where they were and what they were doing when they heard about the September 11 terrorist attack, I relived that moment when my sister and I first told our parents about what our cousin did to us.

I went downstairs and poured myself a cup of coffee. Dad was already up and reading the paper. Every time my mom glanced at me, she looked as if she were going to burst into tears. I was so glad to see her going to work. When she left my dad looked at me and said, "What is going on?"

Gulp. "What do you mean?"

"I heard your mother sobbing her eyes out last night. It sounded like she got devastating news. Is everything all right with Caitlin?"

"She's fine. Mom and I were having a rough night. I needed a listening ear, and we got very emotional."

I sipped my coffee; he resumed reading his paper.

A few minutes later he lowered his paper. "Is everything okay with Allie?"

"Everything is fine with Allie."

I eventually showered and got dressed and drove into Chicago for my interview for a possible internship at the Chicago Children's Advocacy Center. As I drove I thought to myself, "Here I am trying to get an internship working with abused children, and just the night before I broke my own childhood secret of abuse." My goal of working with abused kids is to empower them at a young age to use their voices and not be ashamed.

While driving, I missed a call from my mom. When I arrived at the center, I listened to her voice mail message. She had spoken to the school psychologist, Jeannette Ardell, about everything. I can only imagine that between my mom being hysterical and hearing this sickening news, Jeannette's Friday had not started off on a cheerful note. I am sure she remembered the days I used to be in her office, trying to sort out my life. Believe me, there were times I came close to spilling it all to Jeannette, but I always held back because I was too afraid to open that door. I had been through too much agony. Dealing with flashbacks of my cousin's abuse and panic attacks, I did not need to open that door and expose an even darker past. I believe a lot of the pain I suffered from Brian only helped cover up and push the rape and sexual abuse I endured as a little girl down deeper. I knew that one day I would be doing what I am now, putting it all out there and dealing with the ugly truth.

Jeannette told my mom she needed to talk to the school detective about this; he would know how to handle it. My mom walked down to his office and told him.

He leaned forward. "There are ways to track down this guy. Ashley's school records will state who she lived with, her doctors, and where she moved so that her transcripts could be sent."

He did a quick computer check to see if she had gone to any of the high schools in the district, but nothing came up. He called the police department, and they told him the best thing is for me to come in and file a police report. They wanted me to get the address of the house Ashley used to live in.

I called Mom back. "I'll drive over and get the address on my way home after my interview."

"How do you feel about filing a police report?"

"Well, it makes me nervous." I would have to let authorities know all these years later. I would feel horrible if I found out he had hurt other children. And a part of me did not want to know this. Deep down, though, I knew it was important to expose this man. After all, he could have hurt other kids by now—maybe he was still hurting children. Just the thought of that made me sick.

My mom called me throughout the day. Although learning of what happened was difficult for my parents, I could not allow myself to take in any of their pain and emotions. My main goal was to get this out, no longer hold it in, and do what was best for me. I had to begin my healing process by focusing on my own pain and finding closure to this chapter of my life.

After my interview, I drove into my old neighborhood. I passed my grandparents' street, and the park and tennis court Ashley and I used to play at, then I turned up the hill toward Ashley's old court. Many of the homes in my old neighborhood had been torn down and brand-new beautiful large homes replaced them. The house that had brought so many painful memories was gone, replaced by a large two-story, three-car garage home. It felt so good to see nothing left of that house.

I passed the corner of the sidewalk that lead where Ashley's house used to stand. Ashley had stood there and begged me not to tell because she might lose her house and we exchanged our pinky promise. I had kept my promise until now.

I drove into the court and turned around. Being there again sent chills up my spine: all the years of nightmares of my running through that court from a sick man, just going in circles and always ending with his tackling me to the ground. It was the only reoccurring dream I had of that man.

I remembered me as a small innocent child walking home after being raped, and being so confused and sad. "I am taking back control," I told myself.

When I got home my mom explained that the school detective suggested I go in tomorrow and file the police report. She sat in the kitchen, staring at the images I drew as a child. She got teary eyed. I closed the folder and told her to stop looking at them. It was obvious that these pictures only brought up her own pain.

When Dad came home, we sat in the kitchen talking for a while.

I kept praying my mom would keep it together. I was leaving soon to volunteer and did not want to ruin my dad's weekend. At one point, my mom looked right at me as her eyes filled with tears. I decided to bring up something funny my sister Allie had told me earlier that day. I wanted to do anything to get my mom's mind off the news.

Eventually, Mom and Dad kissed me good-bye, and my mom gave me a hug before they headed for our house in Wisconsin. I could tell she did not want to let go. She asked me again if I was going to be okay about filing a police report the next day by myself. I told her I would be fine, that I could handle this.

That evening I volunteered for the Children's Advocacy Center's annual dinner/dance fund-raiser. I sold raffle tickets to a trip to Disney World. I also was in a video presentation given during dinner, talking about my experience at the Children's Advocacy Center and their importance in the healing they do for children.

Once dinner started, the video began and different clips showed me talking about statistics on child abuse, the different people who help abused children in the advocacy center, and how they helped me. The evening's event planner approached me and asked if the master of ceremonies, Anita Padilla from Fox Chicago News, could let everyone know that the young lady they saw on the video was here tonight. I agreed, and in a matter of seconds, Anita introduced herself and asked if I would say a few words of encouragement and how the center helped me. It was crazy how I went from the night before telling my mother of the awful rape I had endured at six to a well-known news anchor introducing me on stage—with only seconds to prepare what I would say.

I stood before the audience and told them how much I appreciated their supporting such an important cause. I briefly explained I was abused by a family member and was brought to the Children's Advocacy Center. I pointed out the forensic interviewer, Meghan, who had interviewed my sister and me. I told the crowd how the center helped me break my silence and believed my experience, how they provided such wonderful support group services for my family and me, and how they helped me turn a negative in my life into something positive. I honestly believe my life would have been a complete mess had I not received the services I did when I first broke my silence about my cousin. I added that I travel the country and speak to groups and organizations, telling my experience. I pointed out that every dollar spent is well spent and that their donations are what keep these centers running and providing families with vital services. I told them that with their continued support another child would find her voice, begin the healing process, and might one day be standing here before them sharing their story. I ended by telling them all to give themselves a round of applause for helping abused children find their voices and keeping Children's Advocacy Centers funded.

When I walked offstage to my seat, Meghan stood up and gave me a big hug. I figured she never imagined one of the children she interviewed would one day stand on a stage in front of strangers, sharing her journey back from abuse. I hoped the words I spoke that night showed her how important her role was in helping me find my voice when I was thirteen. If it were not for her empathy and support, I do not think I could have done it.

Looking back now, I wish I'd had the courage to speak up about my rape. Then maybe Brian would never have abused me, I would never have developed an eating disorder, and I wouldn't be dealing with filing a police report at age twenty-two. While talking with Meghan, I knew deep in my heart that if I were to tell her about the rape, she would tell me the same thing my mother was urging me to do: report it to the police. So I made a decision. I would find the courage to make that police report.

The next morning Mom left a voice mail on my phone. She had told my dad everything and wanted me to call her.

I called her back to hear how it went. She told me that while they were going out to dinner, she had asked if he wanted to know why she was so upset.

"Erin told me that you and she were talking and you both got emotional."

"Well, that's not the whole truth."

Concern etched his face. "Is Allie pregnant? Has she been hurt? Or is Caitlin pregnant?"

"No, Allie and Caitlin are fine, but if I tell you now, it will ruin your weekend."

"I don't care. I have to know what has upset you."

"It happened over fifteen years ago, but it's liable to change your life."

She told me he'd had an idea what she was talking about and began thinking of all the people we knew back then and wondered if one of them had hurt me.

By the time they had arrived at the restaurant, Mom had told him the horrors I had endured. My father was sick. He could not eat his dinner. When they got home, she showed him the pictures I had drawn. It only made his stomach turn and enraged him. He went to bed that night only to toss and turn. Mom said that my father was very angry and they both wanted this monster dead.

"I told him you were going to the police to file a report. He thought it was a very good idea but wondered about the pain you might have to go through if they found him and you then had to face him in court."

"Mom, I can't even think that far ahead. I doubt anything could be done at this point. I don't even know the monster's first name." I wondered if Ashley's uncle was really her mom's boyfriend and they told me he was her uncle because her mom would look bad if she had a live-in boyfriend. If it really was her uncle, he might have a family of his own now. Maybe his children have been abused. It makes me sick to think that I could have told someone long ago, but instead I broke beer bottles and held in the truth. Yet I could not fall into the same trap I did when I learned my sister had been abused, blaming myself and feeling guilty that I could have saved her from Brian. I had to remember I was just a little girl being hurt by a large grown man who overpowered me and took from me, a precious little girl, my innocence.

"Are you still going to make the police report?"

"I am really nervous about doing this."

"You know that if you do and they catch him, you could help save other children from the pain and agony you endured."

That is all I needed to hear to remind me that I am all about people finding their voices and speaking out. Because it is so hard, some people wait until they are in their thirties, forties, fifties, or even older before breaking their silence.

"Do it only when and if you are ready for that step, Erin."

It was a beautiful Saturday when I pulled into the police department lot. I parked my car and just sat. I stared at my old high school, which is next door to the police department. I asked myself over and over, "Why did I not have the strength to do this when I was in high school?" It is how the healing process goes. I honestly thought I had escaped ever facing my earlier childhood experiences of sexual abuse and rape—until they began haunting me when I got to college. I sat frozen with fear. Then I started shaking because I was so nervous to finally report what I had carried in my soul for so long. I could not quite figure out how I had no problem getting up in front of hundreds of people and sharing graphic details of the abuse I endured at the hands of Brian but found it so difficult to speak to one police officer. Then I realized my inner child, who had been hurt so badly, was showing her fear that was so great it was consuming me. It was like feeling a mixture of being a strong, determined, and courageous woman and a scared, innocent little girl. I had to do a lot of self-talk to empower the child within me to be brave. After a half hour of this,

I decided I would not waste another minute being afraid. "You have nothing to be afraid of, so go in there and do it," I told myself.

I finally opened the car door and made my way toward the front doors of the police department. I prayed the entire time. The automatic doors slid open, and I walked up to a big glass window where three officers sat, two men and a woman. They stared at me, but the woman spoke. "What can I help you with?"

What could she help me with? I did not even know what to say. How do you say "I was raped fifteen years ago and I am finally coming in to report it?"

I took a deep breath. "I was assaulted many years ago by a friend's uncle who lived with her."

"What kind of assault? Did he physically beat you up?"

"No, he sexually abused me."

"What's the address where the abuse occurred?"

I was so uncomfortable standing there, speaking through a glass window with two male police officers staring at me. She finally buzzed me in through a door and told me to come around and follow her so she could take the report. She took me down a hall and into a back office where I sat at a table. I suddenly felt the tears forming in my eyes.

She sat down, took one look at me, and said, "Oh, let me go get you a box of tissue." When she came back she asked me to tell her everything I remembered, which I did and then showed her the drawings.

She looked at one. "Are those devil horns you put over the rapist's head?"

"I have no memory of drawing these pictures, but I assume they are, just by the looks of them."

After sitting there for over an hour and overcome with emotions flowing through me, the police officer got up and went to speak to someone about the drawings. She came back and said, "We need to hold on to the drawings."

When we were done, I followed her back to the front desk, where she called in the report. I listened as she gave the person on the other end of the phone the location of the crime and reported it as a sex crime.

She hung up, then gave me her contact information and a case number. "Your case will be handed over to a detective who will contact you within the week. If you remember anything else, give me a call."

After thanking her for everything, I left knowing I had done the right thing even if nothing came of it. Leaving the police department brought back memories of when I went to the Children's Advocacy Center when I was thirteen. I broke my silence for the first time there. The difference now was that I was the adult taking the little six-year-old trapped inside me and letting her be heard.

The event was documented and in the hands of the authorities. I wished it had been documented years earlier. I called my mom when I got out of the police department and told her I felt physically and emotionally exhausted, like I had not slept in days.

I went from carrying this all alone for years to suddenly sharing it with my mom and then the police. Yet no matter how much time had gone by, the horror and pain had not faded, it still felt raw and as though it had just happened yesterday.

Sunday morning I went to my church for the first time in months. Living in Wisconsin all summer and away at college, I did not get to go regularly like I did throughout high school. I attended church with my sister every Sunday at college through a campus ministry.

I needed to feel God more then ever that Sunday morning. I had no idea what the service was going to be about, but as I drove there I prayed that God would speak to me through the service. I walked through the doors into an auditorium that seats seven thousand people. I found a seat, and looking down at my program the usher had given me, I read. "Questions for God in Tragedy." Boy, was I in for the service I needed to hear. I was reliving my own tragedy that entire weekend. The service began with teaching pastor Nancy Beach talking with actor Jim Caviezel. Jim played Jesus in the movie *The Passion of the Christ*. Jim talked about the pains he suffered while playing the role of Jesus. He told everyone in church that life is short. We all have crosses we must carry in life and some are bigger or shorter than others. He added that no matter how hard it gets, we should not forget that God has rewards for those who suffer. He made a clear statement that we should not live for tomorrow; rather, we should live for today. His message was powerful and uplifting. These were words I needed to hear, and I knew God was speaking through them.

The next message started with a story about a grandma and her grandson who died in an early morning fire one February morning. A neighbor could not understand why bad things happen to those she described as the best people. A question all of us have asked at least once in our lifetimes: Why do bad things happen to good people? One of the teaching pastors said, "You may be sitting here wondering, 'Why did my parents have to get a divorce?' 'Why did my son or daughter get killed by a drunk driver?' 'Why did child abuse occur in the childhood I grew up in?' 'Why did my dad get cancer?' 'Why was I the victim of a violent crime?'" He went on to ask, "If God is great, why did he allow suffering and evil? What good can God bring out of tragedy?"

He raised some good questions. Questions I knew thousands in the service were asking, seeking answers to their own tragedies. These people all came to church to worship the same God, and we all carried different painful tragedies in our lives. The pastor explained that God created a perfect, flawless world. It was not evil. God included in this perfect world people who were made in His image and who were given freedom. With that freedom came the ability to choose right and wrong, to do good and evil. He pointed out that it frosts us to see drug dealers, wife beaters, and child abusers getting ahead in life. We live in a sinful, toxic world. One in which rain falls on the just and the unjust, the righteous and the unrighteous, the good and the bad. The cross of Christ is a reminder of taking what looks like the worst thing and turning it into the best thing; dark days do not last forever. I felt like his message was directed right at me, showing me that I have watched those do evil acts to me, and in return I have turned it into something tremendously good by speaking out and helping others. The message that came across to me is that I needed to take this horrible past and turn it into something positive.

When I prayed to God on the way to church to speak to me through the service, I did not expect a message as powerful as the one I received. It was clear and direct. I needed all the encouragement I could get. I felt like I had gone from standing up and speaking out to having my feet kicked out from under me, feeling knocked down and vulnerable. I exposed a past I never thought would come back to haunt me. I exposed the Devil's deeds. Yet God gave me the message that although I may face dark days, the rewards for speaking out are far greater, and that He will be by my side to turn to in times of need. I honestly believe that God is showing me that many more doors holding back painful memories will open when I am strong enough to handle them.

That same Sunday I made dinner for my parents when they got home from Wisconsin. Later that evening, while up in my bedroom, I turned around and saw my dad coming into the room.

He walked up to me and wrapped his arms around me. The first words out of his mouth were, "I am so sorry. I just want to take away the pain you went through."

I looked up to him. "I am sorry I lied about why mom was crying. I just could not break it to you."

"I know. I understand." He continued to hug me. "Erin, I want to kill this motherfucker. I want to take a baseball bat to his head."

I felt my eyes grow big. "I bet you do, Dad."

You have to understand, I have never heard my dad swear or even raise his voice. I never saw or heard him express anger, and he never punished my sisters and me for anything. When we wanted something as children, he always responded, "Ask your mother." Only once did I hear about a time he showed his anger. It was right after learning Allie and I had been abused. His father had made light of the situation, indicating "kids will be kids." It angered my father, yet he hid it from my sisters and me to protect us.

That Sunday night he had tears in his eyes. In my twenty-two years, I had never seen my dad shed a tear. "You are my precious little girl."

I felt the tears forming in my eyes as I hugged my dad.

"Maybe things would have turned out differently if I had been more focused on you girls rather than on my business."

"Dad, don't blame yourself for what someone else did. You are an amazing father who has provided me with so much."

"You cannot even let your kids in their own backyard or go to the park. I try to make myself feel better by telling myself that it could be worse. You could have told us you were terminally ill and I would lose you forever."

I saw how much of an impact this was having on my dad. It seemed everything that he had pent up was now pouring out of him. I did not want to see him and mom hurt anymore. It was enough to see their pain over what Brian had done to us. I tried to get him to understand that I did not want them to blame themselves, or think they had failed me. They had no way of knowing I was being abused unless I had said something, or they walked in on it. Abuse is the last thing parents think would happen to their kids.

After the longest hug I have ever received from my dad, we sat down on my bed. "Erin, we can hope for two things: he is already in prison, or he is dead."

"For years I had hoped Ashley would break her silence and tell the authorities. Then they would knock on our door, asking if it was true."

It was much easier to talk to my dad now that I was older. I could never talk to him about the abuse my cousin put me through. I love my dad with all my heart, and he is the only man in my life so far I trust and can share anything with. "Remember when I put my hand through the glass door when Caitlin was taking my shoes and socks off my feet back when I was six? Well that is what Ashley's uncle did to me when he could not get my jeans off. He tried to take off my shoes and I kept kicking, but he eventually got them off."

"I want to take a baseball bat to his head!"

Obviously, hearing the horrors I went through at such a young age was killing him. It broke my heart to see him so upset, but at the same time I knew I was finally taking care of myself. I felt he deserved to know. In a sense, I thought that this might be healthy for my dad to finally let his emotions out. Now that I was an adult, he did not need to hide his anger about his girls being hurt.

"You do not know how many times over the years I wanted to tell you and Mom. I can name off so many different situations and places where I was so close to telling you, but the timing just did not feel right."

"Truthfully, there is never a right time for news like that; no one can be prepared to hear that kind of horror."

We eventually made our way back downstairs.

"Erin, I am just glad you are okay and I still have you. I bet you are never going to let your kids out of your sight."

"I will never allow my children to go to overnights, and if they want to play with their friends, they will do so in my house under my supervision." The truth is when I become a parent, it will become my full-time job. From the moment they utter their first words, I will begin teaching my kids about the bad people in our world who hurt others. As much as I want a huge family, part of me does not even want to bring kids into a world that has so many sick monsters out there. I used to tell my dad, "I think I am just going to raise kittens and dogs." My hope is that by the time I have kids, every school in America will be required by law to teach to children as young as preschoolers the Safe Touch program.

Mom, Dad, and I talked about what would happen if the police find this guy. Dad said, "Most likely he will be questioned and deny it all. But maybe the police could get a confession. Hopefully, Ashley would back you, but sometimes people will protect the perpetrator out of fear, especially since it is family."

I nodded. "Much like how our relatives protected Brian. Ashley is all I have to go on and, of course, the other little girl in the bedroom, but I have no clue what her name is. Other than that, it is my word against his."

The next morning I had to head back to college, a four-hour drive. I hugged and kissed my parents good-bye. They both hugged me like they did not want to let go. They told me to call when I got back to school and to let them know if I heard anything from the police.

I had told Allie the night before that I needed to speak with her when I came back that night. We had planned to meet at a coffee shop at six near our college campus, but when I picked her up in front of the library, we decided to go to a park near campus where we could sit and talk.

As we drove through our campus to the park I asked, "How was your weekend."

"Great! How about yours?"

"Actually, it was draining."

"Because of all the interviews for your internship?"

"No, it's because of something I need to tell you."

I parked my car and we walked over to a picnic table. The sun wouldn't set for another hour and a half, and it was still quite warm.

We settled ourselves and when I looked at her, the words just rolled off my tongue. "Allie, I wish I didn't have to tell you this, but when I was home, I had a long talk with Mom, telling her something that I've been holding on to for a very long time. Brian was not the first person to abuse me."

Her eyes widened and she blurted out, "What! Who?"

"Do you remember my friend Ashley?"

"Yes."

"It was her uncle."

"What did he do to you?"

I took a deep breath and mustered the courage to continue. "He did not just molest me, he raped me."

Tears filled my sister's eyes and spilled down her cheeks. "Erin, I am so sorry. Why did you never tell anyone? You wrote a book and never told anyone about this." The shock and disbelief that covered her face had as much to do with speaking out nationwide on this epidemic yet still living in silence as it was about the news I just dropped on her.

I explained to Allie, as I had to my parents, that it had never affected me until recently. I had buried the rape, the most painful thing I ever went through, but I never forgot it.

I had to stop and take a deep breath; I fought the tears forming in my eyes. "I can still feel the pain from being raped as if it occurred yesterday, and I still remember trembling inside after it was over."

She covered her eyes with her hands then put her head down on the picnic table. "I cannot believe you lived through this. How can you date anyone after living through that?"

"I struggle with it every day. I have trust issues with men."

"It's sick, just sick. How can someone do that to a child? All I can think about are the home videos of you as a little kid. You were so cute and yet you were carrying that horror."

I told her more details of what I went through. I recounted the times I came close to either telling our parents or telling her. I became overwhelmed with emotions and closed up when I felt tears filling my eyes, a reaction due to the man who, while he raped me, told me to stop crying like a baby.

I took a few deep breaths and told her about the drawings. "I filed a report with the police department and gave them a copy of the pictures I had drawn."

She cried more when learning how close someone could have come to finding out what I was going through by taking a look at my artwork.

She paused then looked up at me. "How are you so strong? I would be in a mental hospital the rest of my life if I lived through that. Did you repress it? Is that how you coped?"

"I did bury it, and once we moved away I used that as a way of trying to forget the past. I was always aware that it had happened. I just pushed it way back and covered it up. I was consumed in the pain from being sexually abused by Brian and I never allowed it to surface until now. It was like I dealt with my pain from what Brian had done, and once that was settled, memories and nightmares of being abused and raped started to pop up periodically.

"I often wanted to play with my friends only at our house, or have overnights at our house. If I'd go to other friends' houses to spend the night, I was scared because I'd have to trust others. It was out of my comfort zone of feeling safe in my own home."

My sister began crying again. "When I have kids, they will never go to overnights. I do not even want to bring kids into this world now. I am too afraid of their getting hurt."

"I know; I understand." I was numb from all the crying I had already done that weekend.

She wiped her eyes. "Thank God we did not go to the coffee place. I would not want to have this conversation in public. Look at me." Then she added, "I take back everything I ever said or did to you. Please forgive me, Erin."

There was no need to forgive because she had done nothing

wrong. "Do you understand now why I suffer from an eating disorder? It allows me to have control, since so much of it and power was taken from me throughout my childhood. I feel disgusted with my body. It has been used and abused by two men for their damn, sick pleasure."

"Please forgive me every time I got on your case about you being anorexic or your eating habits. Forgive me for everything I have ever said. I take it all back. I feel awful."

Allie kept crying into her hands, saying over and over, "I cannot believe you had to go through this."

"In the end it is only going to make me stronger. I am letting that little girl who has been trapped inside me out. It is not easy, especially feeling so weak and vulnerable right now, but one day she will stand before a crowd and share her courageous story. I am going to honor the little girl I once was and no longer keep her story a secret buried away. From now on she comes with me and her story will be heard. She will save the lives of other little girls. I have nothing to be ashamed of."

I told her of Dad's reaction to this news and how much anger and rage he has toward this monster who did this to me. Allie began sobbing even more, so I got up from the picnic table, sat next to her, and wrapped my arms around her. "It is okay; I am okay."

Through her tears she said, "I should be the one hugging you. You're the one who went through this."

I smiled. "I did the same thing with Mom, hugging her and telling her everything will be okay." The social worker in me was coming out, showing the empathy I had learned over the years. I guess the difference is that I have known about this event my whole life. I have carried it with me every day since I was six. But it is new information for my family, and hearing that kind of news about someone you love is crushing. I cannot imagine either of my sisters telling me something like this. It is devastating, and I prepared myself for months before telling my family. I knew they would get emotional, and I needed to be strong if they fell apart.

Two weeks before I made the trip home and broke this heartbreaking news to my parents, my family and I had attended my cousin Kelly's wedding in Michigan. Allie and I were bridesmaids. At the end of the night my parents, sister, and I were all out on the dance floor, dancing and laughing together. It was a joyous moment. When I danced with my dad, I thought about the pain I carried. This joyous moment might be the last one before he learned of an even darker past I carried.

On the way home from Kelly's wedding dad drove us through our old neighborhood and drove past Ashley's old house. Now, sitting at the picnic table with Allie, I told her that driving past the court Ashley used to live in had churned me up inside. "I am really numb right now from all my emotions. Many memories have really been haunting me. But I know in the end I will come out stronger. I overcame this once in my life; I can rise above again."

One look at Allie and it was evident she had cried her heart out. "I need comfort food; let's go get ice cream."

Usually, anything I ate came with negative thoughts of calories and fat, but this particular night I did not think twice about it. I think we both needed something sweet after that conversation to cheer us up a bit. We got up to leave and walked toward my car. I knew that sitting at that picnic bench in the park with my sister would live in me forever, just as the day she told me Brian was abusing her is as clear as if it happened yesterday.

"I always tried to imagine where in life I would be when I told you this, and I sure did not imagine sitting here in our college town at a park. I pictured myself telling you when I was a mother with kids."

We took our ice cream back to her dorm room and locked the door. I did not stay long; I was really drained and just wanted to get some sleep before class in the morning. As I got up to leave and hug my sister good-bye, she wrapped her arms around me and we just held each other. She started to cry again.

"It is okay. Don't worry about me. I am only going to grow stronger now that I have exposed the little girl inside me. One day I will soar higher than ever."

I made my way out to my car and convinced myself that while the days, weeks, and months ahead may not be easy, in the big picture, something incredible will come out of this, allowing me to continue to heal and grow.

chapter six

PUTTING THE PIECES TOGETHER

I did not sleep through the night. Nightmares woke me up, similar to what I went through in high school. Except this time it was not Brian's face that haunted me, but that of a man I had not seen in sixteen years. I tossed and turned, struggling throughout the night to fall back asleep. I had not experienced any nightmares in the three years I had been at college, and suddenly I found myself thrown back in time.

It did not stop there. My anxiety throughout the week was nerve-racking. I jumped every time the phone rang, thinking it would be someone from the police department getting back to me about the report I had filed. I lost my concentration with my college work. After thirteen straight nights of waking up with nightmares and no word from the police, I decided to call them to see if anything had been done. I became my own detective, searching the Web for anything that would lead me to Ashley's whereabouts. Finally, a sergeant called me and explained that my case had been handed to a detective who had been on vacation and that he would be in contact with me by Monday or Tuesday of the following week.

The next morning was a Friday, and I woke at 8:00 to my phone ringing. I missed the call, but when I listened to the voice mail, it was Detective Morgan, who would be handling my case. I called him back immediately.

He began our conversation with "What are you doing with your life?"

"I am at school in my senior year."

"I'd like us to get together and discuss your case. We need to find this man who did this to you."

"I will be back there next Friday."

"Okay, then call me on Thursday, and we'll set up a time to meet on Friday."

Knowing I had the support of the authorities would make it much easier to deal with future events.

I believe that God gives you only what you can handle. Had I broken my silence about this back when I was thirteen or in high school, I am convinced I would not be here. The pain of dealing with the memories of Brian abusing me and reliving the abuse and rape I suffered at six and seven would have been unbearable to process because I was not emotionally stable to handle all that pain at once. It would have killed me.

I love children, senior citizens, and animals. I have always been able to soothe a crying baby, comfort an upset child, communicate through my soul with a disabled girl, hold the hand of an Alzheimer's patient and listen as she repeats her wedding day story six times in one hour, or provide a home to a stray kitty. The same love, comfort, and patience I express to others is exactly what I want to show the little girl I left in a back bedroom so many years ago. Each time I addressed a crowd and was a voice for every little kid that that has been silenced, I was also speaking on behalf of the little girl inside me still trapped and afraid to open that door, not knowing if that monster would be waiting on the other side to hurt her again. Though he physically would not be there, the power of haunting memories had kept me from opening the door for years.

God has a purpose for my life, just as He does for everyone. He carried the pain and memories of the rape for me until He knew I was strong enough to face it. I never forgot what happened, I just never let myself go there and face it. I had a vision for years of myself standing in front of the bedroom door where I was raped, but I never went in. I did not want to traumatize myself all over again. I was too weak and afraid of what might come out of that bedroom.

I am no longer weak and afraid. I have years of courage, strength, determination, and empowerment behind me now. I am going back into the house of horror and rescue the little girl trapped in the back bedroom. Though years have passed, I can close my eyes and envision myself standing in front of a house that in reality has already been torn down. I do not knock; I just walk through the front door into an eerie silence. I head straight down a dark hallway, where I can hear cries coming from behind the door. I have waited all these years. I cannot waste another moment, so I turn the knob.

I am about to open a heavy door to emotions that I thought I would keep closed forever. Behind that door is the face of a little girl who has haunted me in my dreams—a girl so sad, confused, angry, scared, lonely, hurting, silenced, and patiently waiting to be rescued.

I push open the door. I carry her to the light at the end of the tunnel. I have walked through this tunnel once before. I come out stronger when I get to the other side, and the little girl whose voice was silenced by the dark monster who came out in the night will finally be heard. I release all the anger this man caused me.

The passion and drive inside me wants answers. Though I had finally spoken out about the rape and brought it to the police, I still could not sleep at night. I wondered who and where my rapist was. One night I came upon a website that allows you to get property reports. Enter the address and you can obtain all the property records of the house: people who lived there, value of the home, taxes, neighborhood and town background, and, of course, a list of sex offenders in the area. I thought, "This will provide me answers to unlock more of the past." I purchased the property report. It was worth the $15. I became my own detective in my own case, trying to put the pieces together that would lead me to the answers I needed.

The report gave me a list of sixteen names, either a resident or someone associated with the property. I scrolled down the list, looking for Ashley's last name. There, the very last one. Number sixteen was the name of a woman in her forties who had Ashley's last name. I knew it was her mother. I continued my search and found her current address, which was in a town thirty minutes away from my hometown. Still, though, it did not give me the name of Ashley's uncle. I typed her mom's name into several search engines, but each time I came to a dead end.

I set aside the property owners report for a few days, but it was never far from my mind. I was driven to find this man. I was an advocate for the little girl within me, with no plans of giving up until I found something.

My determination to hunt this monster down who raped me would allow me to stop at nothing until I found him. Had I known this scumbag's name and his current address, I would show up at his front door with every media reporter I could find, break down the door, and show them the face of a child rapist. I would look into the eyes that once terrorized me and show him he messed with the wrong little girl; she is back and is his worst nightmare.

Two days before meeting with Detective Morgan, I sat at my computer writing a paper for a class. I was getting tired and decided to check my e-mail before going to bed. My inbox had a new message from a girl named Ashley on MySpace. I had received e-mails like that for the past eight months because I had written to so many Ashleys, looking for my friend. But each one answered that she had not grown up in my hometown. I opened this one: "I did grow up in Schaumburg; did we go to school together?" My heart raced. It had to be her. She did not recognize my name because I used my pen name. I checked her profile, but it did not have a photo; however, the town she currently lived in was the same one that came up for her mother's name. I sent her this message:

Ashley, I sure hope you have not forgotten me because you have been on my mind and heart for many years. I do not even know where to begin. I have been looking for you for some time. I am shaking sending this because I am confident it is you, and I really need to talk to you asap. You probably know exactly why I am contacting you all these years later . . . at least I hope you do. Although I do know how the mind works and you may have repressed it like I did for so many years, I hope bringing this up does not freak you out, since I have no clue what has gone on in your life over the years. I am talking about things that happened when I used to spend the night at your house when we were little. I am talking six- to seven-year-olds. We never talked about it except when you stopped me outside on the sidewalk when we were little and made me pinky promise I would not say anything. I hope I do not have to explain any more and you know exactly what I am talking about. I really need to talk to you. I wish I had the confidence back when I was thirteen and ran into you in the halls of junior high to talk to you about this, but I did not. Please get back to me as soon as you can.

Erin

I did not want to give away that police were involved, thinking "What if she protects her uncle and gives him the heads-up that I turned him in?" Nor was I about to give her my phone number, because I did not want her uncle to get it and contact me. Now I waited to hear back from her.

I told Mom I had found Ashley on the Internet. She then told the high school officer. He told me not to respond to any of her messages because Ashley could back her uncle and he could learn the authorities were on to him.

I went to the police department that Friday at 2 PM. I stood behind the glass window, where I had first come to report the rape, waiting for Detective Morgan. He came around and opened the door for me. I followed him down a hallway. Walking in the opposite direction toward us was an officer who was the resource cop from my junior high school. He remembered me and asked what I was doing there.

"Taking care of some things."

He joked with Detective Morgan, saying he knew me when I was a little stinker. I laughed and told him I still was. It lightened an awkward moment for me.

The detective led me back into an interview room. I seriously felt like I was reliving that moment when I was interviewed at the Children's Advocacy Center. I sat in a small room at a table that faced a mirror. He joined me at the table and put his notebook down. "Tell me what you found through your research."

I pulled out the papers and showed him. He took down the information.

"I found Ashley on MySpace. We made contact."

His eyebrows shot up. "It's important that you have no further contact with her. If she contacts you, do not respond."

Detective Morgan then asked me to think back and remember any specific details about this man. "Did he have any tattoos, scars on his face? Was he fat, or skinny?" He did not expect me to remember much, since I was only six and seven when this happened.

But I had not forgotten my rapist. I closed my eyes and immediately felt as if I were thrown back in time into that room the day of the rape, staring this man in the face and looking into the whites of his eyes. "He was a dark African American man who seemed very muscular to me, with large eyes and hands." I know a young child's interpretation of a man will seem large no matter what.

"Do you remember any kind of truck in the driveway that would tell who he worked for?"

"I have no memory of that."

"I'm sorry to make you relive this by sharing all the details, but for me to make an investigation, I need whatever details you can remember. Take your time and tell me everything that happened."

So once again I relived the horrible events of my childhood. Over the course of the past three weeks I had done this several times. It was draining. As I began pouring out everything, I felt as if I were a mother reporting the crime that had happened to her child, trying to stay strong yet feeling like breaking down at the same time.

Before Detective Morgan would take any action, like calling someone in for questioning, he wanted to make sure he had all his ducks in order and was going after the right man. He asked many questions throughout the interview. One question stood out. "What has caused you to come forward with this now?"

Giving the same answer I had told my mom, dad, and sister, I said, "I kept this hidden for years. It was always with me, but it wasn't until recently that it began haunting me. When I was younger, I could not handle facing it. But now I have begun having flashbacks and panic attacks. The time is right for me to speak up now." Then I added, "I do not know if you know this, but my sister and I were sexually abused by our cousin many years ago."

He must have found the information in the police records he received when he got this case because he was aware of that. "I understand what you are saying. There is a difference at the age when you were raped and when your cousin abused you. I can see how you could bury the earlier abuse because of how young you were."

"I apologize for being so graphic, but did this man ejaculate on you?"

"From what I remember during the rape, he grabbed my hand and made me feel his penis, which was wet. I don't know if it was wet from my hand being sweaty, from wiping my tears, or from him. Those memories all blend together."

"What did your family doctor ever discover when he did pelvic exams when you were a child?"

"My sisters and I were all born at home, and our doctor was the kind you would find during the *Little House on the Prairie* era. He never did pelvic exams."

"So he never checked to make sure everything looked okay?"

"Nope, not that *Little-House-on-the-Prairie* doctor."

His first priority was to get a current picture of Ashley by going through yearbooks and finding the high school she went to. He said he would speak to her, hoping that by bringing her in to the police department, she would break down and share her own story of abuse. "Maybe she will have similar stories to what you have told me. She may have no memory because young children repress things. Or she might deny everything, protecting her uncle like so many families do. After talking to Ashley, I will bring her uncle in to be questioned."

"What if you have both Ashley and I saying he did this, but no physical evidence? How do you prove it?"

"I can't lie to you, this is going to be tough. As an American citizen, Ashley's uncle could come in and not say a word; he has the right to remain silent. So he can either deny it completely or not say a word."

"What happens if he denies it?"

"I will try to break him down and get him to confess by asking him questions like 'Did you brush up against them?'"

I knew exactly what he was talking about. When Brian was brought in for interrogation, the police used this kind of question to get him to confess. After that Brian began sharing more details. I realized it was a long shot, but more than anything, I just wanted to make sure he was not hurting other children. Justice does not come only from a conviction. I was getting my first sense of justice from a rape that occurred when I was six just by coming forward.

We finished up and Detective Morgan gave me his card and told me to call him if I had any questions or just wanted to talk about this. He said he would be in touch and let me know what was happening.

The whole weekend many thoughts ran through my head: *What if out of fear Ashley stands by her uncle, denying anything ever happened to her? What if she does not remember anything? What if he lives in another state? Do the police go there and bring him back? If he were to deny it and has children, could they interview his children? The little girl within me will heal if we cannot get this guy to confess, but if he is still hurting little girls he needs to be stopped and prosecuted.*

When I got back to my apartment at college after meeting with the detective, I checked my e-mail. I opened my inbox and found a new message from Ashley. I panicked and immediately logged into my account and opened her message that had one bold sentence all in caps: "WHAT THE HELL R U TALKING ABOUT?" At once, all my fears came true. I had not told Ashley that I had gone to the police nor had I gone into detail about anything. I just said I needed to talk to her about things that had happened when we had sleepovers.

I stared at that one sentence statement, trying to interpret it. I had felt that if she did not remember anything she would write me back and tell me she is confused and want to exchange phone numbers so we could talk. This response seemed to be her way of telling me to shut up. It was as if I had opened an old wound for her by sending her that message. The door I was just opening to my life, she seemed to be trying to keep tightly closed. I immediately e-mailed Detective Morgan with her response. Because I was to have no more contact with her, I would allow him to handle this in his way.

Ten long grueling days went by before I heard from Detective Morgan. He called on a Monday evening, asking me if I had heard any more from Ashley and if she had given me a phone number to contact her. She hadn't, and he had discovered that the number listed for her mother's house was disconnected. He had investigated another guy who shared the same last name as Ashley's. His leads with that name were not getting him the information he was looking for, so he decided that the next day he would drive out to her house, which was a half hour away from the town we both grew up in.

That day had started out unusually calm. Now I felt as if I were jumping out of my own skin. The thought of Detective Morgan showing up at Ashley's door and her having to face the awful past we both had lived made me feel like I was making her relive a horrible nightmare. But then maybe she had no memory of it, and the conversation would only get the true identity and location of her uncle.

My mind raced with these thoughts. After calling home to tell my parents, I struggled to fall asleep. I lay in bed in the dark for an hour and a half just staring at the ceiling. By 12:30 I had eventually fallen asleep but woke up at 2 AM in a panicked sweat. My mind was racing and I could not fall back asleep. A small amount of light poured into my bedroom window from the lights outside my apartment. I lay there staring at my half-opened closet door and without warning a flashback hit me. I was a little girl in my bedroom, waking in the middle of the night. I was staring at my closet doors, fearing this monster who hurt me would come out of the closet.

I sat up in bed and thought of doing homework to distract these tumbling thoughts. I looked to the edge of my bed and saw Chance in a deep sleep and my cat, Bailey, passed out next to Chance.

I sat there and just thought for a moment. Oh, to just be able to relax, to fall asleep feeling physically well and not tense with racing thoughts. I pet the top of Chance's head. I tried thinking positive thoughts, looking beyond the anxiety and panic. I thought about when I would be past this, I would be stronger then ever before. I thought back to when I put the pieces of my life together after Brian's abuse of me. I struggled with self-injury and had to work hard to gain control and power of my life again. I'd had that lightbulb moment, when I poured all my anger and pain out in that first letter to my cousin; it was the start of a huge transformation in my life that ended in forgiveness.

The hardest thing for me was knowing what is on the other side once I work through this chapter of my life and put the pieces back together. I have gained insight through the trials I have faced in my life. Though I may not have all the answers now, one day I will. I took the risk of exposing myself to the anguish that comes with acknowledging a painful experience. I knew it would not kill me—what does not kill you only makes you stronger.

I sat in bed for the next three hours thinking about what I could do to take the control and power back for that little girl within me who had been hurt. An eating disorder was my current unhealthy outlet that had allowed me to have control and power, but it had taken over my life and consumed me. Anorexia had me go from a healthy woman to wasting away. I starved myself to ignore the little girl screaming inside me to be heard. I finally had let her voice be heard, but anorexia had already taken such a toll on my life. I controlled so much of my everydayness. I already knew how hard it was to break loose from it because I had tried many times before to reverse my negative thinking patterns about my body image. Saying it is so much easier then actually doing it.

I would have to learn to accept myself for who I am and muster empowerment from within to fight off the negative, unwanted thoughts. In the darkness I began to make sense of what the eating disorder was doing to me. By denying myself the nutrients I needed to survive, I was slowly allowing myself to spiral out of control, which in the end could kill me. If anything, I was allowing this child rapist still to control me all these years later through an eating disorder. It was as if he still had a tight grip on me. But now I was seeing a clear picture of the jeopardy I was putting my life in. This was a moment when I needed to lean on others for support so that I could pick up the pieces of my life.

Reaching out for help is not a sign of weakness but a sign of strength. I was sent to the park with a dustpan and broom at seven to sweep up the pieces of my shattered childhood. I have carried those pieces alone for many years. I am putting those pieces back together and am going to make myself whole again. This time I am not doing it alone. The little girl within me has been dormant all these years, and to be suddenly brought out in the open, exposed to several emotions, makes me feel vulnerable, yet so alive. My body, mind, and soul cannot thrive if I do not give it the energy and fuel to push forward. Like a car whose tank is not kept filled with gas, it eventually empties and cannot get to the intended destination. If I continue to burn 1200 calories a day working out and consume only 300 to 500 calories, I cannot fulfill my destination in soaring in life but instead will hit rock bottom. I will not rise to the top of my crusade and legacy if I am not physically well.

Struggling with an eating disorder and grappling with sleeping through the night because I woke to the recurring nightmare of this monster chasing me was taking a physical toll on me. Yet within my own soul lay the strength I needed to grow. I was strong enough to recognize my eating disorder and I knew the steps I needed to take to overcome it. I had been hiding behind a door of denial, but that door has opened. There is nothing worse then denying the truth. I am proud of myself for finally coming out and saying it. I am as human as anyone else; I am not perfect and have faults. I have an overwhelming amount of insight to know that I will conquer this and something beautiful will come out of it. One day I will reach out to others who are struggling with an eating disorder and let them know they are not alone. With every struggle I have faced, a blessing has come from it. I hold on to that.

What is worse than denying you have a problem is acknowledging it but refusing to try to overcome it. So many times the battle is in the mind. I have always struggled to look at myself in the mirror because each time the little girl within me tried to show herself to me. That image first appeared while I sat in a chair and broke my silence in 1998 at the Children's Advocacy Center. I saw myself in the mirror as I relived the horrors Brian put me through but denied the other abuse of my life.

While speaking in Houston, Texas, for the Children's Assessment Center, I stood before hundreds of people. I am usually right on track and my story flows out of me, but as I began to share my story, in my mind's eye I saw the little girl still trapped in that back bedroom, crying to be heard. I had to get a grip of myself. It was the closest I ever came onstage to breaking down and shattering my entire story. I know exactly why this occurred. The evening before my speech, while at dinner, one of the staff from the center had mentioned she had interviewed a girl that day, one she had interviewed years earlier, who had been victimized again by another individual. Just hearing her say that struck me, yet I was still carrying my own silenced story.

After sitting in bed for three hours, reliving my past, I finally decided to get up and head to the gym. Working out was an outlet for my anxiety and stress. But between getting little sleep and thinking about Detective Morgan going to Ashley's house, I could barely keep my eyes open all day throughout classes.

Two days later, in my Abnormal Psychology class, I experienced my first panic attack in years. My legs got tingly, my first sign of an impending panic attack. I felt like I was going to faint. I tried catching my breath. As my professor continued to lecture, I worked to stay composed, gripping my seat and trying to ground myself. I became hot and struggled to calm my racing heart. I got out of my seat, left the classroom, and made my way down the hallway to the bathroom. I turned the cold water on and stuck both my hands under the running water to snap me out of it. I had not had to do that in years. I stared at myself in the mirror, talking myself through the panic. Once I was grounded, I went outside for some fresh air. Then I slowly made my way down the hall back to my class. I felt like crying. I was so frustrated that this had to intrude into my life this way, but in the back of my mind I knew there was a purpose behind it, and I just needed to keep that in focus to push me forward.

A week had passed since Detective Morgan had told me he was going to talk to Ashley. I could not help but wonder all week how she would respond to his showing up. I could only pray for the best. Tuesday afternoon, as I walked to my 2:00 class, I got this weird sensation that Detective Morgan was going to call me that day. I had been in class fifteen minutes when I looked at my phone and saw I had a new voice mail from an unknown number. I knew it was him because every time he called me, his number came up as Unknown Caller. I had another hour of class before I could listen to the message—one hour of dreading what he would say.

Once class was over I listened to the voice mail, returned his call, but got his voice mail. I could not go through another night not knowing what had happened. I waited half an hour and called him again. This time he picked up.

We exchanged pleasantries before he got to the purpose of his call.

"I went to Ashley's house last week. We sat down and talked for a while."

I held my breath, not sure what he would say next.

"When I asked her if she was ever abused, she denied anything ever happening to her. I asked her if she remembered a friend named Erin. She mentioned your message but said the Erin she knew had a different last name."

The last name she gave Detective Morgan was very similar to my last name, which would be easy for a seven-year-old to confuse.

"I asked her about having sleepovers. She said she barely ever went to sleepovers because her mom would not let her but that she mainly only had sleepovers at her house for birthday parties."

I did not understand why she would say that when I spent the night at least four times at her house. Maybe she did not remember or want to remember.

"What's your opinion, Detective Morgan? Could you tell by her responses if she really had no idea what you were talking about? Do you think she was trying to protect her uncle?"

"She seemed afraid and nervous, but that could be just because I was questioning her."

Detective Morgan had spoken with her mother. She provided

READER/CUSTOMER CARE SURVEY

HEFG

We care about your opinions! Please take a moment to fill out our online Reader Survey at **http://survey.hcibooks.com**.
As a **"THANK YOU"** you will receive a **VALUABLE INSTANT COUPON** towards future book purchases
as well as a **SPECIAL GIFT** available only online! Or, you may mail this card back to us.

(PLEASE PRINT IN ALL CAPS)

First Name _____ MI. _____ Last Name _____

Address _____ City _____

State _____ Zip _____ Email _____

1. Gender
☐ Female ☐ Male

2. Age
☐ 8 or younger
☐ 9-12 ☐ 13-16
☐ 17-20 ☐ 21-30
☐ 31+

3. Did you receive this book as a gift?
☐ Yes ☐ No

4. Annual Household Income
☐ under $25,000
☐ $25,000 - $34,999
☐ $35,000 - $49,999
☐ $50,000 - $74,999
☐ over $75,000

5. What are the ages of the children living in your house?
☐ 0 - 14 ☐ 15+

6. Marital Status
☐ Single
☐ Married
☐ Divorced
☐ Widowed

7. How did you find out about the book?
(please choose one)
☐ Recommendation
☐ Store Display
☐ Online
☐ Catalog/Mailing
☐ Interview/Review

8. Where do you usually buy books?
(please choose one)
☐ Bookstore
☐ Online
☐ Book Club/Mail Order
☐ Price Club (Sam's Club, Costco's, etc.)
☐ Retail Store (Target, Wal-Mart, etc.)

9. What subject do you enjoy reading about the most?
(please choose one)
☐ Parenting/Family
☐ Relationships
☐ Recovery/Addictions
☐ Health/Nutrition
☐ Christianity
☐ Spirituality/Inspiration
☐ Business Self-help
☐ Women's Issues
☐ Sports

10. What attracts you most to a book?
(please choose one)
☐ Title
☐ Cover Design
☐ Author
☐ Content

TAPE IN MIDDLE; DO NOT STAPLE

BUSINESS REPLY MAIL
FIRST-CLASS MAIL PERMIT NO 45 DEERFIELD BEACH, FL

POSTAGE WILL BE PAID BY ADDRESSEE

Health Communications, Inc.
3201 SW 15th Street
Deerfield Beach FL 33442-9875

FOLD HERE

Comments

him with more pieces to this mystery. "Ashley's mother said that her brother lived with her back then, and at another point her fiancé lived with her."

"Yes, her brother is Ashley's uncle, the guy I've been telling you about."

"The problem is, Erin, if two different men lived there at different times I have to be positive I'm questioning the right guy."

I totally understood what he was saying, but because her mom said her brother had lived there matches up to exactly what I said, I did not understand why he could not just find the uncle and bring him in for questioning. But I also knew Detective Morgan had to check every detail before bringing anyone in. Because he had tracked down my childhood friend, drove to her house, and spoke with her and her mother had my head spinning. I just could not believe what I was hearing.

But the next words out of Detective Morgan's mouth took me by complete surprise. "Ashley's uncle is still living with her and her mom."

I could not believe it. All these years I wondered if he had moved on with his life, married, and had children. Then I wondered if he hurt his own children. Now I learned that he was still living in some back bedroom of his sister's house. Of all the different scenarios I had imagined, this was not one of them.

"His name is Richard."

Hearing this man's name sent chills over my body. It moved me that much closer to putting all the pieces together. For years he was just known to me as this piece of scum who took so much from me. The monster in my dreams, the rapist who stole my innocence, and finally a name to go with the haunting eyes in my nightmares.

"Tonia, Ashley's mom, said that Richard had worked the midnight shift at the gas station up the street from the house."

"That explains it."

"What do you mean, Erin? You said he came into Ashley's bedroom in the middle of the night. But that doesn't fit the timeframe if he worked the midnight shift."

"I was six and seven years old, and my bedtime was eight o'clock. At the sleepovers, we probably stayed up until eleven—the middle of the night to young children."

"Well, this is true."

"If her uncle worked just down the street doing the midnight shift, he was probably coming into the bedroom after Ashley's mom went to bed and before he left for work, which explains why many times he was not in pajamas or other nighttime clothing, but in jeans."

It all made complete sense to me and just getting the details of his name and where he worked made it all the more real. To now know where he went to work every night gave me the chills. I thought back to the last time he abused me at Ashley's eighth birthday party, after he had trapped me in the bathroom. Shortly after he came out dressed like he was going to work, and he never returned that night.

I knew we had the right guy, but Detective Morgan wanted to be positive and wanted to make sure the fiancé was not the man. Although he was just doing his job, I knew in my heart that Richard was the right guy. All the information Detective Morgan had learned added up to exactly what I had been saying from the initial police report.

Richard was not returning Detective Morgan's calls. I had a feeling Richard was tipped off. What would he think when a detective calls him from a town he no longer lives in, asking to speak with him? A part of me felt he was trying to cover his tracks and come up with a story.

I threw Detective Morgan an idea. "Can we do a photo lineup?

Maybe I could identify him that way." Although I really had no desire to look at this man's face again, I would do anything to prove to Detective Morgan that this was the right guy. I still had Richard's image burned into my memory from what he looked like in the early '90s.

"That's a good idea. I'll continue my investigation and be in touch."

After hanging up the phone, my mind once again raced. Unanswered questions were coming together and I was getting a much clearer picture. I wished the detective had enough to go on that matched what I said and what he learned about Ashley's uncle Richard to call him in for questioning. Everything Detective Morgan had learned matched my story. The words in my childish artwork spoke for me, saying I liked going to Ashley's when her uncle was not home.

A wave of emotions crashed over me. Clearly, this scumbag Richard knew exactly why this detective was calling him. The past he had tried to keep locked away was suddenly in his face. I am sure the minute he heard Detective Morgan was looking for him, he went into a state of panic. I hoped he was shaking in his pants. Maybe he was experiencing for once what it is like not to be able to sleep at night.

Why did I have such detailed memories of being at Ashley's house and spending the night on a few different occasions when she said she never had overnights except for birthday parties? It was not just my word against hers; my parents remember dropping me off at her house to spend the night. Then it dawned on me. The detective had described Ashley as being nervous and afraid, which made complete sense. If my rapist uncle still lived with me and I had a detective showing up at my house asking me if this ever happened, of course I would deny it. Ashley was probably terrified, and her uncle could come home at any moment and find her talking to the police. Of course she would deny it. Another thing occurred to me. If a detective came to my door saying my father had molested or raped one of my childhood friends when I was younger and I had absolutely no memory of it, I would be on the phone or send an e-mail to this person, wanting answers about their accusations. Ashley had my e-mail address. She could easily have contacted me, but she had not.

I sensed she was scared and overwhelmed. This Richard guy all these years seems to have lived a pretty low-key life, still living with his sister. I have grown and accomplished much in the sixteen years since he took my innocence. But he is still living in his sister's house in a back bedroom. It is as if he stagnated.

After getting off the phone with Detective Morgan, I thought of other questions, so I wrote them down to ask him when I called him the next day.

When I talked to him, he confirmed that Richard currently lives with Ashley and her mom.

"Doesn't it seem strange that after all these years he still lives with his sister?"

"Yes, it does. And if he does live there, it would make Ashley nervous to be talking to him, knowing he could've walked in the door while I was questioning her."

"Did you talk to Ashley in front of her mom?"

"No, I took her outside to talk to her."

A scenario formed in my mind. It is one thing if she really had no memory of abuse, but something told me she did what so many sexual abuse survivors do: she stayed silent because of fear and shame. Fear of the perpetrator. And one can only imagine what she may have gone through all these years living with that monster.

"Did she get defensive when you talked to her?"

"No, not at all."

"What about Ashley's mom? Was she defensive?"

"She was completely cooperative. She's supposed to call me and tell me the exact years her brother lived in the house."

I was so glad Tonia was cooperating with him rather than trying to protect her brother. God was very present during Detective Morgan's visit to Ashley's house. I could only pray that God would give Ashley the strength to speak the truth. I really hoped she was being truthful when she said she had no idea what the detective was talking about. Denying anything because she had repressed it would be better than to deny it because her uncle exerted control over her.

More questions popped into my mind: Where does Richard work? Does he have a criminal past? Why does he keep such a low profile living with his sister? Detective Morgan said he was in the process of gathering all that information.

I believed that Richard had some kind of mental illness or was taken over by the Devil. At age twenty-eight this rapist worked the midnight shift at a gas station, which raised several red flags. Was he so scary that he could not work the regular day hours. Now at forty-four, what had he done with his life? It did not seem he did much if he was still living in his sister's home. What a poor, pathetic waste of space.

I had waited a month before telling my older sister, Caitlin, all that was coming out. She lived out of state in Oregon. I waited to tell her until she was settled into her new home and new job. I did not like to have to share this kind of painful story over the phone, but she needed to know what everyone else in the family already knew. I spent nearly three hours on the phone telling her everything. At the outset she began crying, and the more I talked about it the more I broke down and cried.

Looking back now, she was able to understand why I had acted out the way I did while growing up. "When you put your hand through the window and we took you to the emergency room, the doctors and nurses tried holding you down, but you flipped out and were screaming and kicking. You lost it. I was ten and laughed at you, thinking it funny that you were so out of control. Grandpa took me out to the waiting room."

She told me how people could hear me screaming all the way down the hall. Many had stared in my direction, no doubt wondering why this little girl was screaming at the top of her lungs. Now I have another piece of the puzzle. I had no memory of throwing this fit in the ER, but it makes perfect sense why I would freak out if doctors held my hands and legs down. I do, however, remember that once they gave me something to calm me down, I just lay there, overcome with fear and staring at the elevator for Dad to appear.

After Caitlin told me this, I remembered another story. I was thirteen when I had an operation to correct blindness in one eye. Coming out of the anesthesia, I began kicking and swinging my arms. The doctor later told my parents and me that it took eight doctors and nurses to hold me down. These stories only made it more clear the pain I was holding on to inside and the panic I felt when I was not in control. These doctors in both situations had control over something I did not, and it most likely made me feel vulnerable and threatened, bringing out the fight in me to protect myself. I was terrified each time I had another eye operation and an anesthesiologist would explain that he would give me something that would put me to sleep. Internally I would freak out because I knew that a bunch of strangers, not me, would have control over me as I lay unconscious.

As I did with Allie, I told Caitlin all the times I came close to spilling everything to her. As she thought back to those times, she could remember thinking that I was holding back on her. And as Allie did, she apologized for picking on me throughout our childhood, oblivious to my personal horrors. She recounted how I was very cautious and that home was a very secure place for me. She was right. Home was my comfort zone. Nothing bad ever happened in my own home. Any holiday or family party we had at our house, Brian would never come near me. So the walls of my home were my security. It was outside those safe walls that I felt like a target: scared of what might happen to me, not knowing whom to trust, afraid I would be hurt again. The more I stayed home the fewer people I encountered and had to trust. That is why I made only a few close best friends. These select few I hung out with at their houses, and the rest of my friends I kept within the boundary of school.

After a long deep talk that brought up many memories and emotions with Caitlin, she thanked me for sharing everything with her and told me over and over how much she loved me.

I could not ask for such incredible parents and sisters, who have surrounded me with love and support. Without them I would not be the woman I am today. They are my rock. Little did I know that just months after breaking my silence and starting an investigation into this abuse and rape, my world would once again be flipped upside down in an instant. I had desperately tried to gain control over me, but I would see I had lost complete and utter control.

chapter seven

THE ACCIDENT

I was in my final semester of my senior year of college in January 2008. I had just spent the past three and a half years living in my college town of Macomb, Illinois. It is a small town that has more headstones and cornfields than it does people. I found peace and joy here. I loved seeing the sign WELCOME TO MACOMB every time I returned after summer or a school break. The four-hour drive is the most boring drive I have ever made. The biggest attraction in the town besides the university is its Super Wal-Mart. Even at that, this small college town brought me so much comfort and provided me with a new environment in which to grow and mature during my college years.

In December 2007, as I prepared to move home to finish off my final semester doing an internship in a crisis center near my hometown, I began to feel anxious about moving home.

For the final year and a half of college, I had lived in an apartment off campus with my college friend Nikki, my dog, Chance, and my cat, Bailey. Nikki counted down the weeks we had left to hang out together before I left, wanting to use what little time we had to really bond. I expressed my fears to her about moving home. My high school years were difficult, so my biggest goal when I graduated high school was to move away. At the same time, though, I always knew I would one day move back in with my parents while I established myself in my career. It was different now that I had grown and become independent.

Macomb held no painful reminders of my past. In my hometown I was surrounded by daily reminders of my childhood and had the fear of running into unsupportive relatives at a restaurant or grocery shopping. This concerned me as I faced moving home. I felt vulnerable moving home, but then I realized I was identifying with the girl I was before going away to college. I was no longer that fragile, silent teenager trying to find my place in life. I was moving home with a new reality, a chapter of my past was now opened and exposed, making me feel like a target for triggering reminders. Living on my own, I could easily hide my eating disorder, not so easy to hide under the perceptive eyes of my parents. They would be on my case, making sure I was eating enough. When I left Macomb in December I knew it was not good-bye forever. I still had to come down every other Friday for a three-hour seminar class, and I would stay with my sister Allie in her dorm until I graduated in May 2008.

It had been three months since I made the initial police report. My parents and I began to doubt Detective Morgan would have any success with the case. In December, my mother had stopped at a 7-Eleven to get coffee before going to work and ran into Detective Morgan. He had not returned any of my phone calls in weeks. The first thing he said to her when he saw her was, "I will be stopping in to the high school to talk to you. I have some questions."

Mom worked at the high school, which was right next to the police department, so it was easy for him to contact her. But another week passed before he stopped by the school to talk to her.

His first question was, "When Erin was a child, did you ever take her to be examined by a doctor?"

She told him what I had already explained to him. "Our family doctor was very old school. He did not do pelvic exams on children."

"Richard has a history of run-ins with the law, and he's not returning my phone calls." That came as no surprise. Richard obviously knew why this detective wanted to speak to him. "Also, this man is on kidney dialysis."

"Detective, has the Department of Children and Family Services been contacted, since Ashley's nine-year-old sister is living in the same home as Richard?"

I believed the first thing to be done was for the Department of Children and Family Services to check on the well-being of Ashley's sister. My biggest concern was to make sure he was not hurting other children, especially children who lived in the same home he did.

"I'm working on it. Ashley's mother assured me that her nine-year-old is never left alone with Richard. If she's not in school, she's in an after-school program until she's picked up. Her father, Tonia's husband, also lives in the home. He's gone on record as saying he does not like Tonia's brother living with them. I'm just waiting to speak with Richard."

I sent Detective Morgan an e-mail telling him I am not looking for him to lock this man up for my sake, because I will find my own justice by speaking out; rather, my concern was that Richard might be harming other children, especially his nine-year-old niece. Just because a mother says her daughter is never left alone with him does not mean he cannot be abusing her. Many times I was in a home filled with over forty relatives and my cousin still found ways to get me trapped behind some door and abuse me. So it was very possible he was doing the same.

A month went by, and after a week of intense domestic violence and sexual assault training for my internship at a crisis center, I received a call from a woman who worked at the Department of Children and Family Services. My name was on the contact for a report made. She said they were investigating the report and sending someone to the nine-year-old's school to speak with her. They would check to make sure she had not been abused in any way. It was refreshing to hear that someone would check on this child's well-being, but on the other hand, I feared learning this child was abused and that I could have said something sooner to prevent it. I prayed that whole night that she was safe and had not been hurt, and if she had, she would be brave enough to speak out.

The following day was a beautiful yet cold Saturday in January. I went out shopping and had just left a store to head home. It was nearly one in the afternoon as I came upon a busy intersection. The light had just turned red as I made my way into the left-turn lane, putting my foot on the brake.

Without warning, I was overcome with feeling as if the world were going in slow motion. Everything seemed to be closing in. I began tilting my head back and forth, feeling like I was about to faint. It was a much different feeling from a panic attack. I turned my head to look to the back of my car, and everything I saw was closing in. I saw what appeared to be a white light. I remember saying out loud, "What is happening to me?" My voice sounded so faint, as if I was miles away. I remember speaking, "I need air. I cannot breathe." That was the last thing I remembered.

When I awoke, I was in the back of an ambulance with three paramedics surrounding me, one man taking my blood pressure, another man asking me my name, and a woman appeared in my line of vision. I panicked. "What happened to me? Where am I?" But they did not answer me.

One of the male paramedics asked, "What day is it?"

"Wednesday."

"Try again."

"I don't know."

"Where were you coming from?"

"I don't know. What happened to me? Please, tell me what happened."

The back doors of the ambulance were open, and I could see cars on the busy intersection passing by.

The female paramedic finally answered me. "You've been in an accident. You had a seizure." She asked if I had any seizure-related conditions.

I was so confused and disoriented and kept asking them to let me go home.

"Honey, we need to take you to the hospital and get you checked out."

As I became more aware of my surroundings, I noticed that my pants were soaking wet.

Another paramedic who was talking to a police officer came back into the ambulance and saw me looking at my pants. "Oh, did you pee your pants?"

When this young paramedic pointed out that I had peed my pants, I asked God to wake me up from this nightmare. I was so confused and just wanted to wake up from this terrible experience and discover it was not really happening.

I asked for my phone so I could call my parents. My mom picked up on the first ring. I began crying. "Mom, I don't know what happened. I am so confused."

Of course, she panicked and I handed the phone to the female paramedic, who could explain what I could not. I listened as she told my mother that I had hit the man in front of me because I'd had a seizure at the wheel. The man I hit had looked up in his rearview mirror and saw me violently shaking. He jumped from his car and came to my aid. He reached over me to put my car in PARK and called 911. He said that from the time he reached me until I stopped shaking, it seemed to be thirty seconds.

When my parents arrived at the scene, they expected to see my car smashed up. But since I was at a stop light with my foot on the break when the seizure began, I rolled into the car in front of me, only tapping it. Neither car had a scratch on it.

When I arrived at the emergency room, I was crying and confused as to why this happened to me. My parents notified both my sisters. Allie was in the area and went straight to the hospital. Caitlin, who was moving home in a week from out of state, called to hear what happened. As I relayed the sequence of events, I began remembering more. The entire aura I got before I had the seizure and blacked out came back to me. I then remembered waking up when the paramedics and fire department first arrived at the scene of the accident. I saw the flashing lights and hundreds of cars around me. I must have passed out again, because the next thing I remembered was waking up in the back of the ambulance. I had no memory of being transported from my car into the ambulance.

For the next seven hours I was in the emergency room. I had an EKG, and a CT scan of my brain. We could not figure why I'd had a seizure when I had never had one before. Was it because I was worn out from the stress of my intense, weeklong training? Was it because I had gotten so few hours of sleep the night before because I was up late with my sister, her friend, and my boyfriend?

The doctor said all the tests came back fine so he discharged me, but I could not drive until I was cleared by a neurologist. He gave me the name of one and I was to call in the morning to set up an appointment.

Once again I found myself in a situation not in my control. My brain had done something I had no way of controlling. I wondered if I was putting too much on myself. I became very emotional not knowing why this freak thing had happened to me. My parents kept saying it could have been a lot worse: I could have been traveling at a high rate of speed, lost control, and ended up in a coma or even dead. I had to be thankful I had no serious injuries.

The next morning when I woke up, every muscle in my body ached. It was worse than the day after I walked the Chicago marathon back in 2003. The seizure gave my muscles the biggest workout they had ever had. Every little movement hurt for the first few days, and I had a headache that lasted days.

I had an appointment five days later with a neurologist, who felt maybe it had to do with stress and not getting enough sleep. He needed to make sure everything was physically okay with me, so I set up an appointment with a heart doctor for an EEG and an echocardiogram.

The neurologist also told me I could not drive until these tests all came back fine. He explained the state normally does not allow you to drive until six months after you have had a seizure. Just the thought of that made me want to cry. Not only did I feel I was losing complete control of my life, but also my independence.

I soon became dependent on my family. They took turns driving me to doctors' appointments and my internship at the crisis center. In the midst of my own health crisis, I did a good job hiding it when I entered the doors of the crisis center. I worked with several kinds of people: shelter mothers and children, walk-in clients who needed food assistance or clothing, homeless people who just wanted a blanket to sleep on that night. Helping the less fortunate kept me focused while so much of my life was unknown. I tried my best to hide the confusion, fear, and pain I was feeling inside. I let that show behind closed doors when I got home. I felt as if I was on top of the world and then suddenly pushed to the edge of a cliff, about to fall into a dark hole. I searched my soul for meaning in what was happening to me. Turning to God like I have throughout my life, I asked Him to show me what I could not see. I could not bear to take on any more pain and grief in my life.

I had to do the one thing I struggled with most: trust these doctors.

Sitting in the cardiologist's waiting room, I felt out of place because I was surrounded by people who appeared to be sixty-five or older. The doctor did an echocardiogram. Sticky patches called electrodes were placed all over my chest to track and record my heart rhythm. While lying down, a cold gel was applied to my chest and a device called a transducer was placed over my heart. The transducer sends and receives high frequency sound waves and the monitor shows pictures of my heart beating. The process took about forty-five minutes. Then I was hooked up to a heart monitor that I had to wear for twenty-four hours and return the next day.

How could a healthy young adult like myself need to have my heart checked out? "Nothing is wrong with me," I told myself. I felt like there was a hidden message I was not picking up on that God wanted me to see in everything that was happening in my life.

With each passing day I grew more depressed and desperate for answers. One day a letter arrived in the mail from the secretary of state, informing me my driver's license had been revoked due to a loss of consciousness at the wheel. A doctor would have to fill out paperwork to say I was medically okay to operate a vehicle. I wanted to rip the letter up; instead, I threw my hands in the air, looked to the skies, and asked God to come down and comfort me. I needed to feel His love.

When I was not interning at the crisis center three days a week, I spent my off days in bed sleeping. I wanted to wake from this nightmare that had trapped me. My drive to be thin and obsessing over my image went out the window, and I looked to food for comfort. Doctors ruled out anorexia as the cause of the seizure; most people who are anorexic faint. I had eaten a turkey sandwich right before the seizure occurred.

Back in November I had spoken to high school students about my journey. A young female student approached me afterward and asked if the abuse I had endured had caused the eating disorder. The students I was trying to educate were teaching me something I needed to know.

She could not know that she made me realize what kind of example I was setting for students by not taking care of my body, giving it what it needs to function well. I was being a bad example and needed to find a new healthy outlet to find the control I desired. I made an effort to get to a healthy weight, even though I knew it would not be an easy process. Overcoming an eating disorder is a huge challenge in itself. It sucks the energy out of you and fills your head with negative, unwanted thoughts. I often played mind games with myself, trying to make myself believe that the working out I did was healthy. I needed to fill my soul with positive, good thoughts, and it would start with getting back on track with a healthy body image and accepting myself for how God created me. I had gained weight before, only to be consumed with negative images and I fell back into starving myself. What I did not know yet was that I was starving myself of what I could not yet see.

Many sexual abuse survivors fall into unhealthy sexual activity like prostitution because how they view themselves and their bodies and their perception of love is skewed. What many fail to realize is that having sex with numerous men or selling their bodies is just another unhealthy way of coping with the pain they have yet to work through. For many sexually abused victims, someone else taking control over their bodies is all they have ever known. So they continue to use their bodies for sex—prostitution or going from one man to the next—looking for love in unhealthy ways. It is when they finally come to terms with their abuse and shatter their silence that they actually find the true meaning of love and a healthy relationship. Once they work through the abuse, they can understand that sex is more than lust, more than two physical bodies coming together; it is an emotional and spiritual connection between the souls of two people who are expressing love for each other.

Some abuse survivors often walk the difficult road to recovery using drugs. It is a way to avoid feeling the pain of sexual abuse. Using drugs numbs the pain but does not deal with it. The source of the drug addiction lies deep beneath the surface.

It is easy to point to someone and say she has an eating disorder or drug problem, she is a prostitute, he does self-injury, and so on. But the outsider cannot see the invisible scars on the inside that caused them to fall into these unhealthy ways of coping and living. You can never judge a book by its cover until you know what is going on inside and get the full story.

In the midst of my health crisis that was taking an emotional toll on me, I began to get answers. The heart doctors gave me the good news that my heart was in great shape and there was nothing to cause concern.

My next test was with the neurologist for my EEG test. It is a sleep-deprivation test. I had to stay up most of the night except for two or three hours of sleep. Then I went into the doctor's office and a medical technician attached wires to my head, which measured my brain's electrical activity. This test would show if there was any spiking or firing activity in the brain. The process took over an hour.

Less then a week later, Caitlin drove me to the neurologist to get the test results. I wanted closure for myself and my family on this mysterious seizure. We all assumed everything would come back normal, so I was not prepared for the look on the doctor's face when I asked him if everything looked great. It was that look that says "I have life-changing news for you."

The doctor got up to close his office door. "Your EEG and MRI both show problems in the temporal lobe. It's called mesial temporal lobe sclerosis."

Panic bubbled within me. It was a bunch of foreign nonsense to me. "What is it? What does that mean?"

"You have temporal lobe epilepsy."

My head started spinning. "That can't be right. How is this possible? This cannot be happening to me!"

The neurologist spent the next twenty minutes explaining that I would need to take seizure medication for life, I would not be able to drive for six months from the date of the seizure, and that the kind of epilepsy I have is best treated with brain surgery. "You most likely developed this kind of epilepsy when you were coming out of the birth canal."

"Does being born without a sense of smell have anything to do with it?"

"No, it doesn't."

It was all too overwhelming. I cried hysterically in the doctor's office. I went in with the impression I was under too much stress, and I walked out with the news that I had epilepsy. The neurologist made the diagnosis and prognosis worse when he warned me of the birth defects the medications cause. It only made me cry more. I had wanted to create a large family, but the doctor told me my children would have a higher risk of mental retardation and cleft lip.

He offered two different kinds of medication. Keppra works

immediately, while Lamictal takes weeks to gradually build up in the system. He strongly suggested Keppra so that I would be protected immediately. I could only cry, but I followed his suggestion.

He came off as being very cold and ignored how I was reacting to this news. I sensed my crying made him uncomfortable and he didn't know how to respond. You'd think medical school would teach doctors how to show empathy when they give patients life-changing news. He obviously missed that class. He was not reassuring at all; he only made things sound worse. Before I even grasped the idea of having epilepsy, he was spewing all the warnings of birth defects from the medication.

Before getting me sample medication, he asked me one last question: "Do you struggle with any anxiety?"

"Yes, I take medication for it."

"Hmmm. One of Keppra's side effects is increased anxiety. Because you have that, it's liable to make it even worse. You might do better with Lamictal."

I made an appointment to see him in a month. I left his office sobbing and walked through the waiting room, going right past Caitlin, who sat in the waiting room, to the parking lot. She caught up with me and asked what happened.

Just as we were pulling out of the lot, my phone rang. My mother was calling from work to find out the results. She knew just by the sound in my voice that it was not good. I cried into the phone and told her I had epilepsy. She told me she was leaving work and coming home.

The entire way home I kept saying that I could not handle any more pain and confusion. I felt defeated, weak. What control I had been taking back seemed to be ripped away again. I had just been told that I have a disorder I have no control over. I rested my head against the window and tears streamed down my face. I said to my sister, "I have only so much strength. My heart cannot carry any more pain. I cannot handle another hurdle."

She reached over and held my hand. "Erin, look how much you've overcome. Yes, this is a blow, but you can rise above this, too."

"I don't have the energy to find meaning behind all this pain. I've done enough of that. I just want to give up on life."

The news traveled quickly to Allie, who was away at school, and to my Dad, who was working. At noon I had a previously scheduled phone meeting with my editor, Michele, to discuss my manuscript. I was in no shape to talk about it when I was struggling to see beyond this all. When Michele called, the first thing she asked me was how I was. I told her immediately what I had just been told hours earlier in the doctor's office. I tried to keep myself from breaking down on the phone with her. Unlike the doctor, Michele expressed empathy to me and rescheduled a time for us to talk about my manuscript.

I spent the rest of the day lying on the couch and crying. So much uncertainty ran through me. I won't lie. I did not know if I had the will to survive to discover what the future might hold. I did not know if I would spend my life worrying if and when I would have another seizure, how frequently they might occur, and if I would ever have my independence back.

While I went between crying and sleeping, my mother called a good family friend Nancy, whose daughter has epilepsy and works with some of the best doctors in the state of Illinois at the Epilepsy Center at Rush Hospital in Chicago. My mother relayed the news, and Nancy suggested getting me in to see the doctor her daughter, Megan, goes to and for whom she works. Nancy was able to set up an appointment for me to see Dr. Rossi, an epileptic specialist.

I realized I needed to turn to God and ask Him to take away my pain and confusion and help me make sense of this life-changing news. I needed His guidance to help me find the meaning behind it. I believe everything happens for a reason. I just did not know if I had the energy to search for the meaning and purpose behind this. I felt as if I had fallen into a dark hole.

As the days progressed, I grew more depressed. I was the most emotional I had ever been in my life. I began having horrible headaches—a side affect of Lamictal. I put my guard up and tried the best to hide my emotions when I went into the crisis center to work. I felt like a hypocrite. I counseled people who called a crisis line. They faced different crises in their own lives, some sharing thoughts of suicide. I would try to get them to see a purpose beyond their pain and encourage them not to give up. Yet when I went home each night, I would crawl into bed and cry or sleep. I still had not found my purpose beyond the pain I was feeling. I slept all day on my days off and turned to God to hold my pain for me. My family did the best they could to help me through this, but like I have done so many times throughout my life, I kept pulling away, hiding my pain in darkness behind closed doors. My family saw me spiraling into a deep depression and made sure I talked about what I was feeling. I could not talk without getting emotional, so again I cried. It continued like that for weeks.

I usually broke down and cried every night. Crying was not like me, and I was uncomfortable feeling so weak and defeated. One particular night in February, my mother and sister wanted me to talk about my feelings.

"I don't want to talk about it because I feel I've lost control over my emotions and end up crying."

"You cannot carry this alone. You have family to lean on, who want to help you carry this load."

I looked at them both and once again the tears welled. "I just don't know if I have the will to live. I was knocked to the ground when I began to lose my vision when I was eleven. I've had to deal with the horror of Brian molesting me and overcome the pain from that. I had to fight to finally find my voice and get back on my feet again."

I wiped away the tears that streamed down my face. "If that is not tough enough, I have to live every day haunted with the image burned in my head of the young child I once was lying on a bed as a grown man used his force, power, and control to rape me. I had no one to rescue me or hear my screams, so all I could do was cry. I abandoned that child I once was. I cannot turn back time and change the past. I am trying to allow that little girl to grieve for what was taken from her."

I could no longer find words to express myself. We were all quiet. Then my silence turned to crying like the little girl I once was as a man forced himself on top of me. I suddenly felt like I was six again, but instead of suffering in my pain alone, I showed both my mother and sister what I had carried alone all these years.

Allowing myself to go back to a place when I was so vulnerable, scared, and frightened brought up much of the same feelings I had about the seizure and the diagnosis of epilepsy. Once again I was in a situation where I had a loss of control and power. It also left me feeling vulnerable, scared, and frightened. Two completely different situations, yet they both brought out the same emotions.

My mother and sister were on either side of me, comforting me as I cried. All the crying gave me a pounding headache. Crying in front of my family and letting them see the emotional roller coaster I was on was something I had never done before. I had always held it in out of fear of what would pour out of me.

When I finally went to bed that night, I lay in the darkness and spoke up to God. "Hold the six-year-old that I once was in the palm of one of Your hands, and hold the twenty-three-year-old I now am in the palm of Your other hand. Then bring Your hands together and pull me close to Your heart so I can feel the beating of Your heart filling me with Your insight, love, comfort, guidance, confidence, strength, courage, and determination.

I woke up the next morning with a new vision for my life. I had been searching since I was six to trust people and be in control. The more I searched, the more hurdles I was thrown: vision problems, sexual abuse from Brian, self-injury, eating disorder, and now epilepsy. I was forced by circumstances to put my trust in others. When I did, it seemed that I was betrayed over and over. It was a constant struggle. Time and again I would find myself in a situation where I would have to put my control in the hands of others, and at the same time I would fight for it back.

The next morning, after crying like I had never cried before, I had an epiphany: I do not need to be the one in control. Instead I need to give my trust to God, recognize that He is in control at all times, no matter what circumstances life throws at me, and He will not leave my side.

The seizure and subsequent diagnosis of epilepsy rocked me to the core, but it did more than just that. It is what allowed the walls I had surrounded myself with to come down, and it pulled the pain from my childhood out. I never realized crying would give me such a release, but it allowed me to let out the many emotions I had carried inside for sixteen years. I let them all go and understood that no matter how many times I had faced another hurdle, each time I somehow found inner peace and strength from it. Pain once again allowed me to grow, drawing me back to my soul where my spirit thrives to reach the skies and soar.

We humans are all different from one another—different ethnicities, disabilities, beliefs, morals, and values—but one thing we have in common is what no one can see: the soul. Our souls allow us to live life to the fullest. Those who are fully engaged in discovering their full potential, no matter what circumstances come their way are listening to their hearts and souls. These are the people who overcome anything and accomplish whatever they put their minds to.

Even on some of the darkest and gloomiest days, my soul still bursts with light. The light within me is like a burning torch that keeps me pushing forward to see what this life is all about. Everything else is in God's hands.

By mid-February, just a few weeks after I received the diagnosis of epilepsy, I received a second opinion by Dr. Rossi, an epileptic specialist from Rush University Hospital. After reviewing my medical history, MRI, and EEG, he questioned the diagnosis of epilepsy. It was bittersweet news.

My parents, Caitlin, and I gathered in his office as he showed us on his computer screen the MRI image of my brain. It was bizarre to see the different areas of my brain. He spent over an hour showing us the abnormal area in my brain. He pointed out a dark cluster that he believed were cells that had developed in my brain while I was in the womb. These cells caused irritation to the brain, which triggered the seizure. It was like watching Discovery Health channel, but it was much closer to home, since it was my own brain I saw. Dr. Rossi explained the MRI was poor quality and wanted a better image to determine exactly what the dark image was. My father was concerned it could be a brain tumor, but Dr. Rossi assured us it was not.

Dr. Rossi admitted me to the hospital to run better tests. He also took me off the Lamictal medication that was causing horrible headaches and placed me on Topamax, another antiseizure medication. Within a day of taking it, my head was spinning. No matter if I stood up or lay down, I had a constant spinning feeling. It is a common side effect, and it continued for five days. I called Dr. Rossi, and together he and I decided to give Keppra a try. It was the drug the neurologist who diagnosed temporal lobe epilepsy wanted to first put me on but decided against because of the increased side effect of anxiety. I started off on a very small dosage of 250 milligrams. The good thing about Keppra, unlike the other two drugs I tried, was that it took effect immediately. After a week I had no side effects, other than being tired. Dr. Rossi prescribed two pills a day. It seemed to work for me.

On March 11, 2008, I was admitted to Rush University Hospital in Chicago. No sooner had I gotten into my hospital room, when I was once again hooked up for an EEG. Twenty-four wires were glued to my scalp, recording my brain waves and looking for any kind of spiking and firing activity. I was videotaped, along with audio, during the test. My activity was monitored. The purpose is that if a patient has a seizure during the EEG, doctors would be able to review the tape and brain activity of what the patient was doing right before the seizure occurred.

Allie was home on spring break and stayed the night with me in the hospital. Dad had taken me to the hospital, and after I was settled in my room, he made sure I was okay with his leaving me. I laughed and told him I was not a seven-year-old anymore. I reassured him I would be okay and told him to go home and get some sleep. He did not need to sleep in my hospital room like he had when I was a little girl. I pointed to the small uncomfortable couch my dad would have slept on if he were to stay the night with me. We both laughed at how some things never change in hospitals.

After Dad left, my sister and I watched television and played cards as nurses continued to check on me or draw blood. I felt like I had a helmet attached to my head because of all the glue and wires on it. I got very little sleep throughout the night because the nurses woke me up regularly to see how I was doing or to take my vital signs. At one point I looked at my cell phone to see what time it was after being woken up three times and saw that was only 1:30. Allie slept through every nurse coming into the room, but I could not fall back asleep for over an hour. I knew someone was watching me on a video monitor, and it made me uncomfortable. I felt like my privacy was violated with every moment being monitored. Once again I closed my eyes and imagined myself on the soft sand of my safe island with the sun beaming down on me and the ocean waves crashing on shore. It allowed me to remove myself from the icky feelings of a dark hospital to the safe comfort of nature's beauty.

The next morning I awoke to a wonderful nurse giving me my morning pill of Keppra and bringing me breakfast. She introduced herself as Lindsay; she would be my nurse throughout the day. After getting an IV in the morning for the MRI I would have later that day, Lindsay spent some time getting to know Allie and me. Allie mentioned to her how I had turned my childhood diary into a book. Lindsay asked me all sorts of questions. Then it dawned on me that it had been ten years ago, during spring break, that Allie had broken her silence to me about our cousin. Here we were ten years later during our college spring break spending it at Rush University Hospital. It made me wonder where I would be ten years from that very moment.

After lunch the EEG wires were finally removed, which took a good deal of time because they had to rub acetone into my head to remove the wires. It would take a few showers before I scrubbed all the glue completely off my head.

In the afternoon, a nurse arrived to take me down for my closed MRI. It was the part of the hospital stay I was dreading the most. The fear of being trapped in a closed, tight area often brought on panic attacks. These kinds of things reminded me of being held down and unable to escape when I was abused.

Lindsay, who was only two years older than me, turned to me in the hall before I was pushed into the elevators. "Erin, after everything you have already overcome, the MRI is going to be a big nothing."

Hearing her say that boosted my confidence. And I reminded myself that I can just keep my eyes closed and go to that safe island I have always escaped to when I was afraid.

When I finally made it to the MRI room, I was left alone with an African American man who would be going over everything with me. His presence reminded me of Richard. He explained he could put a washcloth over my eyes if I thought I might open them once inside and freak out.

"I trust myself enough to keep my eyes closed."

"Would you like to listen to music during the procedure?"

"That would be wonderful."

The MRI was loud, so the tech gave me earphones to listen to a local station I liked. I closed my eyes and was backed into the closed machine. I kept myself calm the entire time, and the music was soothing. Instead of reminding myself where I was, I imagined once again being on the beach, listening to my iPod. Toward the end of the procedure, I was pulled out then pushed back in for the final part of the MRI. I decided to open my eyes, and I discovered I had nothing to fear. No panic set in. Instead, I stayed calm and relaxed, realizing the end of the MRI was near.

When it was all over, I was brought back to my hospital room, where Allie was waiting with both my mom and dad. I filled out discharge paperwork, and then we were on our way home. It took us over an hour to get through Chicago traffic. A half hour after returning home, I received a phone call from Dr. Rossi. He had looked at my EEG and MRI. He said the EEG showed a couple of extra large spikes and the MRI clearly showed the problem. He determined that I was born with scar cells near my temporal lobe, but that it was not temporal lobe epilepsy. These scar cells are called astrocytes. They can irritate the normal, surrounding brain cells. He explained that because I have had them my whole life and experienced my first seizure at nearly twenty-three, I could go the rest of my life never having another one again. Dr. Rossi explained the medication Keppra keeps this irritation from spreading through brain pathways beyond this local irritation. Because there was a small amount of activity, he would like to keep me on Keppra for two years and then take me off it. Dr. Rossi went on to explain that the MRI clearly shows these scar cells are blocking the area that controls my sense of smell. It finally made sense all these years why I could never smell anything. It was crazy that the neurologist I first saw said it had nothing to do with my not being able to smell. The lesson I learned was getting a second opinion is a must.

Dr. Rossi said to send him my medical forms to fill out so I could get my driver's license back. It was such a relief to hear. After going through so much confusion, misdiagnosis, and being told I may need brain surgery to stop having future seizures, Dr. Rossi's diagnosis and prognosis finally gave me some clear answers.

He also said that he was pretty certain that from what he could tell in my MRI, my memory, speech, reading, and writing that is normally developed in the temporal lobe went elsewhere in my brain when I was developing as a baby. These kinds of scar cells would normally affect my speaking and writing development, which would mean that I should have been struggling to do these skills. It would be impossible for me to have developed the ability to speak, write, and memorize had the cells that control these areas not developed in some other area of the brain. I am gifted at speaking and writing, and unfortunately my memory is so sharp that I often wish there were things I would not have to remember, so what he said made sense. At some point Dr. Rossi can test to see in what part of my brain my speech and memory developed.

I had never been able to smell because the scar cells blocked my sense of smell. But something incredible happened to me toward the end of March 2008, when I splashed a bit of perfume on me. I suddenly had a strong reaction and was overwhelmed with this amazing aroma. Living my whole life unable to smell, I was truly taken by surprise. Over the course of the next few months I began to notice different smells. I stuck a piece of gum in my mouth and for the first time could smell its strong straw-berry scent. My sister laughed at me as I freaked out over being able to smell it. I went through the perfume departments in stores, trying all the testers to smell the different fragrances. My entire life my parents and sisters had always told me how won-derful lilac flowers smell, and I longed to know what it was like. When my mom brought in a bunch from the bushes in our yard, I took one sniff and understood why they all loved the scent. I began associating the tastes of things with how they smelled. I remember putting on vanilla hand lotion. "It smells like it tastes!"

So far I am not able to smell everything, but of the few things I can, I have not once smelled anything with an awful odor. I have smelled only wonderful scents, and I hope it stays this way. I am probably the only person who could say they do not mind clean-ing out the cat litter every day. My favorite aroma so far is hazel-nut coffee.

I do not know why I suddenly could smell, but I am sure my doctor might be able to explain it. I assume it has something to do with my medication, since I began to be able to determine scents shortly after I began taking it. Maybe the cluster of cells that have blocked the area in my brain is changing due to the medication.

I am no doctor, so it remains a mystery to me for now, but I wake up every day looking forward to what new smell I will discover. I realize for the first time what I have been missing.

The entire ordeal of my seizure opened my eyes to seeing God's grace. Maybe this was His way to show me that I needed not only to let go of my need for control and trust but also to see that I have had this birth defect my entire life in the area of my brain where many childhood memories were stored away, just waiting for the right time to give me the wake-up call I needed. Maybe that is the true miracle in it all, the wake-up call it gave me. These cells are something I have carried with me my entire life that I had no idea existed, unlike the secret of rape that I was always aware of.

Throughout my life, I have tried to be bold and strong, never allowing myself to feel the pain from when I was raped. In the big picture, maybe this seizure saved me from going down an even darker road. Because of the seizure I pulled the emotions from my soul to the surface and grieved what I was never able to grieve as a child. As I have learned in life, if you are willing to search, you can draw meaning from pain.

I was so concerned and worried about my health, the entire investigation slipped my mind. It was not until after riding a roller coaster of emotions that what came out of the investigation of Richard sank in.

chapter eight

JUSTICE THROUGH MY VOICE

In January, four days after having the seizure and the evening I was released from the emergency room, I received an unexpected phone call from Detective Morgan. I had not heard from him in nearly two months and had settled with the idea that there was nothing that could be done because the rape had taken place too long ago.

Detective Morgan apologized for taking so long to get back to me. He explained the process of the investigation, which took time. He had made several attempts to contact Richard through the telephone, but Richard would not return his calls. When he had finally gotten through to him, Richard said that his attorney advised him to remain silent and he had nothing further to say. Our only real hope was having Richard come in and speak with Detective Morgan in person. This way he could hopefully break Richard down and get a confession. It sounded as though Richard was not about to say a word because he knew the truth of what he had done. Unfortunately, that meant it was my word against his, and it would go nowhere in court unless I had Ashley backing my claims.

The Department of Children and Family Services went to the elementary school Ashley's nine-year-old sister attended, and someone had talked in private with her. She had not revealed any abuse.

"Thank God. Let's just hope she is not being silenced, and if she were being hurt that she would have the courage to tell her mom. I hope her mom is extra cautious with her daughter when she's around Richard."

"You'll be glad to know that Tonia forced her brother to move out after all these years of living with her. Once she learned why I questioned Ashley and her and wanted to talk to Richard, she kicked him right out."

His words were like a blessing dropped from the skies. If that was the closest thing I could get to justice, I would be satisfied.

"That surprises me. I have not seen Tonia since I was a child. Considering Ashley said she had no memory of being abused, yet she sent her brother packing, Tonia must believe what I said is true. That's a sense of justice for me."

I have lived many years with an extended family that did not support my sister and me even when Brian confessed to the police. And yet this woman I am not related to kicked out her brother based on my report to the police that he had raped me sixteen years earlier. I surely did not see that coming and was stunned.

I expressed to Detective Morgan over and over how much happiness that brought me. "I have my voice; I can find justice through speaking out. Maybe with Richard no longer living with them, Ashley can find her own voice and break her silence."

Tonia's husband did not like Richard living with them. Maybe other things I did not know led Tonia to the decision to kick Richard out of her home.

"The last time I talked to Tonia, she told me she is a survivor of childhood sexual abuse."

I gasped and the hairs on my arms rose. The pieces to the puzzle were coming together. No wonder she kicked him out; she knew exactly what I lived through. Of course she is going to protect her children. It dawned on me that by breaking my silence, I might have helped Ashley's mother find her voice. An overwhelming sense of compassion for this woman came over me. Not only had she opened up and shared her own pain, but also made sure her children would be safe. She had no idea the justice she gave me.

I wondered that if Tonia had been sexually abused as a child, could it be that Richard had also been sexually abused? Are secrets hidden deep beneath the surface in that family like so many others? Was I getting a clear picture that what this man did to me had been done to him as a child? Too many things alarmed me: Richard's working night shifts at a gas station, his still living with his sister when he was in his forties, and learning of the sexual abuse in Tonia's childhood. I believe Richard and Tonia's family had secrets, just like mine did.

Tonia told Detective Morgan that Ashley would be getting counseling, and if Ashley remembered anything, they would contact him.

The detective reminded me that I could bring charges against Richard until I am thirty-eight, giving Ashley plenty of time to find her voice. At the same time, I believe Richard's days are numbered because of his kidney failure.

I honestly think it would take a miracle to hold Richard accountable for his actions. I think even if Ashley were ever to come forward, it would still be our word against his. There is no physical evidence and so many years have gone by. The miracle would be Richard confessing, and he seems too much of a coward ever to do that.

I received the closure I needed, I am glad I found my voice, and

Richard lived to know that the little girl he hurt did not forget. The little girl he once silenced with his hand over her mouth found her voice, even if it took sixteen years. It empowered me to know Richard knew I did not spend the rest of my life in silence the way he had hoped.

The cries of the little girl silenced inside of me have been exposed, no longer under his power and control. Richard may have taken my innocence and filled my head with unimaginable images, but he was unable to take my soul, which has allowed me to grow. The light that pours out of my soul is so much more powerful than the darkness I have encountered. I went back and rescued the little girl trapped behind closed doors. There is no way around the heartaches we face in life. I used my pain to fuel the push that moved me forward.

When I decided to go public with my story, I placed on myself the lifetime responsibility to educate others about abuse and to work to prevent it. I hope people will follow in my footsteps to end the silence of sexual abuse. That does not mean that all I ever think about is my past and what my next step will be to heighten awareness of abuse. I hope to one day travel the globe to educate millions. For now, I balance my life's mission of traveling the United States and still take time to enjoy life, including escaping not to an imaginary beach in my head but the real thing. I have pushed myself to strive for the best in life.

We cannot change the path God has chosen for us. We can accept it and learn to overcome life's obstacles. Though it may not make sense now why certain events occur in your life, one day you will get a clear understanding. Take my life thus far as an example: keeping a journal of the good memories from my childhood and remembering them helped keep everything in perspective—the bad I endured as well as the good. Start writing down your dreams for the future, then begin turning them into reality. With time you will replace the nightmares with the dreams you hope to accomplish.

To find out what life is all about and to get a clear understanding of why things happen the way they do, you must begin to put the pieces of your life together. Sometimes the pieces do not fit the way we want, or pieces are missing. Finding the answers to my past was like a job. I could not just sit back and expect the answers to fall into my lap. I had to work to find the answers, put the pieces together, and forgive. With a little self-determination and motivation, you can begin to get a clear picture of your life. It suddenly comes full circle and the pieces begin to fit together to form a picture.

By finding my voice and speaking out, I found my purpose in life. Pain can make people stronger. No matter how great the pain you experience, at some point in your life you will find the strength and meaning behind the events that caused your pain. The biggest obstacle many people face is looking past the pain and searching inside for a purpose. It is like driving for miles on an unfamiliar road in darkness with no map. You feel lost and alone. Suddenly the road goes uphill and becomes filled with potholes. You are tired and just want to give up. Pain in our lives makes us feel this same way, like every day is an uphill battle. To gain a good perspective of the life we have been given, we have to trust that whatever troubles fall on us, with time and strong faith, the path will become clear again, allowing us to move forward in life.

I know the feeling of not wanting to get out of bed and face another day. If you find your inner strength and search for God's purpose for your life, you will make it through the forest and over the hills to see the true beauty waiting on the other side. When you hear of a child being killed by gun violence, a mother paralyzed from a drunk driver, a man ending his life, and a parent not returning from war, all four tragic events can be turned into positive messages that may one day save the life of someone else. In any tragic event a purpose can be discovered, even when that purpose seems far outside of your reach, with so many layers to peel away and work through. It is discovering that purpose that allows people to find their strength again. I believe God created a world that was not perfect so we would experience pain and see how we handle what life throws us. Some turn toward God when in pain, some turn against God. I have done both, and I can say it was when I turned toward Him that I saw Him working in my life. Even when I turned my back on Him, He did not turn His back on me. Today might be that day you need to open that door in your life and allow Him in.

Think of how long you have suffered through your pain. Has it been weeks, months, years, or decades? Has anything changed from yesterday to today? Allowing yourself to suffer is like never moving forward. Each day you let time slip by, never resolving the deeper meaning to your pain but instead becoming numb to it. It is like picking off a scab over and over again, never giving the wound a chance to heal. You have a scab on your mind and soul that needs to heal, but it cannot heal until you are ready to deal with the pain you buried deep within yourself and recognize it. The sand in your hourglass is slipping away and the clock is still ticking. Do not let another moment slip away; you cannot get it back.

To find your purpose you must first start off by exposing the wound. Whether that is opening up to a friend or family member and breaking your silence or taking that first step and seeing a therapist. Healing does not happen overnight. You must be patient. Building a support network around you is healthy. The sooner you begin the healing process the sooner you will realize you are not alone. Support groups exist throughout communities and churches that help sexual abuse survivors. You might be surprised by how many other people in your life may have had similar experiences they never shared. There is nothing wrong with asking for help. It is a sign of strength, not weakness.

Every day we encounter people who have been affected by sexual violence and do not even know it. It may be the person ahead of you in the supermarket checkout, the bank teller, your boss, the cop pulling you over, your child's teacher, a neighborhood child who plays with your kids, or, as in my case, a loved one. Sexual abuse victims cannot be picked out of a crowd. A sexual abuse survivor bears no physical signs. It is the invisible scar no one can see. Spending another day suffering is letting another day of your life be taken from you. It is allowing your abuser to continue to have control long after the abuse has stopped.

Take all the negative feelings you have toward the person who abused you and turn them into something positive. I spent far too many years of my life sucked into the pain, allowing the past to haunt me. Not a day goes by that I do not realize how much happiness I allowed Brian and Richard to take from me. I cannot change the past, but I can live for the moment, knowing their actions no longer rob me of my happiness.

Wake each morning as if it were your last. Turn your dreams into realities: turn your past into something positive you can use to teach others about. The hardships we face in life have been placed there for a reason. It is our purpose to discover the reason behind it. I am not saying you will wake up tomorrow with all of life's answers, but you will be one step closer to finding closure and meaning in your life. The tools you need to heal your life may come from books, therapists, awareness, but the answers come from within. It takes self-discovery to find it. You are the only one who can choose happiness for yourself; no one else can. It starts with standing up, looking at yourself in the mirror, and identifying what you are running from and how you are going to conquer it.

Seek and discover your full potential. You may be surprised at just how much strength you really have; don't sell yourself short. Challenge yourself and step outside your comfort zone. I promise you it is not as scary as it seems. It will push you to continue to move forward. Many survivors of sexual abuse continue to be victims long after the abuse has stopped. One of the first steps in moving forward is instead of dwelling on the pain you carry or the memories that haunt you, turn it into something you can learn from. Turn all the negative energy into positive energy.

When you begin to look at life with a positive perspective, you will be surprised at how many new doors will open in your life. When I began opening new doors in my life, I found a voice that had been trapped for so long and a will, not only to live, but also to thrive each new day. I gained a new confidence to achieve anything I put myself to. I will not lie, I still have doors in my life that need to be opened, and I will get them opened in time because I move forward each day.

I went from a little girl raped, molested, and silenced to a teenager haunted daily by my silent past. Now I stand at podiums and classrooms or stare into a camera and share my life to thousands of people. I am the same woman who use to take razor blades to my wrists in high school to handle the pain, who lapsed into an eating disorder as a young adult in college still searching for control. I live in amazement to see the transformations that have played out in my life.

In mid-November 2007, when the investigation was underway, I had been asked to speak for two days at my old high school health classes. On the second day, the health teacher I had in high school approached me and informed me a mother had called him, wanting to know about the guest speaker who had spoken to students the day before. The teacher's first thought was that this mother was calling to complain and that she did not want her son being educated on sexual abuse. But as he talked with her, he learned she had called to ask if the teacher would give me her number because she wanted to talk to me. I promised the teacher I would give this mother a call. When I sat down a few days later to contact her, I did not know what to expect.

When I introduced myself over the phone as the one who spoke in her son's class, she shared that I was the first person to break through to her son. For the next hour this mother informed me that a year prior to this, she had learned of the sexual abuse that her eight-year-old and fourteen-year-old had suffered at the hands of their dad. After hearing me speak in his class, her son had told his mother that a guest speaker had talked about sexual abuse and shared her story about not being ashamed and speaking out. He broke down and shared his pain with his mother. She thanked me over and over for being able to reach her son and make him understand that this happens to boys, too, and he has nothing to be ashamed of or any reason to blame himself.

She asked if I would be willing to talk with her in person. She felt the justice system was failing her kids, who had been interviewed at the same Children's Advocacy Center my sister and I were taken to. When we decided on a time and day in December, she gave her address to me. When she said Walker Court, I literally gasped. It was the same court Ashley used to live in. It was the same court I use to have the recurring nightmare of running through each house. It hit so close to home. Her house was one of the houses in my nightmare I would run through, and while all the lights were on, no one ever seemed to be in them to hear my cries.

A month later, when I pulled into the familiar court, I was overcome with emotions. It was around the same time of year when I was raped, so the feeling in the air felt much the same as when I made that long trek home on a cold January day. As I walked up to the front door of this woman's home, I looked over at where Ashley used to live, where many childhood memories were created: where I left my little pink bike on her driveway; where we used sidewalk chalk and drew flowers; the backyard where we would play house or use our imaginations to create our own games. Even all these years later I remembered so clearly. I stared at the corner of the sidewalk where Ashley locked pinkies with me, and together we made a promise not to tell anyone. It was a landmark in my life, where my innocence was taken and I had abandoned the little girl for sixteen years. As I pondered all this, I realized it was a message sent from above, allowing me to return to that place and rescue what I left behind. It was like déjà vu walking into a home I used to run through in nightmares as a child.

I spent over two hours with this mother. With many tears, she shared the horrors her two young children endured. She felt utterly helpless when she learned the man she had married hurt her children. They struggled with nightmares and flashbacks. Her nine-year-old constantly wet the bed or had accidents around the house. Her husband began stalking her and the kids. She eventually got an order of protection. She installed alarms throughout her home and cameras outside her house to help her sons feel safe in their own home. These boys feared their father would come back and hurt them. I promised this mother I would do whatever I could to help support her through this process, whether it was using my resources to help her children, or just being someone to talk to. I assured her that she and her children were not alone, and she, too, could get through this.

I am living proof that you can rise above pain and turn all the bad things around for the good. All the strength, courage, and determination I found came from within. It was always there, I just had to do some digging to find it. As you begin digging into your past and facing the obstacles you have experienced, it will not be easy. I do not recommend doing it alone. Get support from friends, a counselor, a spouse, or someone you trust. While the immediate reaction might be too hard to deal with and stir up a lot of pain, if you do not give up and push on, even through the potholes in the road, when you reach the top of the hill, you will get a clear picture of everything. You have to be driven, motivated, and not willing to give up. In the end it will be worth it. The results have changed my life in ways I could never have imagined.

I often wanted to give up, not move forward because each new day was unpredictable. I never knew if I would have flashbacks or panic attacks; sometimes my day would start at 2 AM, waking to nightmares. It seemed so much easier to quit. The pain was emotionally, physically, and mentally exhausting. It affected my schoolwork and threw me into a dark depression. I was sleep deprived and often hopeless.

To move on and grow I needed to believe that God had the power and control to make my life everything I ever dreamed of. It would be like planting seeds and watching them grow. If I did not water the plants they would die. Traveling down the anorexia path was slowly killing me. I honestly believe if I had continued to starve myself a year longer, it might have killed me, and I would have taken my secret to my grave. I needed to nurture my soul and comfort the pain I was avoiding. Anorexia was just an escape for me to avoid my pain.

Find something in your life that will help you focus on your own growth. Whether it is a new baby, new puppy, flowers in your garden, or changes of the seasons. Life is about growth and change. Part of that change requires us to say "I am not a victim." I will never tell people I am a victim of a crime or a victim of sexual abuse. I am a survivor of sexual abuse. Victims are people who do not live on. Someone who was murdered would be a victim—not able to use his or her voice to fight for justice. A major step to getting out of the victim mentality and into survivor mode is reaching a place of recovery and being healed.

A part of moving forward is not about taking one large step but instead several small steps. It is more like two steps forward and one step back. You cannot expect everything to go smoothly; you will hit bumps in the road along the way. If you have the perspective "I am going to overcome my obstacles by tomorrow," you are very optimistic but not realistic. You have to set small manageable tasks for yourself. If you have not broken your silence, that should be your first goal. Letting out your experience and not holding it in will be one of the first very courageous steps you will take. Healing is a process, and you can decide if you want to make it a negative experience or a positive one.

For many survivors of sexual abuse, talking to someone who cannot relate to your experience is difficult. I often struggled to talk openly with my close friends who had never experienced sexual abuse. I often wondered if they truly understood what I went through or if they were just listening to be supportive but were really thinking, "She just needs to get over it." You learn who your true friends are by those who support you no matter what.

It is always easier to connect with people who understand the life you have walked. So when you get to the point where you are ready to speak out, connect with others by joining a support group. Talk to your church, talk to your local hospital, many towns either have sexual assault centers where can get involved in a support group or can give you references to one. People are out there who are willing and ready to help you. You may not connect with the first counselor you work with, but do not give up. If you feel the person is not the right match for you, try someone else or ask someone for a recommendation. It is always a good idea to find a counselor who has had experience in working with sexual abuse. I would give the same suggestion to others who are dealing with emotional pain that is not related to sexual abuse—find someone who has experience working in the area that is currently affecting their lives. When someone is in physical pain, they see a doctor to get better. Emotional pain affects you in a different way but should not be ignored. Do not deny yourself the right to heal.

I took ownership over my past and no longer allowed it to run my life. To continue my healing process I needed to keep talking. I would not allow myself to stay silent. Staying silent let evil win. I found my platform through finding my voice after confronting my cousin. That platform was going to no longer live in silence; instead, I made a commitment to encourage others to speak out and not be shunned by society's stigma of sexual abuse. I knew by speaking out it would be life changing for some, and others would rather I never mentioned the topic. Even if you personally cannot relate to my story, believe me when I say that someone you know—even if you are not aware of their story—can relate.

The question asked so often by sexual abuse survivors is "Where do I begin healing?" It begins with telling your story. Each and every survivor of sexual abuse has their own story and a way of expressing it. For me, telling my story was writing about it. I turned my diary into a book for my own therapeutic process, to help me heal. For you it may be through art. Painting and drawing can be a very therapeutic way to tell your story. For others it may be through singing or poetry. Often a starting place is finding a therapist or someone you trust. Any way you choose to tell your story is an important step in breaking your silence. It is taking that first step that scares people.

I think of the stages of healing as going in a circle. Picture a globe. Before ever being abused, you were a carefree child, on top of the world. When someone took your innocence and abused you,

you were suddenly no longer grounded but free—falling through the circle. As a child, you may start off healing through a state of shock and confusion at what has happened, trying to make sense of the wrong that has been done to you. Then you experience a phase of guilt and blame yourself. Often the person who abuses children blames them, tells them this is their fault, and they will be in trouble if they tell anyone. Others tell children they will hurt them, or no one will believe them. It is a way pedophiles often brainwash children to stay silent. I went through the phase of guilt and blame for a period of time after learning my sister was abused. I felt I could have prevented it, but I later learned I had no way of controlling the actions of another person.

Then you may reach the stage of denial. Here is where many get stuck, not knowing how to process the pain they have endured. They often try to ignore the effects of the abuse because they do not know whom to turn to or how to get help. It seems much easier to pretend the abuse did not happen than to go through the grieving of what was lost.

Once you have acknowledged the abuse and are no longer burying it, you will enter a stage of mourning for the childhood robbed and grieving innocence lost. The stage people most often get stuck in is when they have reached rock bottom. Still picturing the globe, the South Pole in healing is often cold, empty, and lonely, an isolated place of despair and depression. I look at it this way: You have been walking on thin ice and suddenly you fall through and are struggling to keep your head above water. Each time you try to pull yourself up, it is a battle, and the ice around you continues to crack. You panic. This is the stage in healing where people often turn to unhealthy coping and experience suicidal thoughts. You just want to give up. You feel stuck, like you are frozen in a moment you cannot escape. It is the darkest phase in healing and one of the most difficult to get past. At the worst, you may encounter recurring flashbacks, nightmares, and panic attacks. Though flashbacks and nightmares can happen at any stage in healing, it is at this stage where survivors feel trapped. They make progress but may fall back into the darkness. That is why this stage fits best at the bottom of the globe as you imagine yourself traveling around its circle.

To move forward in healing, you must connect with yourself and seek out the help of others. You cannot heal on your own because it is extremely difficult to go through it alone. You must work through the pain, anxiety, and fears that are holding you back from moving forward.

I use the image of the globe because of how I look at landmarks in healing. Treading the ocean currents, washing up on a deserted island, climbing mountains: these represent hurdles we must overcome to get to the other side. Healing seems so fragile, like walking on thin ice. Sometimes it feels like you are lost in the thick woods, unable to see where you are going. The journey may be a bumpy one, but in the end the path clears and you can find meaning from your past.

After climbing out of depression and despair, you come upon anger and rage. It is the place in healing where you let out all the pain done to you, the anger toward the evil you experienced, the rage you want to scream at the person who hurt you and those who did not support and help you. Working through anger and rage is a healthy part of healing. It is healthy to vent your anger toward your abuser, whether writing a letter, confronting the person, or expressing your feelings to a therapist. Keeping it bottled inside will only cause you more harm later in life. Staying stuck there is unhealthy. The stage of anger is often a hard place to move past. You may need to revisit it time and time again as you move forward in life. It is very difficult to let go of the anger you have toward someone whose evil acts have haunted you and changed your life, but there comes a point when you can find peace in that anger. I came to a point where I realized I was not going to let the men who abused me and the family that did not support me rob me of another day of my happiness. My anger consumed me, but by letting it go and moving forward, it allowed me to start living my life to the fullest. I would not allow evil to define me; instead, I moved forward and rose above it.

In healing you may get past a certain point then fall back into a previous stage and feel stuck, or you may revisit one or more of the healing stages at different times in your life. One day, as I marry and become a mother, I will have to face the emotions these changes will elicit. My fears of trusting a man enough to spend the rest of my life with him seem huge to me, but I know God has a plan, and that special person will come into my life when God knows I am ready for that step forward. When I have a child who is the same age I was when I was raped, I am prepared to deal with those emotions. Once my children start speaking, I plan to educate them on safe and inappropriate touch and teach them not to keep secrets. I will be very cautious about whom I allow to watch my children. That being said, I do not plan on making my children live a sheltered life because of the childhood I experienced. I will once again leave it in God's hands to watch over my children and keep them from harm's way.

I think back on other situations throughout my life where trying to stay in control was something I searched for. For example, I feared flying. It took me until I was sixteen to finally get on a plane. Looking back now, my fear was not about crashing but about not being in control. The person flying the plane had my life in his hands. It was another defining moment in my life when I realized God is in control at all times, so I had nothing to be afraid of. Once I let go of that, flying became a breeze, and now I enjoy soaring above the clouds.

chapter nine

THE FINAL STAGE
IN HEALING

It is that *F* word people struggle to say. No I am not talking about the four-letter swear word people slip out in anger and frustration. I am talking about *forgiveness*. It is the stage in healing that seems unimaginable. It is a word I never thought I would come to say about the men who hurt me. For many years I was consumed daily by feelings of anger and rage toward Brian and Richard. There came a point in my healing that I realized I cannot change what happened, but it did not mean I had to stay stuck in an unhappy place either.

Everyone in life has been hurt in one way or another through the actions or words of someone else. We can choose to stay angry and bitter toward those who have hurt us, or we can let go and live fulfilled lives, not being tied down by our pain but instead rising above and growing from it.

Forgiveness is a choice we humans can make. There is no time limit to reaching the point of forgiveness. For some it may take decades; for others it may seem impossible. I do not judge those who cannot forgive, nor do I preach forgiveness to survivors. I only share the gift I have found in my own journey to forgiveness.

Through the trauma I have endured, I found treasure waiting for me on the other side by not allowing my past demons to taunt me.

Forgiveness begins with picking off the scab and exposing the wound no one can see but you. For that wound to completely heal, you must be able to let go of the bitterness and anger and allow empathy and love to fill your heart and soul. When I was able to forgive, it was like the grand finale fireworks going off inside me. Forgiveness and healing go together. I learned in my healing that forgiveness was one of the key ingredients I needed to turn that wound into a scar. Holding on to my anger and rage was like toxic poison filling my body. I was continuing to allow the evil in Brian and Richard to hurt me. Forgiving them allowed me to let go of the anger I felt toward them and instead pray for the darkness of evil that wrestles inside of them. Forgiving them took away the weakness I felt and empowered me.

I am not suggesting that if you are in a stage of anger you need to hurry up and forgive. It took me many years to work through my anger. There came a point when my anger boiled over. Instead of seeking revenge, I allowed my anger to fuel me to speak out and not live in shame and guilt. Instead of allowing pain to hold me back, I used it to fuel me to push forward and to enrich my life.

Just because you can forgive those who have hurt you does not mean you justify their actions. For me to move forward, I needed to start with forgiving myself for blaming myself because I had kept silent for years, for carrying the guilt of not protecting my younger sister, and feeling like I had abandoned Ashley. I use to blame myself for giving up too quickly and not fighting back long enough. Turning the blame inward for some-one else's actions is a pattern many sexual abuse survivors get themselves into. I had to come to the realization that I was just a child, that I had done nothing wrong. I had to make myself see that the people I trusted took advantage of me, and I did the best I could to protect myself.

While I had been making continued progress moving forward, my letter confronting Brian was one huge leap forward. It was the step in the right direction to come to the ultimate decision of forgiveness.

I rode a roller coaster of emotions reading the letter Brian sent me. First, it was much longer than most of his letters in our seven months of corresponding, so I knew he gave it some thought. I read it over a dozen times the first day I received it, trying to replace that image of the cousin who had held me down and abused me with the man expressing remorse and apologizing in this letter. It was the first time I felt like I was hearing from a different side of Brian than the monster he had represented in my life since I was eleven. I began having empathy for him, feeling like he was letting me understand how his actions affected him. It was crazy to go from anger and rage to empathy, and it made my head spin. But in his letter he acknowledged that what he did was wrong and how his past continued to haunt him.

November 5, 2003

Erin,

For the last four or five years I have wondered if you really had accepted my first apology at Bill's house. I was pretty certain that you hadn't due to all the looks that have been exchanged between you and me at family parties. Over the last four or five years there has just been a complete lack of comfort and true enjoyment at family parties. That is one strong reason that I wished you had forgiven me a long time ago. Every time before a family event I always hoped that you were not going to be there because I just did not want to feel uncomfortable. It was not that I minded you, what I hated was the stale air between us. But that is something I could probably stand to live with the rest of my life. What I hate living with would be knowing that I destroyed your life.

I would assume that if you never had forgiven my apology for my actions, that over time you would build this hate for me, and this rage would in turn spark a need or want for revenge. I do not know if this would have happened but I do know that if it did, it would consume your life and mine. All I want is for us both to go on living a much happier life as well as a more satisfying one. And I know that when you [think] of me, it probably consumes your thoughts and feelings for a long extent, because when I used to hear your name or if I was talking to someone about my cousins, my thoughts and emotions would rip into me for more than a day because I really felt that I had fucked up your life and as well as mine. I pray that someday this feeling goes away. I hope one day that I feel satisfied enough that I haven't destroyed the rest of your life. And I believe that will only come when you have accepted my apology.

A long time ago I apologized and will do it again. Erin, I am sorry for what I did to you a long time ago. My actions weren't thought out, I was confused and disoriented, and I acted on the behalf of just plain stupidity. I wish that I had never hurt you the way that I did. I wish I could go back into the past and stop myself and teach myself what was wrong with my actions, but I had to learn the hard way, and unfortunately you were the one I abused. I apologize for the past and I hope that you can forgive me, but if you can't I can understand. I am sorry.

Brian

I struggled with the idea of forgiving Brian. I felt by forgiving him that meant I was sending the message that what he did was okay, that he was not responsible. Over time I came to realize that forgiving him would not diminish his actions but would allow me to let go of all my anger and hate and find the peace and joy I had longed for.

Forgiveness takes time. It is not a decision one makes overnight. I questioned whether Brian's apology was sincere or if it was just a cover because of his own guilt. He had tried to show me through letters a changed man, but at the same time I did not trust him. He had taken so much from me, so I struggled with being sucked into believing something he was not. How could I trust him all these years later when he told me he was sorry for abusing me? Getting these letters created some confusion for me. Brian's letters tried to make me understand his abusive behavior, but as I read them, memories kept popping up of the evil I had seen in him. That is when I knew I only had one choice: turn to God. If I could not trust what Brian was saying, I could trust God. He would guide me in the right direction. I prayed for God's strength to help me forgive. Of course, whenever I turn anything over to God, He works in a big way. I did not realize how big He would work in my heart in forgiving my cousin.

November 11, 2003

Dear Brian,

I have struggled over the past week to write this letter to you. I never imagined the day I would be faced with writing this letter. It has taken a lot of thought and soul-searching to finally put it on paper. I will begin by saying no matter how many times I tell you the pain you caused me, you will never be able to understand the depth of your actions on my life. No apology can erase the effects of your actions, nor can it bring back the precious years you took from me. Although the abuse may have ended when I was thirteen, the memories will last a lifetime.

You may have taken my innocence, ability to trust, an incredible family relationship, you even robbed me of my childhood, but, Brian, you have not destroyed my life. If you have destroyed anyone's life, it is your own. For you must live with yourself the rest of your life knowing what you have done.

I've spent countless hours in therapy trying to unravel the mess you put me through. I am at a point where I will continue to look back and put the pieces together of my childhood, but in the end I will still be left with questions I may never get answers to. I am going on with my life and no longer living as your victim but instead as a true survivor. I will hold on to the precious years when I knew no evil and my childhood was anything a child would want.

As for the person you tell me you are today, I am hearing a man who feels terrible for his actions and wants to move on with his life, a man who wants to be forgiven. Brian, only you know in your heart if you are honestly sorry and a changed man. I cannot trust your word that you are a changed person, nor will I ever trust you. Only you know the true you. So I hope if you ever feel the urge to hurt someone again you will do the right thing and get yourself help— probably the best thing you could ever do for yourself. I will leave it in God's hands, for He knows the real you that I do not.

I will take the pain you have caused me to my grave some day, as for the anger and hate I will not. For I forgive you!

Erin

Forgiving will not erase what happened, but it can heal a great deal of the pain. Survivors often tell me that it is too late to forgive the person who abused them because their abuser is deceased. Just because the person who abused you may no longer be living does not mean you cannot forgive them for what they did. You can forgive them in your heart and know you no longer harbor anger.

Finding forgiveness has many of the same feelings as getting justice. Getting to the point in your life where you can forgive is a huge accomplishment: you let go of all the anger and hate you may be holding on to; it transforms you; it gives you an incredible release. Getting to that point is worth the effort. It is a process you have to be ready for, and you will know when you are at the point of forgiveness.

When you can openly say, "I do not hate the person or persons who abused me and I let go of the anger," it is as if a huge cloud hovering above you has cleared. The rays of sunlight come into your life. You feel a glimmer of hope.

When I forgave my cousin, an overwhelming sense of joy came over me. I was in control of the entire situation, and it helped me to feel powerful, something I had not felt since I was a little girl. I no longer harbored anger and hatred toward Brian. It was a powerful experience to go from being consumed with anger to suddenly feeling sympathy for the man who abused me.

Some may wonder how I can have sympathy for the one who terrorized me, laughed when I fought to get him off me, and cut my childhood way too short. It has been through therapy, a good support system of friends and immediate family, and building a relationship with God that have helped me look at Brian in a different way than I had ever before. When I turned to God for guidance through my process of forgiveness, I did not realize He would continue to place my cousin in my heart long after.

Through God's guidance and strength, my anger and hate turned to sympathy. I tried to avoid the feelings at first because it did not seem right to have sympathy toward Brian—I never in a million years would have guessed I would have sympathy for a man who locked me in rooms for his own sexual pleasure. The sympathy did not disappear. I asked God, "What are You trying to tell me?" I did not ignore God's message and began praying for

Brian's well-being. I prayed that he would make good decisions the rest of his life and never hurt another person again. It was at this point I realized the choice I made no longer allowed toxic feelings to take over me. The anger and hate were only consuming me and taking over my life. Letting go of the ill feelings allowed me to close the door to anger and hatred and open the door to forgiveness. As crazy as it sounds, praying for Brian helped me grow. It turned those negative feelings into more positive ones. I grasped the idea that he is a creation of God who made some terrible mistakes in his life. Jesus died on the cross for Brian's sins long before he ever committed them. I had a choice to make: not forgive Brian and stay weak; or rise above the situation, which took immense strength and courage, and forgive him. I must say it was not easy, and getting to the place of forgiveness took me years of emotional work. I feel so blessed that I chose to forgive. I no longer have the haunting image of my cousin. I no longer wrestle with the painful memories of what he did. That has been laid to rest, for I have conquered his evil. Forgiveness is a long, physically and emotionally draining process.

We all make choices. Forgiveness has by far been the biggest choice I have ever made. What happened to me as a child was out of my control, but how I choose to respond was in my control. It was not easy to forgive a man who I believed had walked away with barely a slap on the wrist for the nightmare he put my family and me through, but I could not go back and change the outcome of what happened; instead I look forward to the future with hope. I was moving forward not backward and by forgiving the man who caused me many sleepless nights, I became empowered. Forgiveness does not mean you have to reconcile with the person who abused you. Forgiveness is a gift you give yourself. You will experience different waves of anger throughout your life, but holding on to the anger and allowing it to consume you is the unhealthy part.

Empathy is an important tool to help you identify with the person who abused you. By trying to understand what made Brian and Richard hurt me, I began to think about what might have happened to them in their childhoods. I have reason to believe they both could be keeping their own childhood secrets of sexual molestation.

I believe behavior is learned. I do not think Brian decided one night, "I think I am going to sexually abuse my cousin while she sleeps." Though I might never know the truth behind my cousin's actions, I believe he had been struggling with his own demons of abuse he endured as a child and finally could not keep it in anymore. Stories came out when my sister and I broke our silence that suggested someone might have sexually abused Brian. I asked Brian once in a letter if he had ever been sexually abused. He never once said he had, yet he never denied it, either. Nothing is worse than living in your own silent hell of secrets. The same way Brian silenced me through the abuse, someone might have silenced him. If so, instead of finding his voice, Brian may have acted on what might have happened to him. I am only speculating, and if my intuition is true and Brian was abused, I can only hope that he got the help no one could provide him when he was a teenager. While being abused and then becoming the abuser is no excuse for his actions, nor is it for anyone who does, my heart is heavy knowing what he might be silently carrying. I would hate to walk in his shoes with not only the guilt of his actions but also a past he may still be hiding. The shadow of his past will always follow him, but I hope he never repeats it.

By allowing your heart and soul to empathize with the person who abused you, you are serving yourself a sense of justice for their actions because it allows you no longer to be consumed by their actions. I know that idea sounds crazy, but in all honesty I would not say this unless I had experienced the good that has come from empathy. Allowing yourself to feel empathy leads you down a path that is not filled with anger, rage, and hatred; instead, you will no longer identify the person who hurt you as strong and powerful, who still has a tight grip on your life. Empathy releases you from that emotional grip because you look beyond the power and evil you experienced and replace it with the idea that the one who hurt you is no longer in power, is very weak, and is battling a sickness of demons. Empathy will eventually lead you to the next step of forgiving whoever hurt you.

Forgiveness does not undo the damage, minimize the pain, or make an abuser's behavior acceptable, but it can change your life tremendously for good. I believe forgiveness has been the greatest tool in my own recovery. It allowed me to look at the driving force behind the abuse I endured: I absolutely believe it was Satan at work.

Ask yourself, "Am I willing to waste any more time and energy on the pain someone has caused me?" The sand in your hourglass is slipping away. Do not let another moment pass caught up in anger and bitterness. I am not suggesting you not feel anger, only that you not hold on to anger. Get it out of your system by journaling, screaming, venting, crying to your therapist, pounding your fist into a pillow, but do not hold on to it because it will only consume you, take away your happiness, and haunt you the rest of your life. Do not allow it to make you fall into destructive, unhealthy coping.

Forgiveness allows you to find peace after surviving abuse and it allows you to grab hold of the good memories from your childhood. I think a lot of the memories that haunted me throughout my childhood and early adulthood were due to anger that I was holding on to, stirring up emotions and issues I had yet to address and bring to the surface.

The day I forgave Brian I began a new chapter in my life. I felt as if I had reached the top of the mountain I had been climbing since I broke my silence. At eighteen I suddenly saw my purpose. Everything became crystal clear. Though I may not have reached the journey's end of complete healing, I was no longer wandering scared in darkness. I had overcome depression, self-injury, and suicidal thoughts—barriers I had to overcome to continue to move forward. Confronting and forgiving my cousin were by far two of my greatest challenges and accomplishments thus far in my life. I took all the negative feelings I had experienced through the abuse and turned it into something positive. I channeled all the pain, anger, and grief I have experienced and put it into action. I spent far too many years of my life sucked into the pain, allowing the past to haunt me.

When I was twenty-two and broke my silence of being raped at six and a half, I was able to connect the dots and discover why I still harbored so much anger and fought to gain control. Now that I had been courageous enough to use my voice and speak out, I wanted to drive to Richard's home, knock down the door to his bedroom, confront him, and show him how strong I was. I decided to work through the anger I felt toward him by picking up a pen and journaling what I would like to say to him. I put all my feelings and emotions into a letter, similar to the way I confronted Brian, but this time I was doing it just for me to work through my own anger. I tell many survivors to try by writing a letter, even if the person who abused them will not receive it. The process you work through while writing the letter is the important, healthy, nondestructive part of healing. Pouring all the anger onto paper instead of keeping it bottled up is what I call good anger—letting out the pain. This letter gives you an idea of the emotions I was going through when I wrote it.

October 2007

Dear Richard,

For sixteen years I have carried an image of you coming out of the shadows of the night and taking something so precious from me. You took a little girl's smile and replaced it with tears, a beautiful soul and filled it with anger and rage. At six I shattered beer bottles in the street and sidewalk as my only way to express the pain you caused me. I would love to take a bottle and smash one over your head for every single year I stayed silent carrying your dirty, disgusting, secret, you selfish, sick bastard.

While my classmates were learning how to use twelve-inch voices, you silenced mine. Because of your actions, at age six I knew more about sex than I did reading, writing, adding, and subtracting combined.

Over and over again I relived those moments of you with that disgusting grin on your face forcing yourself on top of my small fragile body. The emotional scar you left on my life is just as painful as the physical pain of your forcing your way inside me. With your hand over my mouth, you silenced my cries as you raped me. The whites of your eyes pop out at me in my nightmares, glowing in the darkness. Your shadow is all I see in my dreams as I run through the court, house to house in the middle of the night screaming, but my screams always went unanswered, always ended with you tackling me to the ground. I honestly do not know how you have gotten up every morning the past sixteen years living with yourself. I hope the shame and guilt consume you.

My twelve-inch voice is no longer silenced; in fact, I have turned it up. Your weight is no longer holding me down. I am standing tall now. I am no longer trapped back in that bedroom, suffering. The cries of the little girl silenced inside of me are being heard, no longer victim to your control and power. I am no longer running in fear of you in the night, afraid of being captured. You have been on the run all these years, now it is your turn to be captured. You can run, but you cannot hide.

If justice is not served in this lifetime, there is no doubt you will be held accountable to your actions in the next lifetime. You will face the consequences for your actions at some point. If I ever have to look into the whites of your eyes again, it will be you running in fear, not me. You will realize you messed with the wrong little girl, who is all grown-up and no longer silent. The little girl you hurt is full of anger and rage and ready to take it out on [who] she should have sixteen years ago instead of [acting out] at school, at home, or in the park. I wish for a moment you could feel the pain I endured as you raped me. I would then break every one of your fingers you held over my mouth to silence me as I tried to catch my breath. I would take the shoes you struggled to get off my feet and knock out your front teeth, wiping that disgusting grin off your face.

Finally, those eyes, they are filled with death and so much evil, looking into the face of an innocent girl and taking something precious from her. I would make sure the acid I throw on your face would never let you see the light of day again. I would then leave, slamming the door behind me, leaving you in that back room to think about your actions, allowing them to sink in and consume your every thought of the horrible decisions you made in taking children's innocence.

Someday I will return when the burning anger and rage inside me simmers down and the grown woman I am can help the little girl within find the ability to forgive you for your sins. Then that door and chapter of my life will never need to be opened again.

Erin

Many emotions poured out of me when I wrote that letter: anger, rage, and grief—and always the tears. I had to get up and wash away my tears. As I stood before the bathroom mirror, for the first time I could see that I had been running away my whole life from facing the little girl who needed me, of all people, to rescue her. I mourned for the precious little girl I once was. I decided to embrace the heartache in my soul and comfort the pain; it will be the fuel to push me forward in this journey for the rest of my life. I am at a different place in my life now than when I wrote that letter.

That anger and hatred toward Richard is gone. I have not allowed evil, pain, and anger to consume and keep me in the dark. Instead, I have taken the lessons I learned and used them to fuel my push forward, to make something positive from what was negative, and to speak out with my once silenced voice. I can forgive him in my heart for his acts of evil and sickness. That might seem unbelievable to some after reading the horror and tragic events I lived through.

The same way I forgave the men who abused me, I hope others will forgive me if I have ever said or done anything hurtful. Sometimes we hurt someone without even knowing it by the way we say something or act. Many of my relatives think my decision to expose family secrets was my way of hurting them. It never was and never will be; I hope one day they will understand. If only they could understand my purpose for speaking out and see how my message has helped many others.

I am sure both Brian and Richard have no idea I pray for their souls every night. Some may tell me there are far more deserving people in this world I could be praying for than two sick men who stole my innocence. The way I see it is that these men do not have many praying for them. While my cousin may have an entire extended family that supports him, most are in denial about what he confessed to, leaving that door wide open for evil to come right back into his life. I believe in the power of prayer. The same goes for Richard. After forgiving both these men, I feel called to pray for their souls. I pray that evil will leave them alone and that they will never hurt another child again. I believe that by keeping them in my daily prayers, it reduces the chances of their hurting another child. I am more at peace, keeping these two in my prayers than allowing anger to consume me, wishing they would both just die and burn in hell.

I have learned a valuable lesson that I want to pass on to others who are facing their own heartaches or are trying to bury them. There is no way around the pain. No denying it. While we may be able to bury it one day, it will surface at some point, and your past will stare you in the face. The light pouring out of my soul is so much more powerful than the darkness. Everyone is capable of forgiving. Though it seems unimaginable, when you are at the right place in your healing, past the anger is a forgiving heart. More important than forgiving Brian and Richard is forgiving myself for allowing that little girl inside me to stay trapped, suffering alone.

You can decide to forgive when you realize you are stuck in pain and anger and not moving forward. You can discover forgiveness in the stage of guilt and blame: forgive yourself and realize you are not at fault. When you have come full circle in healing, you will reach the final stage of forgiving those who have hurt you.

For many, forgiving is not easy, and you have to be ready for it. It is a process I struggled to come to terms with, but once it happened the emotions poured out of me as I released all the anger, rage, and hate I felt toward Brian and Richard. When I said, "I forgive you," in my letter to Brian, I meant it. Forgiving does not erase the scar, but I carry it with strength not anger. It took strength for me to expose the wound and eventually it led to my healing. My forgiving Brian and showing empathy demonstrate that I am stronger than the force behind his actions.

Because apologizing is humbling and exposes guilt, it acts as a deterrent, reminding my cousin not to repeat the act that he has been forgiven for. In the same way it takes strength to forgive the person who abused you, it takes courage for sinners to own up to and take responsibility for their actions. From what I saw in Brian through our letters and one telephone conversation, he has shown me that he has taken responsibility for his actions.

The difference between Richard and Brian is I knew the side of Brian that was good before he ever hurt me. We grew up together, and many good memories were formed before he began acting out on his sexual urges. I never knew Richard before he began sexually abusing me. In a sense he was that stranger danger I was warned about in school. I do not have any good memories of Richard, only painful ones, making it more difficult to see any hope of good in this man. While the chances of standing up to Richard are very slim, I had to find a way to rise above the pain and anger I felt toward him and his actions.

I found my own way to work through the trauma, which took a lot of courage and self-talk. I could no longer allow fear to take over me or shut off the memories as I had before. I made myself close my eyes, and instead of envisioning a warm beach, I would imagine myself going back into Ashley's house, going down the hallway, and standing outside Richard's door. I had to make a decision: I could pound my fists into this now weak, pathetic man, asking him over and over, "How could you?" Or I could fearlessly open his door and reclaim the young, frightened, crying child I had left behind. Then looking into the eyes of evil and exclaiming, "I've conquered you, I forgive you, now go find God, for He is your only hope to save you from the darkness of hell!" I would turn around, close the door, and never look back. The first choice would get me no closure. So instead, I chose to put Richard's fate in God's hands. Only He knows where his life is headed and where he will go after this lifetime.

Forgiving has transformed my life. Whereas before I forgave, I took out my anger on the people I loved and friends I cared about; it kept the happiness I yearned for far from me. But once I was able to forgive, I was set free and happiness returned into my life. Forgiveness is the most important thing in my life that has allowed me to move beyond nightmares, flashbacks, panic attacks, bitterness, hatred, and anger. Forgiveness and empathy filled my spirit and soul with wisdom, strength, determination, compassion, inspiration and drew me closer to God.

Forgiving was the greatest gift I have ever given myself. After years of being robbed of joy and happiness, forgiveness gave me pure joy and love. I am no longer suffering in darkness, but holding my head up high, not ashamed of the past I carry, and not seeking revenge.

My hope is that you do not allow others' actions to steal another moment of your happiness and joy but turn the pain into something positive, beautiful, magnificent, and courageous. Do not let days turn into weeks, months, or years and find you are still in the same dark place you were in when you were first hurt. For years, when I refused to forgive, it allowed the men who hurt me to hurt me all over again through the memories that haunted me. By holding on to my anger and hate I kept myself stuck in a foggy haze every day, allowing Brian and Richard to still have a grasp of my soul.

I experienced two ways of forgiving. My cousin came to me, admitted his wrongs, apologized, and asked for forgiveness, which I gave. But if I were to sit around and wait for Richard to apologize and ask for forgiveness, I might be waiting for the rest of my life. In other words, I would be putting my happiness into the hands of a man who once used his hands to hold me down and rape me; I would be allowing Richard to decide when I would be healed. Why allow the person who hurt me to have control over my happiness? Even though Richard has not asked for forgiveness, I chose to forgive so that I could heal myself and live for today.

For some, getting past the anger may be putting all that anger toward the person who hurt them into something productive, like volunteering at church, helping with children, working with the disabled, or visiting senior citizens. Maybe it is giving your time at a nonprofit child abuse agency or rape crisis center that will turn your anger into something positive. It is a choice that only you can make. Your happiness is something you are always in control of. It is one thing no one can take from you. I try not to force my views on people, but if I could get every person to believe one thing, it is that all bad things can be turned around for the good.

I shattered my silence, I no longer struggle with unhealthy coping habits, and in the end I found forgiveness; however, I am working through a difficult area and that is to trust men in relationships. I have feared allowing them into my circle of trust, afraid they might betray me. I will go only so far into a relationship, then when I am faced with a new level of trust, I run away from it, fearing to cross that line. I question whether or not to trust this person.

It took me years to finally get over the uncomfortable feelings I had when a man expressed affection toward me. My first reaction whenever this happened was to feel ashamed, confused, and often sad. I had a hard time separating the wrong sexual behavior I experienced as a child from acceptable affection from a man. Physical affection, as simple as kissing, often made me feel dirty inside, and guilt would consume me. I would try fighting off these negative feelings, but eventually I would end the relationship because I felt so confused and ashamed. I did not experience flashbacks but icky feelings that made me feel it was wrong.

These situations would evoke anger, and I wanted to scream at Brian or Richard for causing me to struggle in relationships and keep me from trusting men, fearing they might hurt me or betray me in some way. If people I love could hurt me, then how could I trust another man? Now, I feel the anger and then I let go of it, not allowing it to consume me.

I eventually learned I had nothing to be ashamed of. Whenever I enter into a relationship with a man, I am up-front about my past and my struggles with trusting.

I had an experience with a guy I dated in high school. He knew my morals and values of waiting until marriage for physical intimacy. I thought I knew him, but I got into a situation where he was trying to get me to have sex with him. I was upset that this boyfriend tried to overstep my morals and values, but I was proud because for once I was standing up for myself. I put my foot down and was able to walk away from the situation, knowing I was not going to be forced into anything.

I dated a guy in the summer of 2007. He respected my morals and values and never tried to force me into anything I was not ready for. I thought I finally had found a respectful, mature man I was really comfortable with. Then one day, toward the end of summer, out of the blue he stopped returning my calls and text messages, and no longer even spoke to me. I was confused and hurt. For the first time I was not running away from a relationship but being dumped, yet I was given no explanation other than some personal problems had come up in his life. I later learned what he had been keeping from me—he was married. Evidently, he was separated from his wife and was going through a divorce while dating me. I was stunned and felt used. This man used me to escape his own problems with his wife. Keeping something like that from me made me question if I could trust men again.

I tell my friends that I need to do a background check on everyone I date from now on. Unfortunately, even background checks will not tell you everything about a person or his character.

I have failed to find a relationship with someone who has a relationship with God. So I decided to leave this in God's hands, knowing He will lead the right person to me. At some point our paths will cross. I no longer live with the fear of being alone the rest of my life. I have faith that the right man is out there. He will respect and support me for who I am, and I can give my trust to him.

So far, my dad is the only male role model I look up to. He reminds me that there are good men out there and not to give up. Someday my father will walk me down the aisle surrounded by family and friends who have supported me throughout life, and waiting at the end of that aisle will be a man who I am in love with, has earned my trust, and is ready to spend the rest of his life with me.

Being honest and open about something so sensitive and personal wakes people up when they hear my life story. I have nothing to hide or be ashamed of, nor does any other person who has been violated. The truth is the tragic events I endured as a child are much more common than most of society realizes. Children right now are feeling helpless, scared, and alone because someone is silencing them. Children today are sitting in waiting rooms of Children's Advocacy Centers across America, about to break their silence. My life's mission is to turn the light back on and allow the souls of abused children to shine and let their voices echo for the world to hear what no one can see inside. I want to turn their cries into the sounds of laughter and give them back what was stolen from them.

My future has already been written. The only person who holds the answers to what lies ahead is God. He holds the keys that will open the doors to my future. My vision of the future is bright. I know God is right here with me every day.

The days of obsessing over calories, fat, and the number on the scale have ended. Hunger pains were once much easier to deal with than the pain in my heart for a little girl crying inside me to be heard. Now that the child within is no longer silenced and hiding, I can heal that little girl, allowing her to cherish the good memories from childhood. Beyond the storm is a bursting ray of light. My soul is a beautiful place that I am letting shine. I arrived at where I am at right now because I used the *F* word on the two men who hurt me most in my life. Author Lewis Smedes once said, "Forgiving does not erase the bitter past. A healed memory is not a deleted memory. Instead, forgiving what we cannot forget creates a new way to remember. We change the memory of our past into a hope for our future."

chapter ten

REFLECTION

The voice that was once locked away for sixteen years I now use to inspire others. With courage, strength, and determination, I raise my voice above the darkness. My crusade moves me into the spotlight, where I will for the rest of my life put a face and voice on childhood sexual abuse. I carry a torch to light the way for others to follow. By exposing my struggles I show that I am like any other survivor of sexual abuse, imperfect and living one day a time.

I do not worry what tomorrow may bring, for I know anything I cannot carry, God will carry for me. I can never erase the pain I have felt, but I shattered the silence. I cannot change the past, but I can use my life to embrace others. I choose not to carry the image of Brian, who terrorized me and abused me; instead I remember the little six-year-old boy who stood next to me at the kitchen table and in his little voice said into the family video camera that he wanted to be a doctor, police officer, or a dad.

I look at the tragic events I endured as a blessing in disguise. That sounds bizarre, but, honestly, I feel so blessed with my life and my purpose. Something positive can come out of every tragic event. A seed was planted the day I was raped. The problems were the roots that stayed hidden in darkness. Breaking my silence allowed the new little plant to burst through the surface and reach for the light. Each step along my journey brought continuous growth. The more I stand up and speak out, the more I blossom like a long-awaited flower. My fragrance reaches others, encouraging them to break through their pain and begin their growth to a life of freedom from the darkness.

I have met and heard from incredible people over the years, crossing paths and connecting with souls I would have never experienced had I not lived through tragedy. By speaking out each day, I get to experience what it is like to have a positive effect on other lives. Each time I speak to a classroom of students, a student breaks her silence. That is why I continue to speak out.

While I may have lost an extended family by speaking out, I gain a new extended family every time I speak for a Children's Advocacy Center, sexual assault agency, conference, organization, community, and school. They are the ones rallying behind me in my mission and supporting the work I do. Whenever I stand at a podium and look out to the hundreds of people listening to my testimony, I feel honored that they have taken the time to hear my story. My courage may help someone in the audience find their own courage. It is my audiences that give me my strength to continue on my legacy of speaking out. While they thank me for sharing my courage, I thank them for taking the time to open their eyes to an epidemic many others would rather look the other way from and ignore.

America is too focused on fighting wars in other countries and ignores the war going on in our own backyard: a battle for the hearts and souls of our children as predators prey on our most vulnerable members, robbing them of their innocence. An invisible caution tape surrounds America as the silent epidemic continues. That same invisible tape stretches around our planet with sexual predators everywhere in this world. If only people could recognize the reality before it is too late and learn the devastating truth that children are abused every day, everywhere.

In the big picture of my life, the good has definitely outweighed the bad: spending a childhood filled with summers in Lake Geneva, Wisconsin, swimming, boating, campfires, pig roasts, shooting fireworks, going on adventures in cornfields, building forts in the woods, walking the lake path, and just sitting at the edge of the pier watching the sunset over the lake.

For years I had begged my parents for a dog. I would cut out sale ads for dogs in the paper and save up my money in the hopes one day they would let me buy one. In April 1997, when I was in fifth grade, I came home from school and found a note on the counter. My mother said that she was grocery shopping. When she arrived home, she asked me to help her carry groceries in and that she had something for me on the front passenger seat. When I made it out to the driveway my eyes locked eyes with a beautiful large one-year-old yellow lab named Chance. I cannot remember a time in my life when I was filled with as much excitement. My mom had found one of those ads I had cut out of a yellow Labrador retriever. I hugged my mom, thanking her over and over. He cost me $200, and he was worth every single penny.

Most of the money came from babysitting, including what I earned watching Brian's younger brothers. While I experienced some painful things with my cousin while I babysat, it did help me earn the money to make my wish come true—a wish that created many more cherished memories. Chance would pull me on snow skies and Rollerblades when he was young. He loves jumping off the pier in Wisconsin into the lake. Say, "You want to go for a walk?" and he creates a breeze with his wagging tail. When I moved off campus into an apartment my junior and senior year of college, Chance came with me. I took him weekly to a dog park in my college town and let him play with the other dogs.

Today Chance is thirteen years old, and he has slowed down. His walks are much shorter, his back hips are arthritic, and some days he cannot make it up the stairs without help. But he still has that spark of life that keeps him going every day. I cannot stop time. One day the door to his life will close and I will have to say good-bye. A day that will be here shortly. Animals can form an incredible bond with their owners, and with Chance I have a healing bond. He has been my companion through it all. I was never ashamed to show him my tears. I believe all dogs go to Heaven, just like the movie. Someday after Chance leaves me, we will reunite in green pastures.

A year after my mom surprised me with Chance, she took my sisters and me to Colorado. She had planned this trip before she knew the secret two of her children were carrying. On the same day my sister and I broke our silence in the Children's Advocacy Center, we pulled out of the parking lot and began the sixteen-hour drive to Colorado, where we stayed in a condo and went hiking and sightseeing. The next year we decided to stay at a campground, where we truly got the campers' experience of cooking over the campfire and sleeping on the ground in tents, some mornings waking up damp from the morning dew or rain that fell overnight. We went hiking, sightseeing, and horseback riding. We were amazed at the amount of wildlife we saw. We always tried to catch these memorable moments on camera; however, not every trip goes as planned, and sometimes disaster strikes.

On our drive to Colorado the second time in June 1999, it was once again just Mom and her girls. Sometime between one and two in the morning, we came upon a hill on the highway. I had just woken up and was sitting up in my seat. Caitlin was still lying down sleeping, while Mom and Allie were both in the front seat.

I was staring straight ahead, looking out the windshield. We were on a four lane highway, and Mom was in the farthest lane to the right. Just as we were about to reach the top of the hill, bright lights flashed into our eyes as a car headed directly at us. My mother screamed for us to hold on as she swerved to the side of the road. She slammed on the brakes and avoided crashing. Everything in the back of the car flew forward. A duffle bag hit me, but firewood and the propane tank smashed into Caitlin's face. She awoke to it all hitting her. She cried out in pain.

Back then we did not have a cell phone. Mom found a gas station farther up the road and called 911 to report the man who had forced us off the road. She gave the operator the information and we hoped the police would catch the man before tragedy struck. Caitlin's eye swelled, and she woke up the next morning with an ugly black eye. It was just the beginning of bad luck for Caitlin on that trip.

We had planned a three-night hiking trip up into the mountains. After we set up our campsite on the first day, we did a little hiking. On our way back, Caitlin wanted to be the first one to the bottom of the mountain. Mom warned her repeatedly to slow down, fearing she would trip on the large roots and twist her ankle. Caitlin did not listen, and sure enough, she twisted her ankle and was on crutches the rest of our trip. Obviously, we were no longer able to go on our three-night hike. We managed to make the most of the trip, staying at our campground playing board games and cards and having campfires.

We decided since we could no longer hike, we would go shopping. We stopped for lunch and got a delicious white sauce pizza; however, even eating pizza was not safe for Caitlin. Moments after leaving the restaurant, Caitlin's stomach reacted to the white sauce pizza. A black eye marring her face and wobbling on crutches, she tried to move quickly to find a bathroom. She did not make it in time, and I will spare you the details of that outcome.

We rented horses and rode them up a trail in the mountains. Caitlin was in the lead when her saddle fell to one side, taking her with it. Allie and I were behind her and could not help but laugh at her "dismount."

The entire list of what went wrong in Colorado made for a trip we would never forget and would talk about for years to come.

The next three years we went with Dad, and instead of hiking, we stayed at a resort and went skiing three days in a row. Caitlin joined us on only one of those ski trips because she was living out of state, and I believe she'd had her fair share of Colorado.

Before the days of making trips to Colorado, when I was a first and second grader, we would take family vacations to the Warren Dunes in Michigan. We would go camping with my aunts, uncles, and cousins from my mom's side of the family. My sisters, cousins, and I spent hours running through creeks, trying to catch frogs at the campground, and climbing the difficult sand dunes only to reach the top and run down on the hot sand.

My mother grew up in Michigan. We often made one or two trips a year to visit family there. I loved seeing my aunts, uncles, and cousins. When I reached my early teens, I especially loved seeing my great-grandma Hildegard. She was born in 1910 in Kassell, Germany. I never grew tired of hearing her story of coming to America. When she was only thirteen, she traveled alone on a ship from Germany to Ellis Island, New York. She came to start a new life in America, and surviving was tough. She spent her first week detained because of mix-up on her paper work. I stared into the eyes of my ninety-two-year-old great-grandma as she shared with me how scared and confused she was as a thirteen-year-old detained in an unknown country. Even at ninety-two she clearly remembered the details, and it was evident how much of an effect it still had on her life. Her journey to America was crucial, for had she not made that rough trip, crammed into a large boat and often sleeping on wooden floors with other children, I would not be here today. I visualized her journey to America every time she told the story. As I often listened to her stories, I would think about my own life as a great-grandma one day, and how I might share with my great-grandchildren the pain I endured as a child and how it, in the end, transformed my life in huge ways.

I cannot help but laugh, thinking back to a visit one summer, when my great-grandma had to have been around eighty-nine-years old but still was living independently and doing what she loved most: cooking. My sisters and I had just come in from swimming on Lake Cora, the lake she lived on. Great-grandma Hildegard had just made a big pitcher of lemonade for my sisters and me. She hated seeing things go to waste and always expected us to clean our plates. When my sisters and I took a sip of our lemonade, the looks on our faces said the same thing: The lemonade was very sour, and there was no way we were going to be able to finish it. But we knew how great-grandma did not like waste. We had no way of getting to the sink to dump it because she was standing in the kitchen. Caitlin came up with the idea of pouring it into our beach towels. So my sisters and I pretended to sip the lemonade but we were actually pouring it into our laps onto our beach towels and trying to contain our laughter. Drinking lemonade will always bring back fond memories of my great-grandma.

She drove up until the age of ninety-two and lived until ninety-three, when she died peacefully at home in Lake Cora, Michigan, in 2003. Her mind was still as sharp during her final years as it was when she docked at Ellis Island, New York. She was just older and wiser. She was remembered at her funeral for her love of cooking, and her meals always filled the soul with happiness and joy. She made a promise to me before she died that when she went to Heaven she would be my guardian angel. Years later, as I struggled with an eating disorder, it was my great-grandma Hildegard I prayed to for help to overcome anorexia. It was the story about the loaf of bread she worked so hard to earn her first month in America only for it to be stolen from her that made me realize I needed to feed my soul and not use food as a way to numb myself of what I did not want to deal with. I believe my angel above continues to help me feed my soul with positive thoughts.

When I was ten or twelve, my friend Emily and I wanted to earn money, so we knocked on a neighbor's door to see if he needed any help. The elderly man, who seemed to be in his late seventies, told us he needed help weeding. His yard was covered with weeds. Emily and I got on our hands and knees and donning gardening gloves we picked weeds for nearly three hours under the hot summer sun. The worst part about it was many of the weeds were prickly and even garden gloves could not protect our poor hands from the sharp thorns. When we finished, we went to the elderly man's door to get paid. The man pulled out a large jar of pennies and counted out 100 pennies for both of us. We both walked away shocked that we had spent three hours fighting the hot summer sun and thorns for 100 pennies each. We truly learned the value of a penny that day. While the elderly man didn't have much to offer us, he gave us a story from our childhood that we continue to bring up time and time again, laughing about getting down on our hands and knees for hours for 100 pennies.

If we were not trying to earn money by pulling weeds, we had lemonade stands. Allie, Emily, and I had done dozens of lemonade stands over the years. This particular day it was just Emily and me. We always had lots of customers—people driving by stopped, those walking and riding bikes also stopped—paying a quarter for each glass of lemonade. This particular summer day, Emily and I noticed a large white truck sitting for over an hour in the parking lot near our home. Inside we could see two guys who observed us as we did our lemonade stand. Eventually, the truck engine rumbled to life, turned toward my house, and slowly came to a stop. Emily and I got nervous and we both knew something did not feel right. The man in the passenger seat had his window rolled down. He pulled out his hand and said, "Girls, we don't want any lemonade, but here is a quarter for you." He had reached out his hand for us to walk up and take the quarter from him.

Something did not feel right and that gut instinct inside told me to say no. "No, thank you, keep your quarter."

The man sounded angry. "Why not?"

I looked at them both as Emily silently watched. "We don't need it."

The driver then hit the gas and accelerated down our street. I think I saved myself that day from what could have turned out to be a very dangerous situation. I immediately ran inside and told my mother, who decided it was time for us to close our lemonade stand for the day. I was warned numerous times about stranger danger, and though we were not asked to look for a lost puppy, it still seemed too risky and definitely not worth a quarter.

Summer camp was always a memorable experience. For three years I went to Van Buren Youth Camp in Bloomingdale, Michigan. It was the same camp my mother went to as a kid and she wanted her daughters to get the same experience. Camp was a weeklong experience of living in cabins and making new friends. The camp was on Great Bear Lake and every morning campers had the opportunity to participate in polar bear. Polar bear involved getting up early every morning before everyone else was required to get up and running down to the lake and jumping in. An announcement would be made over the intercom waking us in our cabins if we wanted to participate. We were given a few minutes to throw on our suite and get down to the lake. If you did it all week you received the polar bear award on the final day of camp. Of the three years I went to camp two of them I accomplished a week of jumping into the lake first thing in the morning with all the other brave souls. At camp each cabin followed a schedule all week. We went to three classes a day where we either did crafts, canoeing, swimming, nature, song and dance, archery, riflery, sports, and low ropes. Riflery caused some controversy outside the camp because some felt teaching children how to shoot a gun was wrong. However riflery taught kids gun safety. Low ropes taught campers problem solving skills and working together as a group in different challenges we were to accomplish as a cabin.

Campers were given two hours a day of what was called choice. Choice allowed us to choose what we wanted to do. Some played sports, others sat along cabin row playing cards, and many went swimming. I often was found going to the nature center playing with the animals. After lunch every day everyone had to return to their cabins for an hour of just relaxation. We could either take a nap, write letters home, or quietly talk to others in our cabin. I always spent that time writing letters to mom and dad telling them what an amazing time I was having. Breakfast, lunch, and dinner always took place with all the campers in the lodge. The food at camp was excellent. Meal time was always interrupted at some point when someone was caught with their elbows on the table and everyone would break out stomping, clapping, and singing, "Get your elbows off the table" and the name of the person who was caught with their elbows on the table. Then everyone would say kiss the moose. The person caught with their elbows on the table would then have to go over and kiss Cleo the moose who has been hanging on the wall since 1920 when the camp used to be a hunting lodge. Cleo was the camp mascot. I could not make it through three years of camp without getting caught with my elbows on the table and had to eventually kiss Cleo.

After dinner all the campers would walk to a place at camp called thought. It was here we would all sit on logs that faced the lake where different cabin groups would put on a presentation that would reflect on our day. Every night everyone from camp would hold hands and walk to the campfire where a different cabin would put on a skit each night. Campfire ended every night like it has for the past fifty years with the whole camp standing and singing three songs: Kum-Ba-Ya, Angels Watching over Me, and Taps.

The first year at camp in 1997 I was still carrying my secret alone, but it was a week in my summer where I knew I was safe and far from my cousin Brian's reach. Camp allowed me to let my guard down and just be a kid. I also made new friends including a girl named Laura who lifted my spirit and made camp so memorable. During one of our classes where we went canoeing Laura was in the same canoe as me. At some point we got separated from the guide and the rest of our cabin. We eventually drifted far from the others and got stuck in a shallow area of the lake. Laura looked at me and said, "We're stuck here forever. I hope you like fish because that is what we will be living on until someone rescues us." Laura and I could not stop laughing and at one point we tried to use our paddles to push us and we nearly tipped over. We decided to sit still until our canoe guide came to our rescue. Little did Laura know that I would give anything to stay stuck there than return to my reality back home stuck behind a closed door with my cousin abusing me.

The second year at camp in 1998 I had broken my silence months earlier and the nightmares were keeping me up at night. Even at camp I could not sleep and would lay in my bunk tossing and turning. My cabin counselor Cindy knew something was not right and on the third night after everyone was in their bunk beds she took me outside our cabin and sat on the steps asking me if everything was all right. I was ashamed to tell her what my cousin did but I eventually opened up and told her about being abused, my family divided, and the nightmares I was having. Cindy did what I wish every person would do when someone discloses sexual abuse. She listened, comforted me, reminded me I was safe now from my cousin, and asked me what she could do to help make the rest of camp a memorable experience. She could have reacted completely different and made the situation difficult for me to talk about but instead she listened and showed compassion. She made the rest of my experience at camp memorable and I did not have one more nightmare the rest of the week.

My final year at Van Buren Youth Camp was in the summer of 1999. I entered my cabin the first day and for the first time in my life I was the minority since almost everyone in the cabin was African American. It allowed me to feel what it was like to be the minority and really opened my eyes. Nothing could prepare me for the new friend I made that week. Her name was Ashley and she reminded me of the Ashley from my childhood. I could not get my best friend from my childhood off my mind and wondered if she was still living in silence. It brought up so many memories that I pushed away and ignored, not ready to deal with them yet. Ashley and I became friends immediately at camp and one day while sitting on my bunk I shared my secret with her about what Brian did to Allie and me. I really opened up to her, which was not usual for me at fourteen, but I trusted Ashley immediately with my secret. Nothing could have prepared me for what she said after I told her my story. Ashley herself had her own secret and had been sexually abused by someone in her own family. She felt safe telling me her story because I opened the door to my own past for her to see and understand that she was not alone. We bonded the rest of the week, and I remember being sad to say good-bye on my final night of camp because not only was she a treasured new friend but someone who shared my pain. We lost touch after camp but I never stopped thinking about Ashley and wondered the path she continued down in her own healing from sexual abuse. Ten years after we shared a cabin together and an incredible bond at camp, I found Ashley on Facebook. I was hesitant about what to say in my message to Ashley and how to express how she had been in my heart all those years after opening up about her own abuse. I did not want to trigger her or bring up anything she did not want to be reminded of. I decided to send a message because I wanted her to know I had not stopped thinking about her. A few days later I got a response back.

Hi Erin,

You caught me off guard but in a good way. Ever since Van Buren Youth Camp I was able to breathe again. I know that might sound crazy but you had an impact on my life. I was never able to share my experience with someone who experienced the same trauma I did. I always thought of it like when soldiers come back from war and rarely tell their stories to others because we do not understand. If we hear their traumatic memories we can show them the type of condolence they deserve. To know there was someone else out there that shared of my experiences made me feel less alone and helped me through many horrifying sweaty nights. Please don't ever think I have forgotten about you because that would be impossible. I must say you are quite unforgettable in my eyes. Meeting you was a breakthrough in my childhood issues and reminded me that I am not alone and to keep pushing forward in life. I am so proud of you

Erin. You have taken a big step for us all. I look forward to getting your book and hearing back from you.

Ashley

Back when I felt so alone in my own pain, I was unaware of the impact I was making on another person, simply by sharing my truth. Little did I know that my need to connect significantly impacted Ashley and allowed her to find her own voice and realize she was not alone, which is why it is so important to let your voice be heard; you just never know who you're helping in the process and the impact you can have on another person's life.

I believe God put Ashley and me in the same cabin for a reason. He knew the healing touch we would have on each other. I opened a door for her to an understanding that she was not alone and that allowed her to open up and share her story with me. In the summer of 2009, ten years after I left Van Buren Youth Camp, I returned to the camp at the request of the executive director and so many wonderful memories from my childhood came flooding back. Every year there is one full week of leadership camp where kids ages fourteen to eighteen come together and learn leadership skills to prepare them to be cabin counselors. Throughout the week they participate in activities and listen to guest speakers. It was brought to the attention of the executive director that cabin counselors wanted to know what to do if a camper discloses sexual abuse. I never imagined I would one day return and speak at the same camp where I once carried my silence and escaped the pain I endured back home. It was a wonderful experience being able to share my story of how I disclosed my own abuse story at camp with cabin counselors. I ended my discussion by emphasizing a very important truth regarding sexual abuse: if counselors never have to use the tools I offered to effectively respond to an account of abuse while at camp, they will one day, at some point in their life, call upon them when someone else inevitably breaks their silence to them.

After speaking to the group, I enjoyed a walk around camp and reflected on the three summers I spent there. I made my way over to the lake and remembered being stuck in the canoe with Laura and how she told me we would be stuck there forever. I learned in 2008 that Laura died a year earlier after a five-year battle with cancer. She left to her family a list of the twelve places where she wanted her ashes to be scattered; one of those places was Van Buren Youth Camp. Laura and I used to sit next to each other in thought during our times at the lake. It was as if I could feel her spirit right there next to me. Just as she predicted so many years ago, a part of Laura remains forever at camp.

The memories with my younger sister, Allie, are endless. We were two years apart in age but only a year apart in school, making that bond we shared even stronger. While our older sister, Caitlin, was a high school student involved in gymnastics, diving, and cheerleading, Allie and I were into playing dolls, going fishing in the backyard, stopping at garage sales, building forts, and creating commercials with the video camera, which we often interrupted with laughter. We frequently came home from elementary school only to play school with each other and our friends. We would take turns being the students and teacher. My sisters and I were all born in February, so Allie and I celebrated our birthday parties together. We would both invite our friends and play games like Bingo or the dice game Bunco and win prizes. Other times we brought our friends to our lake house, but because we had winter birthdays, instead of swimming we took our friends out on our snowmobiles on the frozen lake. There were the karaoke birthday parties where we sang the night away. Our mom was great at organizing parties and always went above and beyond for us girls to make them special and memorable.

Allie and I also had a few very scary moments neither of us will ever forget. We were not allowed to cross the busy intersection by our house, but one day when I was eleven and she was nine, we broke the rule and took our bikes back into the old neighborhood we used to live in. We played at the park awhile and then headed back home. When we approached the intersection, the light said WALK so we *rode* our bikes across. Halfway through the intersection, the light changed and a man waiting at the light did not see us. He hit the gas just as my sister was in front of him. He sent her flying off her bike, and I crashed into his car because I was directly behind my sister. I fell off my bike. Allie and I got up immediately, shook it off. We were both more concerned about being in trouble for crossing the busy intersection. The man jumped from his car, a panicked look on his face, to see if we were okay. My sister and I just ran with our bikes. The man got back into his car and caught up with us. He stopped us to make sure we were really okay. He was really shaken up, but we assured him we were completely fine. Once we convinced him, he drove away and Allie and I swore never to tell our parents. We did not share that story until Thanksgiving dinner 2008—we were both adults, in our twenties. Allie and I started to share stories with our parents that would have panicked them had they known about them at the time. Recently, we shared another one of those close calls, but this one did not involve getting hit by a car. Instead we were chased by a bull.

Up by our lake house in Wisconsin, Allie and I used to spend countless hours going to a farm. A huge barn was filled with pigs, chickens, roosters, cows, sheep, and lambs. The farmer once allowed Allie and me to bottle feed a calf. We also would climb a ladder to the loft that was filled with hundreds of bales of hay. We would run around playing tag or hide and seek with our friends. Our favorite pastime was playing with the litters of kittens that were always being born. We would spend countless hours finding litters hidden in the hay. It was like a scavenger hunt to find kittens every time we went.

One time we found a kitten abandoned in a chicken coop. It was so tiny it could fit inside a wine glass. We brought it home, and, of course, Father said we could not keep her and had to return it on our way home after the weekend was over. Allie and I fell in love with the little kitten and begged Mom to let us keep it. She told us if we could sneak it home without Dad's finding out, then we could keep it. Allie put me up to the challenge. So when Dad stopped in front of the barn on our way home and told us to say good-bye to the kitten, I jumped out of the car and walked toward the barn. Once inside, instead of setting the little kitten down, I put her under my sweatshirt and tried to situate her so she would not fall out as I made my way back to the car. I knew I could not ruin our one chance. I folded my arms looking mad as I walked back to the car, but I was really crossing my arms to keep the kitten from falling. We sang all the way home so Dad could not hear the kitten cry. We eventually named her Chicken because we found her trapped in a chicken coop. Today she is an eleven-year-old cat who bonds the most with our mom. My father has a soft spot for Chicken, yet he loves to terrorize her.

In 1998, the same summer we got Chicken, Allie and I found a new animal that had arrived at the farm: a large bull. The heavy metal gate was kept closed and locked, but the space between the bars of the gate were large enough for us to climb through. We were able to sneak past the bull without his seeing us and get to the other end of the field where we climbed up onto large bales of hay. Allie had her friend Allison with us. Once we were all up, we got the bull's attention. When it came running toward us, we would run along the hay back and forth, teasing the bull as it chased us back and forth. We had a few close calls, almost falling off the hay, which could have been ugly because we had the bull worked up and angry. Then we realized the only way out was the same way we had come in, but now we had a very angry bull eyeing us. So we had to lay low for a while, until the bull got bored of us. When he drifted off toward the grass, we decided to make a mad dash for it. We all jumped from the hay and ran for the locked gate. The bull saw us and charged us. We ran for our lives. He came within feet of reaching us as we jumped through the sides of the metal bars of the gate. We all saw our lives flash before us and learned a valuable lesson: do not mess with a bull. We waited to tell our parents this story until we were adults, too.

"What other close calls did you two get in?" our parents asked after we confessed our bull story.

Allie and I cannot help but laugh, knowing we will reveal more of our shared crazy adventures as the family gathers around a dinner table. These are the memories that fill me with laughter, remind me of a lesson learned, or put a smile on my face.

Of course, I could not forget to share one final memory of so many wonderful ones. I was in kindergarten and came to class every day and stared into an incubator of eggs, waiting to see if they had hatched into furry little yellow chicks. The waiting seemed to last forever and kindergarteners are not known for their patience. But at the moment the first little chick pecked its shell, I happened to be right there. We watched what we had waited so long to see: the transformation of the protected shell cracking open and a little chick appearing.

I remember that moment so fondly, and while I may carry the memories of some tragic events as a little girl, I still have not forgotten being inspired by a living creature breaking out of its shell. I feel that moment gave me a greater appreciation for life. Growing up I was afraid to break out of my own shell and show my pain. The same way I witnessed as a kindergartener the transformation of an egg into a yellow chick, I have seen my own personal transformation from a little girl silenced into a grown, outspoken woman no longer hiding in the darkness of my own shell. You see, even through all the darkness I faced as a child, I still have many more cherished memories than I do painful.

What do you need to do right now so that you can soar and discover your gifts? I urge you to search for the answers you seek. I promise you, they are there waiting to be uncovered. You are carrying them within you, and it may take a little digging to uncover the answers. Go to the root of the problem, for that is where growth begins. Behind whatever pains you might be struggling with, goodness can be found. Set small manageable goals that will lead you to milestones. Give it a try; you may be surprised at what you are capable of. Often, as a survivor of childhood sexual abuse, you might have flashbacks of what you endured. Write down the good memories from your childhood, the way I just reflected on memories that did not involve abuse. It will help you direct the triggering memories into remembering your fond, happy times. Sometimes people can get so caught up in their pain and everything that is going wrong in their lives that often people forget about all the wonderful things that have happened in their lives. It is good to take a step back and reflect.

My image will never be blurred out and my voice will never be altered. I have stepped out of darkness and into the spotlight to be seen and heard. I wish I could slip off the shoes I wore that dreaded winter day I walked home after the rape and allow someone to slip on my shoes and take that painful walk home for me. I wish I could take the horror movie that has played in my memory and put it on the television for people to see the evil in two men staring into the eyes of a precious girl. I wish others could get into my mind so they can understand what it is like to have your extended family call you a liar and then kick you out of the family. If I could do any or all of these, then people would understand why I speak out.

Millions of families across the world have gone through similar situations or are going through them right now. You hear about families being called dysfunctional, yet I believe every family has some sort of dysfunction, whether it is seen or not. There is no such thing as the perfect family.

I hope those who do not understand why I went public can understand that my purpose is to give others a voice, to show the power of forgiveness, and to remove the stigma and shame of sexual violence.

I cannot return to my inner child the pieces of my childhood that were taken; I cannot erase the pain I carry within me. I have, however, used my voice that was silenced and will continue to use it to share my message with others. I am no longer afraid to show my tears because I have learned that grief is a healthy process that allows the human spirit to heal. By bringing down the walls around me, I have discovered that the grass is greener on the other side and the sun is shining past the darkness. Behind my smile is the voice of a little girl who, after sixteen years, is ready to step out into the spotlight and join the grown woman I am. I will not allow the pain to swallow me but make me thrive. Today is the first day of the rest of my life—and yours, too. God already knows the path I will journey down. I trust in Him, knowing He will only give me what I can handle. I live with no regrets, taking each precious day and living it as if it were my last.

My past memories can serve as hope for others to rise above tragedy and find the strength within. I wake each morning with the attitude to go out and make a positive difference in the lives of the people I encounter at work, my family and friends, and the audiences hearing my testimony. Each step I take forward is another step in the right direction. Yesterday is the past, and tomorrow is the future. I cannot save everyone or take away everyone's pain, but I can at least try.

My soul is bursting and ready to walk through the doors that lie ahead, confident that whatever is on the other side, no matter how big, I can overcome it. I am ready and prepared to tackle any challenge. A dark night is always met by the sun rising in the morning, teaching us that even in tragedy, something magnificent can happen. Do not let giving up be an option.

Today in most cars you will find a GPS navigation system that will give you turn-by-turn directions to get to your destination. Unfortunately, life does not come with a set of turn-by-turn directions, so it is our mission to proactively find our purpose. In the process we might take different roads, wrong turns, and encounter dead ends. No doubt we will become lost and confused.

In any direction you go you will encounter fog, storms, and sometimes it will seem as though the rain will never end. Do not run, rather face the storm head-on, for it serves a purpose. If we run away from it, the next storm down the road is sure to be bigger. I can promise you that on the other side of the storm, you will discover much, and you will find a clear, straight path and purpose for your life.

As a child, whether it was sitting in a circle in a classroom or tucked in bed at night, my teachers and parents often read me books. They all ended "happily ever after." As I look back on the tragedy, pain, confusion, and anger in my childhood, in the end I found forgiveness to those who had hurt me and discovered my own happily ever after. No matter what circumstances befall me, nothing will take my joy and happiness. And when I exit this lifetime, I want to be remembered as having found my "happily ever after."

chapter eleven

A NEW PROMISE

In January 2008, I wrote a letter to Tonia. In it I took her through the events of what happened to me with her brother, leaving out the graphic details. I shared what brought me to finally come forward all these years later. I expressed my appreciation to her for the way she handled things by kicking out her brother and working with Detective Morgan. I ended my letter by telling her that I keep her and her family in my prayers. I left it open that if she had any questions not to hesitate to ask. I sensed that Tonia needed to hear from me. I felt I owed her that much.

Winter turned into spring and spring into summer. Six months after I sent my letter, I found a contact for Tonia on the Internet. I sent a simple message asking if it was the right person and if she received my letter. A week went by before I received a response.

Dear Erin,

Yes, you have reached the right Tonia. I did receive your letter. I have been planning to write you back. I am glad you are able to put your life together. I was at first very stunned and horrified when

Officer Morgan showed up and blew apart what I thought was a pretty good life and a great family. Here I thought how great it was at different points in my life, change in jobs, what have you, that my brother has been available to help me out. To think every action of his may have been a lie, a deception to cover his tracks sickens me to no end. That he may have hurt a child, my child, in my own house, under my nose. Please don't thank me for having him move out, there wasn't any question in our minds that he couldn't be in our house until this was cleared up. All these years I thought I was a good mom, how could I have missed this? There should have been some signals. Having been a survivor of sexual abuse myself, I thought I did all the right things, not letting my children stay at anyone's house whose family members I wasn't completely sure of. When I should have been watching my own family.

I can't tell how this has torn my family apart. I've only recently started back talking to my mother, that relationship will never be the same again because she without a doubt believes Richard would have never done anything like this. I can't say that I know that. It pissed me off that he didn't talk to Officer Morgan. If I had been accused of something like this, I would be screaming my innocence from the rooftops. Not, not talking makes me have bigger doubts about him. I don't talk to Richard at all, so needless to say, everyone has taken sides.

Ashley can't confirm or deny anything. She has no memory of anything you claim. I have so many questions.

My husband won't speak to certain members of my family anymore, and my son hates Richard. Ashley and JJ both read your letter. I've never heard my son cry like that in my life. My heart broke for you, Ashley, JJ, your family, and mine. I have trouble sleeping with this on my mind all the time. To say I'm depressed is an understatement. I thought I had put my own pain behind me; I'm having nightmares again of my own abuse. These past months since this came out have been hell.

My daughter is going to be getting married, and JJ is about to be a father any day now. We're having our first grandchild; this should be the happiest time of our lives for my husband and I, and my family. But it's not; we have this cloud of doubt, confusion, and anger hanging over us. I need answers, Erin; your intentions may have been honorable, but the ripple effect sucks big-time.

I don't know if you live in the area still or if you're even willing, but I would like to talk with you. Ashley said she would be willing to meet with you too. I'm including my number. It's up to you if you use it or not, and here is my direct e-mail.

Tonia

I felt great pain reading this letter. I never wanted to turn this family upside down. I had no idea if I was going to call Tonia, and if she was going to be angry with me or sincere. It is hard to interpret a letter. A big part of me felt meeting with Ashley and her mother was the most I could do to bring them answers. I just never expected it would happen.

I was nervous to call Tonia. I knew the minute I heard the tone in her voice I would get a sense of how she felt about speaking with me. I waited a month before contacting her. I wrestled with the words in her letter during that time. Moments before calling Tonia, I prayed hard.

As I listened to the ringing, I wondered if she would be there. She finally picked up, and I told her who it was. Her cheerful voice greeted me. She told me that she had just hung up the phone with Ashley, who had asked her to set up a time to talk with me. She asked me how I was doing. She spent the next twenty minutes talking about being a new grandma and how she had set up Ashley with her fiancé. We never mentioned her brother. We ended the conversation with her saying she would get back to me after talking to Ashley about a day we could all meet.

Two weeks later, on the morning of September 16, 2008, I drove to Ashley's apartment to meet with her and her mom, who lived about twenty minutes from me. The whole drive there was surreal. I could not believe I was moments away from sitting across from my childhood friend I had promised never to tell a soul about our secret. That same secret that was bringing us together sixteen years later. As I walked into her apartment building hallway, Ashley was coming out the door to throw garbage out. We both froze, and then she dropped the garbage and we gave each other a big hug. We laughed as we both agreed we still resembled what we looked like as little kids. Ashley pointed down the hall to her apartment and told me to walk right in, her mom was in there, and she would be right in.

As I entered her apartment, I spotted Tonia sitting on the couch. She stood, hugged me, and said it was great to see me but that she wished it was under different circumstances. When Ashley returned, I sat down on the couch next to Tonia and Ashley sat across from us on her computer chair. I never could have envisioned this day coming.

We drank coffee and talked about the positive things going on in our lives. Tonia was interested in what I was doing as far as school and a career. We talked about the new baby in their family and being an aunt and grandma for the first time as they shared photos with me.

At the same time we all fell silent. The moment had arrived for the conversation we were all dreading.

I finally turned to them and asked, "Where do you want me to begin?"

Tonia responded first. "Take me back to the beginning when this all began, and go through it with me."

222

So I took them back to the very first time Richard had come into the bedroom and sexually abused me. I took her through the time line of it all and tried to place where she could have been—either sleeping in the next room or working while Richard was watching Ashley. When I shared the story about the overnight with the other friend sleeping over, Ashley and her mother went through names of who could have been a family friend who had not gone to the same school as Ashley and me.

As I shared this night with them, I looked directly at Ashley. "You do not remember us lying on the floor in your bedroom, making shadows with our hands on the wall when your uncle came in?"

"I have no memory of that night." Her eyes filled with tears as I continued to share different incidents of sexual abuse.

Then I got to the day I was raped. I leaned toward Ashley. "Do you remember being locked out of the bedroom as I screamed for you, and you kept trying to get the door unlocked?"

Once again, she had no memory of it.

Without getting graphic, I told about being raped on her bed. Tears streamed down Ashley's cheeks. As she grabbed napkins and wiped her eyes, tears began to fall from my eyes. Tonia was right there with us, tears in her eyes, too. I shared the precious moments of innocence being taken as Richard silenced me. I shared with them the blood that stained my underwear and the guilt and shame that stained my thinking. Because I felt I had done something wrong, I hid my underwear in a garbage can in our garage. "So much shame, fear, and confusion consumed me at such a young age. I felt like I had done something bad and could not tell anyone."

Tonia wiped her eyes. "I am so sorry, Erin."

I looked at Ashley as she clutched tissue in her hands. "Do you remember when I put my hand through the window in first grade?"

"Yes, I definitely remember that."

I explained that it was just a week or so after the rape that my sister had pulled off my shoes the same way Richard had, and that caused me panic as that whole day came flooding back, and the immense pain revisited me.

Ashley's flow of tears continued. I brought her back to the day I was raped and how she ran after me and stopped me outside her house, making me lock pinkies with her to promise never to tell or else they would lose the house.

Ashley just stared at me in silence. I focused on Tonia. "Was Richard helping pay bills, or was that just his threat to keep Ashley quiet because she did not know any better?"

"He never helped with the bills; he just helped take care of my kids when I worked."

I took Ashley and her mom through all the abuse I endured. "Ashley, do you have any memories of this?"

She shook her head. "I can't confirm or deny it ever happening."

"Do you think you could have repressed it?"

"I am going to see a therapist to see if any of this comes to the surface. Sometimes I get strange feelings, like maybe I buried things."

"Do you remember pulling the fire alarms in second grade?"

"Of course I do I remember your coming down the hallway after cleaning the classroom erasers. I had just pulled the alarms."

"I was terrified when I learned you had done it because I feared Richard was going to pick you up from school when you were suspended."

Tonia looked like she was remembering something long forgotten. "When I went to the school that day, the principle tried to explain that when a child pulls an alarm it is a cry for help. She questioned me about this, wondering what Ashley's action could be a cry for. I brushed it off, figuring it had to do with problems I was having with Ashley's father, who did not live with us then."

We discussed that it could have been a cry for help because of the abuse Ashley went through.

Tonia clutched the tissue in her hand. "You cannot trust anyone with your children, not even your own family. These sick bastards are everywhere; it's like an epidemic."

I got the impression right away that Tonia and Ashley both supported me completely and believed everything I said. Now I needed them to fill in some missing pieces and give me more answers.

Tonia explained that a week before Detective Morgan had showed up for the first time, Richard had just moved back into her house. He had lived with them off and on over the years. He always struggled to pay his rent. She thought if he lived with them, he would watch their nine-year-old so they would not have to pay for day care. Richard was on disability due to his kidney dialysis, and he was going to start watching her youngest the following week while she and her husband worked.

A knot formed in my stomach on hearing this, and I realized once again that timing is everything. I knew had I not come forward when I did, even if I had waited just a week longer, her little nine-year-old would have been at the hands of a sick monster every day after school alone.

"When Richard moved back into the house, he lived in the basement. The basement is where my nine-year-old, Amy, had all her toys and video games. I sat down with Amy right before Richard moved back in and explain that the basement was now Uncle Richard's room and that little girls do not belong in a man's room. If she wanted to play her video games, she would have to go downstairs to get them and play them upstairs. I talked to Amy many times about safe touch and unsafe touch. I even told her that she was at an age that she should not be sitting on grown men's laps."

It was clear to me that before Tonia ever learned anything about what Richard had done, she was very cautious of her children being hurt. Just listening to Tonia describe this all showed me that she was dedicated to protecting her children.

Tonia briefly shared how a cousin had sexually abused her throughout her childhood. She believed that if her father had lived with her, the abuse might never have happened because her cousin would not have been in the home. But she will never get the opportunity to confront her cousin because he is dead. Her experience made her a very protective mother, cautious of who spent time with her children, which brought up that Ashley spent only one night at my house during the entire time we were friends. I did not remember the overnight at my house, but Ashley did.

The first time Detective Morgan showed up was in October 2007. Tonia was working and Ashley was home with Amy, and Richard was downstairs. Ashley had answered the door and spoken with Detective Morgan.

"The detective wanted to talk to Richard. I told him he was sleeping. He then told me the allegations about Richard. He gave me his card and asked me to give it to Richard when he woke up. The detective wanted Richard to call him. I gave Detective Morgan Mom's cell number. As soon as he left, I called Mom at work and told her to come home immediately."

"When Ashley called me, I got this adrenaline rush, and I could not believe what I was hearing. When she mentioned your name, the person who had made the charges, I remember saying to Ashley, 'Erin? You mean the little tiny petite girl that lived by the park?'"

Tonia immediately took her break at work because the news

had shocked her. When she arrived home, Amy ran to her car, saying a detective had been at the house.

Ashley and Tonia then went upstairs to Tonia's room to talk in privacy, but Amy kept coming in. Ashley assured her mom that Richard had been asleep during the detective's visit. Then Amy had jumped into the conversation and said that he had been awake and that Richard had been staring out the basement window, watching and listening to the entire conversation.

Tonia looked at me. "Without a doubt, I know he heard what Detective Morgan told Ashley. Police showing up at my house looking for Richard was nothing new. He has failed to show up at court for numerous things over the years, so he's had all kinds of warrants for his arrest. In fact, before Ashley ever called me, I had a message on my phone from a man who said he was from Schaumburg police. He wanted me to call him back. I figured it had to do with Richard and some violation he didn't pay or failed to show up at court. It frustrated me that I often got calls or knocks at the door because of Richard's irresponsibility."

That evening, Ashley, Tonia, and her husband had talked things over in private, away from Richard. After that conversation, Tonia went downstairs to confront Richard. He lied, saying he was not awake when the detective showed up. Tonia told him that I had filed charges against him for doing inappropriate things back in the early '90s when they lived in Schaumburg. "His response was abrupt and short, that he did not know any Erin. I told him that he needed to call the detective and clear things up with him. Richard stayed in the basement the rest of the night."

I can only wonder what went through Richard's head that night.

"The following day I spoke with Detective Morgan. He told me all that was going on. I gave him Richard's cell phone number, and we set up a time for the detective to come talk with Ashley and me.

"There was no way Richard could stay in the home with these allegations. I was not about to put my children in jeopardy or have the state take my child away from me. I told Richard the next day to pack his bags and get out."

Before he left, she told him to call the detective.

Detective Morgan and Tonia exchanged numerous phone calls. He came a couple of times to talk with Ashley, Tonia, and her husband. "I was so frustrated that Richard was not returning Detective Morgan's phone calls. So I began calling Richard and telling him to come get the rest of his stuff immediately."

While he was at the house picking up the rest of his belongings, Tonia confronted Richard again about why he was not returning the detective's calls. As more time passed without his calling Detective Morgan, Tonia became suspicious that Richard had something to hide. She began questioning everything she knew about her brother.

"I made a final attempt to get Richard to speak with the detective, and the only thing he said was, 'Just because you say you're innocent does not mean you're not found guilty.'"

I looked at Tonia then at Ashley. "If you knew you didn't do something you've been accused of, you would be screaming your innocence. You wouldn't sit back and say nothing."

"I was convinced he had something to hide, and that made me that much more suspicious of Richard."

I leaned forward. "Well, of course he knows exactly what he did, and he probably could not look Detective Morgan in the eye and keep a straight face while he denied doing anything. Richard had dealt with law enforcement enough that he probably knew Detective Morgan would see straight through him. His deception would be spotted in a heartbeat."

228

"I told Detective Morgan only two things that stuck out in my mind and alarmed me after learning about these charges against Richard. The first one was about you, Erin. It was a day you were at the house playing with Ashley. All of a sudden you took off and you looked very upset. I asked Ashley what had caused you to leave so upset, if Ashley was not sharing her toys. I don't remember what Ashley told me, but I sat Ashley down and told her she needed to share her toys with her friends."

That was probably the morning I mentioned seeing her in the kitchen the morning after Richard had abused Ashley, her other friend, and me. It was interesting she remembered my leaving, and I remembered leaving upset and frightened that morning.

"The second thing I told the detective was about Ashley and her brother, JJ. One day Ashley and JJ were squabbling, so I went to see what they were arguing about. Ashley was telling JJ how much she hated Uncle Richard and that upset JJ. He looked up to his Uncle Richard and could not understand why his sister would have so much anger toward him. I brushed it off and didn't think twice about it. I thought it was a childish argument because Richard spoiled JJ more than he did Ashley, and that was why she disliked him."

Tonia's extended family response seemed to parallel mine. When her family found out about the charges against Richard, everyone took sides. Tonia's mother told her he could never do something like this. She had this idea that a therapist had implanted this all in my head. The mother's statements stirred up a lot of anger inside Tonia. "I reminded my mother that how she was responding was the same way she had when she learned that I had been abused." Tonia's mom said, "What do you mean?" Her mother's comments only made Tonia more frustrated and angry because the mother knew that Tonia had been abused as a child. Tonia had come to her mother when she was in high school and told her mother everything about what her cousin had done. Her mother had handled the situation then very similar to how she handled things with her son Richard.

Tonia was not convinced Richard did not do this; if anything his lack of pleading innocence convinced her right away that he had done this. Things became so intense Tonia and her mother stopped talking. Richard was going between his mother's house, which happens to be two miles from my parent's home, and staying with other family members. Tonia's extended family members began giving her a hard time. They said that she needed to be there for her brother because of his bad health. Tonia and her aunt spent many days going over things about Richard and thinking every lie he could have told. Many thoughts ran through Tonia's mind, one of which was how you think you know your family, then when something like this breaks open, you realize you don't know them at all. "You cannot even trust your own family."

Tonia described herself to me. "I am a Christian woman who goes to church regularly and have always believed God does not get back at people for hurting others, but I cannot help but wonder if Richard got sick because of what he did. He put you through pain, Erin. He has put my immediate family through pain. Now he is experiencing pain. I call that poetic justice."

I knew what she was saying; it was not the first time that same thought had crossed my mind.

Tonia was one of five kids, Richard was the oldest. Most of Tonia's family was either supporting Richard or not saying anything at all. Tonia's aunt was very supportive of her through everything. She convinced Tonia that because her mother's health was not the best, the last thing she would want is for something to happen to her and the both of them not speaking.

"I listened to my aunt. Had it not been for her words of

wisdom, I would still not be talking to my mother. But I decided to start communicating with my mother again. I knew our relationship would never be the same again, and we would not dare discuss Richard because we both had much different feelings about him."

Eventually Thanksgiving and Christmas arrived, and just like in my family, her family did not gather with her relatives; instead, they stayed away. "I would go nowhere in the presence of Richard. The thought of seeing him made us all sick."

One day in December 2007, Tonia received a phone call from her mother. Her mother had said that Richard had finally returned Detective Morgan's call and that he learned I had recanted my entire statement, saying I made it all up.

"I was outraged that Detective Morgan had not called to tell me. So I hung up, then immediately called him. I got straight to the point and asked him why had he not informed me that you had confessed to making it all up."

Of course, Detective Morgan told her that Richard had yet to return any of his phone calls.

"That's when it hit me. Richard was really messing with our emotions now. Making up lies to cover his tracks. I should've known. He's a compulsive liar."

"That's right." Ashley jumped in. "Richard told me lies about a lot of things, even really stupid things. He cannot be trusted."

Then Ashley began getting phone calls from her grandma, wanting her to speak with a lawyer Richard had hired. She wanted Ashley to back him up and report that nothing happened. "I told my grandma there was no way I would do that."

Ashley added, "I need to find a therapist and figure things out. I have struggled with trust issues with men my whole life. I figured I'd stay single the rest of my life. Then Mom found the perfect man for me."

I felt my eyebrows lift. "Why do you think you have trust issues?"

She shrugged. "I honestly don't know. I just don't trust men in particular and people in general."

It was clear to me sitting across from Ashley that she has a lot of pain buried. Though Ashley does not know the answer to why she cannot trust, it is very similar to what survivors of sexual abuse struggle with. I live with that same fear and trust issue with men. Our tear-filled eyes locked. All I could think about was how she struggled with trust issues and how she denied anything happening. "I was really hoping that my coming here today, seeing me all these years later, would spark a memory. I'd thought maybe something I would say would trigger memories. But if you have disassociated any abuse, maybe repressing it was the only way your brain could handle what happened to you. Maybe it was the only way to survive, since you lived with Richard throughout your childhood. I escaped him."

Tears flowed down Ashley's cheeks and her mother's.

Tonia took me to the end of the investigation. She had not heard from Detective Morgan in a few weeks and began leaving messages for him to call her back. "I got a call in January telling me that the case was closed. I was upset and angry. How could it be closed?"

Detective Morgan had told me this same thing in January 2008. Richard's lawyer had him plead the fifth and remain silent, so the detective could not force him to talk. The case would be closed unless Ashley remembered any of this, then it would reopen. We have until we are thirty-eight years old to reopen the case, according to the statute of limitations in Illinois and what Detective Morgan told me.

Tonia folded her arms across her chest. "I went off on Detective Morgan. I said, 'How can you come into my life, drop this on my doorstep, take us through an emotional roller coaster, and now just walk away from it with no closure?' My family and I were very frustrated that Detective Morgan could do no more because Richard was not talking."

Detective Morgan could not force Richard to talk because of his constitutional rights, which sucked because I am sure if Detective Morgan had a chance to talk to him, he would see right through him and that evil grin of his.

I understood Tonia's frustration. "Why is it that he needs both of us coming forward and saying he did this? It is not like we will bring any evidence. Richard is obviously not a good liar and fears Detective Morgan will see through his lies. Richard has dug his hole deeper by the way he handled himself in this investigation."

As I see it, only a guilty man would run from the police. Someone who is innocent does not avoid the police and get a lawyer, especially when there is no evidence to back up the charge. Richard's behavior gave away his guilt. He knew he had something to hide. He was not prepared to face the truth of his actions. He thought he had gotten away with his crime and would never hear about it again, especially sixteen years later.

"I will never speak to my brother again. I dread the day we cross paths again. I make every effort to avoid him, but I know that eventually we will meet. Whether it's at my mother's house or when I'm visiting family, I fear he'll show up."

I pulled an envelope from my purse. "I wrote a letter to Richard. Do you have his address?"

"I don't know where my brother is living, but I'll see that he gets it."

I studied mother and daughter. Then I pulled the sheet of paper out of the envelope and began reading.

Richard,

This is the voice of a little girl you once silenced as you took something so precious from me, my innocence. Sixteen years have gone by, yet I never forgot the look in your eyes, a memory that has haunted me. I was just six and seven when you came out of the shadows of the night, staring into my frightened eyes. You took a little girl's smile and replaced it with tears, a young child's soul and filled it with anger and rage. While my classmates were learning how to use twelve-inch voices, you had silenced mine. I do not have to remind you of your evil, sick, selfish, reasons for silencing me.

My memory is as clear today as it was when I was six and seven of what I endured at your hands. The memories never fade no matter how much time passes. Your image is burned in my memory, a face I will never be able to erase. It has been that disgusting grin across your face and the whites of your eyes that have haunted me over the years. The best way for me to describe you is an evil, selfish scumbag.

I honestly do not know how you can get up every morning and look at yourself in the mirror and not be filled with guilt and shame. Your actions will follow you all the way to your grave.

I assume you thought all these years later I would never come forward. Richard, I have never forgotten for a moment the pain I endured behind closed doors with you. Pain I will take with me the rest of my life. I truly hope you were trembling when you learned the little girl you silenced grew up and found her voice, for you can now understand for a moment the fear I lived with as you locked me behind closed doors. Little did you know back then who I would turn out to be.

I have learned you have pleaded the fifth, using your constitutional rights to remain silent. Where were my rights when I was a child and you raped me? The truth is I do not need metal bars surrounding you to get justice. I already found my own justice, and it is through the voice you once silenced.

I have rescued that frightened little girl you locked behind closed doors. I carry her within me as a driving force to rise above silence and keep the memory of my childhood innocence alive. I have come out of the darkness of your sickness and found a bright light shining down on me. I find poetic justice in the fact that you are now the one living in silence, not me! You messed with the wrong little girl, who turned her pain into a purpose, a purpose to go out there and speak out, exposing your sick, evil actions and to warn society of pedophiles just like you.

We all make choices, and while you may never take responsibility for the choices you made in this lifetime, you will definitely be held accountable in the next life. I have made my choice not to let your actions take my joy and happiness. I am releasing my anger, rage, and hatred toward you and then letting it simmer down and burn out. I will not let something like that consume and destroy me. I will not allow myself to carry anger and hatred around with me the rest of my life. You took so much from me as a child I will not continue to let you take any more from me in this lifetime. I have decided to turn that anger into action, allowing it to fuel me in an unstoppable crusade.

There is another choice I have made in my life that might take you by surprise. I have made the choice to forgive you for what you did to me. I am able to forgive your actions because I have conquered that evil, sickness, betrayal, and power you had over me as a child. I have turned my anger into empathy. What has led me to have empathy toward a man that molested and raped me as a child? It is right there in the word itself. The PATH I have taken has brought me to this conclusion.

Richard, the way I see it is on the outside you may have been this large, strong, powerful man using his force to take advantage of me, but deep down I believe there is something nestled inside of you that you have been running from your entire life. As a little boy if you were asked, "What do you want to be when you grow up?" you would have answered something like a fireman, doctor, police officer, but there is no way you would have answered a rapist. Something happened between your childhood and adulthood that I am completely unaware of that caused you to turn into this sick, disturbed man who needed control and power and found it in innocent little children. I am convinced you did not wake up one day and decide to start molesting children. Only you know what you carry tucked away in your soul, and whatever that may be I hope you deal with it the proper way and get yourself some serious help. There are people out there, believe it or not, who will help those like yourself who have done the unthinkable. Then again, you may choose to do nothing at all, going back to my statement earlier on the choices we get to make in life.

My life is not defined by you holding me down with your body and silencing my screams with your hand, but instead on how I claimed victory, found justice through my voice, and in the end found peace in my life. I will end this by saying it was God's grace that has opened my heart to forgive you. It is through God I have found the strength to confront you and not allow your actions to rob me of my happiness but instead find triumph through tragedy. I am closing this chapter of my life with this letter to you.

For I have conquered you.

Erin

I read the letter just like I would have read it if Richard were sitting across from me. I lifted my head after finishing the last sentence to see the tears pouring from both Ashley's and Tonia's eyes.

"That coward!" Tonia blurted out. "I do not know how you can be so strong and forgiving."

"I have carried this my whole life and have worked through the process of healing and forgiveness. This is all brand-new information to you. Your feelings are completely normal. It would be abnormal not to be angry. For many years I carried so much anger and rage toward Richard. But I have since worked through it. I am not numb to anger. I have gone through the wave of emotions that came ashore in my life and felt like a tidal wave trying to pull me under. If I allow myself to stay angry, Richard would continue to have power over me. The anger was like a fierce storm I had to fight through to keep from sinking in the pain. When I broke through, I found inner peace."

I would be lying if I said I will never experience anger again. Anger is an emotion we all experience throughout life, and I have learned to deal with my anger in a healthy way. When it hits me, I do not hold on to it but instead process it. Then I can move forward.

I looked at Ashley, who sat quietly wiping tears. "I have two choices. Either I can live the rest of my life consumed with anger and hatred toward Richard and let it rob me of my happiness, or I can let go and not let him steal another moment of my life that I can never get back."

Tonia jumped in. "I am at such a different place in my life. Erin, I want him dead for what he did to you and Ashley! That coward!"

Her anger hardened her voice. Her tears flowed more freely. "Erin, when you were at my house you were my responsibility. I should have protected you. I should have protected my own children. I am so—"

"You cannot take any responsibility for someone else's actions. You owe me no apology. Richard is the only one who owes any of us an apology. You cannot blame yourself, and you have to let go of that guilt, otherwise you will beat yourself up the rest of your life for something you did not do."

So much of what we discussed and my sharing how I've worked through my pain pulled up a lot of emotions for Tonia related to her own sexual abuse she endured as a child, which she was able to open up about to me.

I tucked the letter back into the envelope and handed it to Tonia. She told me she would make sure it got into his hands.

Ashley described her running into Richard over the Fourth of July at a family gathering. Her mother had not attended because she knew Richard would be there and could not stand the sight of him. "We kept our distance. I didn't talk to him. I did not then nor do I now want anything to do with him. He definitely will not be invited to my wedding."

Tears burned in my eyes. "I have a new promise to make with you, Ashley, and this one I will keep. I promise never to live in silence again and will keep the innocence of our childhood alive, a childhood you may have buried but has replayed inside of me for so many years."

In a flash of mental images, I saw us playing in the park near my house, riding our bikes in the tennis court and in the neighborhood, and playing for hours with her doll house. I glimpsed memories of eating lunch with her or coloring in our small first-grade classroom. I will never forget locking pinkies with Ashley and promising never to tell our secret. To return sixteen years later and face each other brought me so much closure. I cannot even describe in words the pure peace that settled on me. It was as if I put to rest all the haunting images of our childhood. I was able to replace the image of the little girl Ashley once was with the grown adult I now sat across from.

Four hours had gone by since I first sat down with Ashley and her mother. Four hours that I will take with me the rest of my life as I continue my journey.

We thanked one another for being willing to talk about these difficult things. I hugged them both as we made our way outside. Tonia had somewhere to be and soon pulled away.

I stood on the sidewalk outside Ashley's apartment with her. "I am really sorry this all had to come to the surface, and I am here for you if you ever begin to remember things and need someone to listen."

We stood under a clear blue sky with the sun beaming on us. We hugged once again, but this time Ashley held on tight. It was the kind of hug that reached the soul. So I held on. It was such a healing moment. When Ashley let go, tears once again filled her eyes.

I held her shoulders and looked deep into her eyes. "I conquered him. He no longer has my voice. I promise you the innocence of our childhood will live on, our voices will be heard, and I plan to make sure millions hear the voices of our innocence. I promise." We didn't need to lock pinkies to ensure this promise would hold. I made the promise . . . one that I would forever keep.

I assured Ashley I would be praying for her and her family. Ashley could not deny or confirm anything that I said happened to us, yet without a doubt, she believes she lived through everything I shared. She knows that when I speak out on this epidemic, I am speaking not only for me but also for the little girl she once was.

I will never forget that day, for I found the closure I longed for.

Days later after meeting with Ashley and her mom, I stood at a podium in Columbia, South Carolina, at a national conference of forensic interviewers, detectives, prosecutors, nurses, and others. I shared my pain, confusion, courage, strength, and determination to end the silent epidemic of sexual abuse. Though I have stood before audiences many times and shared my journey to thousands since the age of nineteen, I did something here I had never done before—I shed tears. I let strangers see my tears—

tears Richard told me when I was six years old were only for babies, tears I for so long was too ashamed to show. But now I stood before men and women, complete strangers, and I felt tears wetting my cheeks as I spoke.

No longer did these tears represent weakness and shame. These tears proclaimed my joy of being able to bring a little girl out of darkness and into the spotlight.

When I finished speaking, the audience was on their feet and applauding. Moments later a woman with tears staining her face approached me backstage. She was one of those people who worked in a Children's Advocacy Center yet lived in her own silence of sexual abuse. She thanked me for my bravery in helping her to find her voice. Through hearing of my courage, she was able to break her silence. I wrapped my arms around this woman and hugged her as she just cried her heart out. She had just made a huge step in her life. I thanked her for being courageous and breaking her silence to me. I find nothing more rewarding on this journey than helping people find their voices.

A week later I returned home from Cape Cod, Massachusetts, where I brought another audience to their feet and met wonderful people who shared stories with me about their lives affected by sexual abuse. I have discovered that God has blessed me by bringing some incredible people into my life, men and women I feel so blessed to have met, whom I would never have known had I not survived my childhood.

When I returned to Chicago that evening, I had an e-mail from Tonia. In it she thanked me again for sitting down with Ashley and her and that she is continuing to work on closure. Her son, JJ, would take my letter to Richard that night. She did not want to put it through the mail, not knowing if it would get into Richard's hands. If Richard tried to throw the letter away without reading it, JJ planned to read it out loud to him.

I could not express how much I appreciated the lengths they were going to for me, making sure I knew that Richard would hear my voice even if he did not want to.

I later learned that JJ gave the letter to Richard. He did not throw it away but told JJ that he would read it carefully. I got the last word with Richard as he continues to remain silent. Ashley found a therapist, and Tonia's nightmares ended after I sat down with her and Ashley. Tonia has discovered peace in spite of being sexually abused as a child. She is no longer a victim, for she tells me she sees herself as a survivor. Hearing her share that with me made me smile knowing she is not stuck in a place of being a victim. I hope others can take her positive attitude and become survivors. She truly is one strong woman and has such amazing qualities as a mother. Hearing her talk to her nine-year-old about safe and unsafe touches impressed me. She has a lot to be proud of and is an example for mothers everywhere on educating their children about sexual abuse. God has big plans in the future for her; I can see it.

In January 2009, I came across the "Police Blotter" in my local newspaper, and under the arrest section the very first name on the list jumped out at me. A little more than a year earlier that name would have meant nothing to me. It was Richard's full name, age, and residence. He had been arrested the morning of December 28 by my town's police department for driving under the influence. He also had two arrest warrants in another county. I found it ironic that though he lived a half hour away, he got pulled over by the same police department he has been avoiding all contact with.

I contacted Tonia, but she had not heard about her brother's arrest. Her family knows never to bring him to her attention because she will have nothing to do with him. She has no feelings for him and believes it is God's battle to fight for her. I pray for the best for both Tonia and Ashley. Every few months Tonia sends me an e-mail to see how I am doing. In the most recent she shared the news that Ashley is expecting her first child. I wish her all the best. They helped me reach the closure I needed in my life and for that I am grateful to both of them.

My voice has been therapeutic healing in my life. It is that voice I take with me as I continue to move forward in my life. Knowing I have more chapters of my life I have yet to experience, they will come with a reason—everything happens for a reason.

Many people might believe no army exists that is large enough to tackle this silent evil epidemic taking over our world, but with faith anything is possible. I have been saved by the grace of God.

"He reached down from Heaven and rescued me; He drew me out of deep waters. He delivered me from my powerful enemies, from those who hated me and were too strong for me. They attacked me at a moment when I was weakest, but the Lord upheld me."

Sam 22:17–19

I wish I could give those who struggle with painful pasts of childhood sexual abuse a shortcut to healing. I cannot, however, I can give you hope that if you do not give up and keep processing, you will get there. Mahatma Gandhi once said, "Be the change you want to see in the world."

My voice is the force behind the change I want to see in the world. I am no longer silent but calling the world to move in a new direction that will no longer mark survivors of sexual abuse with stigma and shame but with empowerment and justice. I want mandatory Safe Touch programs as part of every schools' educational goals. Finally, sick, evil pedophiles must be held responsible for their actions and not just given a slap on the wrist.

I am on an unstoppable crusade to pave the way to fulfill these goals. I am determined and devoted never to turn my back on the epidemic of sexual abuse. It is the mission I have dedicated my life to fight for and never give up on. My strength empowers me each day to take another step forward, letting my soul shine in this journey. This journey all began with a promise at six years old that transformed my life and made me the person I am today.

I have had to remove myself from the pain I endured throughout my childhood and go to the safety and security of a beach where I stayed grounded with my feet in the sand for so many years. I have been able to visually escape the horror from my past and allow myself to heal and forgive. In complete quiet and peace I reflected within myself and processed some of the most difficult moments I have endured in my life. When I look into the mirror of my soul, I no longer see a little girl trapped behind a door with a man on top of her, screaming to be saved. God has her tucked safely in His protective arms. In her place, I see a smiling, peaceful young woman.

I have set sail with God as my rudder, directing me as I battle the rough current of this world. I will rescue those along the way who are drowning in their painful pasts, pulling them aboard my ship. And I will take them ashore and lead them in a new direction that will allow them to reclaim their voices and conquer this epidemic.

Today is the day suffering in silence will end and our voices will be heard.

EPILOGUE

With my newly acquired master's degree in social work, I see many possibilities ahead of me. I have many visions for my future mapped out but with one ultimate purpose: I want to see legislation passed that requires all children in public schools across America to be taught safety lessons in a child friendly manner in which children will learn how to say no, speak up, and know who to go to if someone uses unwanted touches. I am not aware of any law that requires children to be taught this. I applaud the schools that already include such lessons in their educational lesson plans. So far I have only heard of a few private schools that educate children on sexual abuse. Children are taught their ABCs so they can spell and their 123s so they can count. Unfortunately schools overall fail to teach children about sexual abuse. It is not the teachers failing our children, it is the school boards that fail to require it. Teachers are obligated by law to report suspected cases of abuse and neglect. Why not reach children before learning they have been sexually or physically abused? While education programs won't stop sexual abuse all together, it will reduce children from staying silent. Why do I put so much emphasis on education in the schools and not on parents? While I think it is every parent's or guardian's responsibility to talk to their children, many parents and guardians fail to discuss sexual abuse with their kids, thinking it won't happen to them, or because they are the actual perpetrator.

For many years I labeled myself as a victim of sexual abuse after years of being ashamed and feeling worthless. Then I discovered I had survived it, and I was not a victim of sexual abuse but a survivor of sexual abuse who was learning to heal. Survivors live through the abuse, but the abuse has impacted their lives. They learn to manage life as a survivor and keep moving forward.

I have survived sexual abuse and rape. I have reached a new place in my life that goes beyond just surviving. I have recently discovered a place in my recovery: no longer healing but completely healed. This wound no longer haunts me. It took exposing that wound to heal it. What is left is a scar that tells an incredible journey of God's amazing grace on my life, of opening my heart to forgiveness, and discovering my purpose.

My memory is no longer haunted with images of evil. Those dark chapters now rest in peace in my heart and mind. I speak freely of them for two purposes: to reach those who are still in the dark and to help them find the light of today; and to educate society and help children who have been abused.

Today I wear the label of sexual abuse and rape survivor with dignity and courage. I have closed the doors to my past, for there is nothing trapped behind them anymore. I look forward to opening the doors to the chapters of my life to come.

I have repeated it over and over in the course of writing *Living for Today*, and I will repeat it just once more: Forgiveness is what set me free. Choosing to forgive has led me to live for today.

"Do not be overcome by evil but overcome evil with good"
—*Rom. 12:21.*

To contact Erin Merryn, please visit
www.erinmerryn.net, or
you can write her at erinmerryn@yahoo.com.

RECOMMENDED RESOURCES

Angela Shelton Foundation is a nonprofit organization whose purpose is to inspire and empower all survivors of sexual abuse and domestic violence to heal and lead joyful lives. Angela Shelton Foundation developed after the incredible journey Angela Shelton made driving across the country to meet other Angela Sheltons—survivors like her. Along the journey she discovered that 70 percent of the forty Angela Sheltons she met were survivors of rape, childhood sexual abuse, or domestic violence. Please contact Angela Shelton Foundation at:

P.O. Box 39702
Los Angeles, CA 90039
www.angelashelton.org.

Darkness to Light is a nonprofit organization with a mission to diminish the incidence and impact of child sexual abuse so that more children will grow up healthy and whole. Their programs raise awareness of the prevalence and consequences of child sexual abuse by educating adults about the steps they can take to prevent, recognize, and react responsibly to the reality of child sexual abuse. Please contact Darkness to Light at:

7 Radcliffe Street
Suite 200
Charleston, SC 29403
843-965-5444
www.darkness2light.org

Girls Fight Back (GFB) is a women's safety and self-defense education company specializing in fun and entertaining seminars as a first step for women and girls wanting to learn more about self-defense. Every year since 2002, GFB seminars have been attended by more than 100,000 women in schools, colleges, corporations, and women's groups around the United States. GFB was created in memory of Shannon McNamara, who died while fighting back against her attacker. In her struggle, she retained physical evidence of her killer, which led police to him. He now sits on Illinois Death Row awaiting execution. Her legacy lives on in the women who are learning to fight back. Please contact GFB at:

4800 Baseline Road
Suite E104 #286
Boulder, CO 80303
1-866-432-2423
www.girlsfightback.com
www.shannonmcnamara.com

National Children's Alliance is a nationwide not-for-profit membership organization whose mission is to promote and support communities in providing a coordinated investigation and comprehensive response to victims of severe child abuse. It is an organization with a vision that will have met success when every child has access to the services of an accredited Children's Advocacy Center. Please contact National Children's Alliance at:

516 C Street, NE
Washington, DC 20002
800-239-9950 or 202-548-0090
www.nca-online.org
info@nca-online.org

National Eating Disorders Association is a nonprofit organization dedicated to supporting individuals and families affected by eating disorders. We campaign for prevention, improved access to quality treatment, and increased research funding to better understand and treat eating disorders. We work with partners and volunteers to develop programs and tools to help everyone who seeks assistance. Please contact National Eating Disorders Association at:

603 Stewart Street
Suite 803
Seattle, WA 98101
Information and Referral Helpline: 1-800-931-2237
Business Office: 206-382-3587

Prevent Child Abuse America has helped build awareness, provide education, and inspire hope to everyone involved in the effort to prevent child abuse for America's children. They provide leadership to promote and implement prevention efforts at both the national and local levels. Please contact Prevent Child Abuse America at:

500 North Michigan Avenue
Suite 200
Chicago, IL 60611-3703
312-663-3520
www.preventchildabuse.org
mailbox@preventchildabuse.org

PAVE is a nonprofit organization that stands for Promoting Awareness, Victim Empowerment. It uses social, educational, and legislative tactics to shatter the silence of sexual violence. Founder Angela Rose was abducted at knifepoint at age seventeen from the parking lot of the mall where she worked and was assaulted by a repeat sex offender on parole for murder. Instead of staying silent, Angela took a stand and worked with the perpetrator's previous victims as well as the community to help enact Illinois's Sexually Dangerous Persons Commitment Act in 1998. Angela has cultivated PAVE into a national organization and continues to inspire others to join the movement to end sexual assault. Please contact PAVE at:

P.O. Box 476991
Chicago, IL 60647
1-877-399-1346
www.pavingtheway.net
info@pavingtheway.net

The Rape, Abuse & Incest National Network (RAINN) is the nation's largest antisexual assault organization. RAINN operates the National Sexual Assault Hotline, the National Sexual Assault Online Hotline, and publicizes the hotline's free, confidential services; educates the public about sexual assault; and leads national efforts to prevent sexual assault, improve services to victims, and ensure that rapists are brought to justice. Please contact RAINN at:

2000 L Street, NW
Suite 406
Washington, DC 20036
National Sexual Assault Hotlines
1-800-656-HOPE
www.rainn.org

The Voices and Faces Project is a nonprofit organization dedicated to giving a voice and face to rape survivors, offering a sense of solidarity and possibility to those who have lived through abuse, while raising awareness of how this human rights and public health issue impacts survivors, families, and communities. Please contact Voices and Faces Project at:

P.O. Box 804295
Chicago, IL 60680-4104
www.voicesandfaces.org